PRINCIPLES OF WORSHIP

A STUDY OF THE TABERNACLE OF MOSES

PRINCIPLES OF WORSHIP

A Study of the Tabernacle of Moses

P. Douglas Small

This manuscript was previously published in 1990 by Alive Ministries as a Bible conference guide. This version includes significant revisions.

Many of the images of the tabernacle that are included with permission from: Points Production, a product marketed by Christian Book Distributors in behalf of Pastor Melvin B. Poe, owner of the copyright; special thanks to Mishkan Galleries/David Hamilton for use of images from www.mishkanministries.org; and also thank you to Dr. Terry Harman of www.tabernacleman.com.

Thanks to Dr. George Voorhis for his critical review of this manuscript.

Layout: Jackie Britton

ISBN: 978-0-9820115-9-1

PUBLICATIONS

An ALIVE PUBLICATIONS Book

DEDICATION

To Annie Laura (Wentz) Small, my mother, who began teaching Sunday School at Trinity Lutheran Church in Kannapolis, North Carolina, when she was only 12. From her I received my hunger for the Scriptures.

And to Luvenia Viola (Kite) Cox who instilled in her daughter Barbara, my wife, a respect for the Bible, not only as literature, but as the Word of God.

CONTENTS

CHAPTER ONE

WHY STUDY THE TABERNACLE?

Years of slavery and personal deprivation, a series of miraculous plagues, and a pair of leaders called Moses and Aaron—brothers bound and determined to go back to an almost-forgotten homeland and take a nation with them—were part of the forces that helped in a slave revolt like none other in human history. It was beyond para-normal it was supernatural in extreme. Every plague was aimed at an Egyptian deity. Egypt seemed paralyzed by an invisible and more powerful hand.

The people of Israel had been eager and hopeful, then reluctant and stubbornly resistant. There had been the proclamations, the increased weightiness of the bricks—and above all, the strange miracles. Laced throughout the long months of negotiation with Pharaoh were the enticing promises of freedom. Freedom awaited them in a new, yet familiar land. It was not a land familiar to their heads or eyes, but to their hearts and souls. It was home. It was the land of their unforgettable fathers—Abraham, Isaac and Jacob.

With the last plague, the death of the firstborn, they were committed to leave. They had to leave. So out of the land of Egypt they came, numbering over two million strong. Pursued by an angry and armed Egyptian war band, they fled. Backed up against the Red Sea, with the mountains on one side and the desert on the other, they were trapped. Moses stood with an outstretched rod and his face into the wind, and they experienced an incredible phenomenon: The waters parted and they crossed the divided sea in victory and triumph. Mysteriously, the sea parted and Israel journeyed into their baptismal grave (1 Corinthians 10:2). Just as inexplicably, the waters surged together again, burying Pharaoh's war party. The first miracle of the sea let them out of Egypt. The second miracle closed the door to their return. It shut them up to God alone.[1] The taste of freedom manifested itself in a celebration dance led by Miriam, the sister of Moses and Aaron. They were free. And they were heading home for Canaan.

THE WILDERNESS—THE LEGITIMATE DELAY!

They came barreling out of Egypt, through the Red Sea and on to Mount Sinai. Suddenly, God stopped them at the foot of that mountain. They could have made the trip up the King's Highway and into their Promised Land in a matter of days.[2]

---

[1]   John Ritchie, *The Tabernacle in the Wilderness* (Grand Rapids: Kregel, 1982) 11.

[2]   Three ancient highways could have been used by Israel. One led along the coast through Philistine territory. Another led west of the Dead Sea through Hebron, Bethlehem and Jerusalem, continuing into what would become the territory of the northern tribes, and connecting with the coastal route north of Nazareth. This second route was called the water-parting route, running between the Jordan and the Mediterranean Sea. The eastern route called "The King of Kings Highway," went northward on the east side of the Dead Sea, proceeding into and through modern Jordan

But God halted their progress and detained them in the wilderness. Canaan was waiting for Israel, but Israel was not ready for Canaan. They needed two indispensable things, both critical to the health and identity of the new nation and to their survival as the people of God in the land.

First, they needed the Tabernacle. This would be the unifying symbol of God's presence around which they camped. Once in the land, this would be their national worship center. Nothing would be more critical to their unity than their worship. The division of the nation after the death of Solomon was driven in part by the creation of an alternative worship site and system that led to idolatry and the subsequent and permanent scattering of the 10 northern tribes. True worship unifies. Idolatry proliferates. The Tabernacle would forever be a model for Israel's worship. It would teach them about approaching and knowing the God of their fathers, the God who had delivered them, saving them from the bondage of slavery. It would accommodate His presence among them.

The Tabernacle was not man's idea. It was God's desire and God's design. Israel appeared content with the golden calf, but God wanted them to know Him, so He decided to live among them and change them—making them a people to and for Himself. Exodus 39 and 40 give instructions for the rearing of the Tabernacle. Seventeen times in those chapters we find the phrase "as the Lord commanded."[3]

The second thing they needed were the tablets. Upon the tablets would be engraved the moral law of God. It, too, would teach them about God, the principles that define Him and were to reform their lifestyles. This moral code by which they would live as representatives of a holy God would shape the

---

[3] W. S. Hottel, *Typical Truth in the Tabernacle* (Cleveland, OH: Union Gospel, 1943) 40.

values of the culture they would create. The Tabernacle with its reflection of God's glory in their midst was to be an awful thing, full of awe. What a God! Unlike any of the gods of Egypt, this God was alive, visibly evident, active, leading, present, a manifest phenomenon. The tablets—the Ten Commandments—were to order their walk with infused values for living. Their worship and walk were being choreographed by the Lord. He would strip them of Egypt's idolatry and its customs.

THE PAUSE IN THE WILDERNESS

In the third month after the Exodus, the nation reached the plains of Er-Rahah, north of Mount Sinai (19:1). The area is a mile to a mile-and-a-half wide by 3 miles long. It is bounded by towering hills on each side ascending 3,000 feet. The central peak is now called Ras Sufsafeh (Willow Top). A small willow tree grows at its peak from a cleft in the rock. Behind Willow Top, somewhat obscured from the plains where Israel camped is a higher peak called traditionally, Jebel Musa (Moses' Mount).[4]

Moses ascended that mountain eight times to confer with God. During his sixth ascent (Exodus 24:12), the first of his two 40-day stays, God gave him the pattern for the Tabernacle (25:8, 9). For six days, he waited. On the seventh day of his prayer vigil on Jebel Musa, God broke the silence, *"Speak unto the children of Israel…. Let them make me a sanctuary"* (vv. 2-8).[5] When he descended, he found Israel in idolatrous worship (32:19). The absence of a legitimate worship center and pattern of worship for the nation had given rise to idolatry. Man is instinctively a worshiper. The question is not, "Will we or will we not worship?" Rather, it is, "What will we worship?" There is a vacuum in the soul of man. That hole, left by sin, can be legitimately and perfectly filled only by the knowledge

---

[4] James Strong, *The Tabernacle of Israel* (Grand Rapids: Kregel, 1987) 15-6.
[5] David M. Levy, *The Tabernacle: Shadows of the Messiah* (Bellmawr, NJ: Friends of Israel Gospel Ministry, 1993) 17.

and presence of a holy and loving God. Israel did not yet know how to worship God. So, in the absence of a correct mode of worship, they created a false god to worship, patterned after the calf worship of Egypt. Moses destroyed that golden calf. Even the gold that had been utilized to construct that calf was considered polluted and was destroyed. It was not and could not be used for the Tabernacle. After that experience, Moses introduced to Israel the legitimate and acceptable pattern for worship that God had given him on the mountain—the Tabernacle.

This was not merely a pattern for worship then—it is God's pattern for worship today. Buried in the rituals of the sacrifices and the holy days, the symbols of the furniture and their elements are the principles that still govern heavenly worship and inform our worship.

THE TABERNACLE

Forty-two days later, four months and 11 days after the Exodus, the construction of the Tabernacle began.[6] It took approximately seven months to construct the Tabernacle. On the first day of the first month in their second year in the wilderness, Israel had a new worship center (40:17).

When it was set up, its priests consecrated and engaged in worship leadership, the fire of God fell and consumed the sacrifices, and the "glory of the Lord" filled the tent of worship. This would be God's tent among their tents—His fire in the center of their family fires. The tribes would camp on each side with God in the center. With His presence (symbolized by the Tabernacle that allowed God to dwell among them) and the tablets (the principles by which they would now live), they were ready for new living places. Fifty days later, the cloud lifted and Israel began their walk toward their new homeland

---

[6] Roy Lee DeWitt, *The History of the Tabernacle* (Chatham, IL: Revival Teaching, 1986) 17.

(Numbers 10:11, 12). The wind never blew this cloud. It moved without wind. Contrary to nature, it stood like a pillar. It was unlike the natural clouds that filled the atmosphere. It stood out against the sky. No meteorologist could have explained it. The darkness caused it to glow, and the brightness of the sun could not evaporate it. It was supernatural.[7]

God's desire had never been to live in a tent. Man was created to be the dwelling place of God—His earthen tabernacle. But sin spoiled man's vessel as a fit dwelling place for a holy God. Sin alienated man from God. Because of man's sin, God had vacated His first tabernacle on earth—the heart of man. Now, with the tabernacle of Moses, God creates an alternative. He will dwell among men because He could not dwell in men. *"And let them make me a sanctuary; that I may dwell among them"* (Exodus 25:8). God would live in a "house of hair"[8]—a tent of goat's hair, just as most of the people did. His tent also had a covering of ram's skins dyed red over the goat's-hair covering. In the covering of ram's skins, two symbols emerge: blood and sacrifice. God is insulated from sinful men by blood and sacrifice. Yet, God is not the one who lives in isolation. Man is the alienated party. Sin has put blood and death between man and God, symbolized by the bloody altar.

This tabernacle would continue for centuries as the worship center for Israel, serving the nation in the wilderness sojourn and up to the time of Solomon's Temple. The Temple of Solomon and even that of Zerubbabel were patterned after this Tabernacle. It is the ultimate house of God—a model for God's encounter with man and man's approach to God. It is a picture of man, who is a temple of the Holy Spirit. And it is a picture of the church, the temple of lively stones mortared together in love. Israel

---

[7] C. W. Slemming, *Made According to Pattern* (London: Marshall, Morgan and Scott, 1938) 56.

[8] Slemming, 43.

is called *"the church in the wilderness"* (Acts 7:38). It is reflective of the relationship Christ would have with His followers. The dealings of God with Israel are so parallel to His dealings with the church. Paul calls the church *"the Israel of God"* (Galatians 6:16). We are the wild olive branches that have been grafted into the tree (Romans 9:1-10; 11:1-17). The things that happened to Israel were written for our admonition (1 Corinthians 10:11).

Here in symbolism is God's plan and procedure to renew the broken relationship with man and to receive man back into His presence. The Tabernacle and its furniture are a road map back into a relationship with God. In the tabernacle, we have a mirror image of worship in heaven, frozen in time. We cannot understand worship without understanding the Tabernacle. And you cannot fully understand the New Testament without this foundation.

The Tabernacle of Moses (Exodus 25–40) is paralleled in the New Testament by Christ, the living tabernacle, and the church made up of lively stones (1 Peter 2:5). The Law (ch. 20) is paralleled by the Christ, the fullness of truth. The priesthood (28:29, 38) finds its fulfillment in Christ, the High Priest of heaven's tabernacle, and in the church as a community of priests. The five offerings (Leviticus 1–5) are fulfilled in Christ, the perfect Lamb, and in our response as living sacrifices. They provide the outline for the Book of Romans. The feasts of the Lord (ch. 23) are a prophetic calendar for the church. Christ is our Passover. Pentecost has come in the empowering of the Holy Spirit in and on the life of the church. The Feast of Tabernacles, the ingathering, is anticipated.

THE TABLETS

Jebel Musa is a mountain covered with bright-red granite cracked into layers as if by fire. At its peak is a thin layer of compact gray granite.[9] During the sojourn at Mount Sinai, Moses

---

[9] Strong, 90.

climbed that mountain and God gave Israel the tablets containing the Ten Commandments. This civil and moral code would govern their new nation. It was the basis of their new faith and their personal value system. This set of guidelines has been the foundation for values and moral government in the Western world for all of its civilized history and for much of the planet ever since Moses came down from that mountain.

WORSHIP AND WALK PRECEDE WARFARE

After the tabernacle and tablets were given, the Lord spoke to Moses saying, "Number the warriors" (see Numbers 1:3). The Tabernacle is representative of His presence and the tablets of His moral law. Supernatural power is essential if victory is to be obtained in *warfare*. So the Tabernacle and *worship* always come before *warfare*. And moral maturity is critical in spiritual warfare. So the tablets, symbolizing God's moral code, also precede spiritual warfare.

In the Tabernacle, we have the principles of *worship*. Here our relationship with God is renewed. Then in the tablets, we have *walk*—the personal practices of a godly life reflected in our behavior. Here is the Biblical pattern: Through worship and repentant prayer, our relationship with God is first restored. Then transformed behavior evidences that we have been in His presence, justified and regenerated, sanctified and edified, and consequently we "walk" differently. Finally, out of the energy of worship, walking in the Spirit, we engage effectively in *warfare*. People who walk in the Spirit have discovered the practical spiritual energy that allows them to experience victory. In both the Old Testament and New Testament, these three concepts—*worship*, *walk* and *warfare*—are an inseparable trio. Of these three, only prayer and worship can stand alone, but they rarely do! Effective spiritual victories (warfare) come out of worship and walk victories. And, the spiritual victory in the walk of an individual or church is traceable to prayer and worship.

Fundamentally, we don't have a spiritual warfare problem, we have a walk problem. And the reason we have a walk (or behavior) problem is that we have a prayer-and-worship problem. Prayerful worship is the fountainhead of spiritual victory in both walk and warfare. Worshiping people walk and behave in a godly and responsible manner, reflecting a commitment to righteousness. They love, not merely with their lips, but with their lives. They are people of light, energized by the Holy Spirit.

WHAT IS WORSHIP?

Worship comes from the old Anglo-Saxon word *worth-ship*. Worship, then, is more than a particular liturgy. It is more than any corporate or personal activity—including prayer and praise, singing and silence, teaching or preaching. Worship is a reflection of my value system. It is making God the center of my life, so that everything I do revolves around Him just as the Tabernacle was the center of activity in the wilderness. God is to be the center of worth in my life. With Him, I have everything; without Him, I have nothing. Worship is wealth. It is the richness that comes to my life from knowing and being loved by God. It is a life perspective.

I am transformed by worship. It is the gateway into the other world on top of this world. It is that place in which you recognize that the things that really matter are not material. They are the intangibles of life—love, joy and peace. So at the gate of the Tabernacle, we drop the tangible gifts we own. We have come upon another world. We have discovered something—no, Someone—of greater value. We give the sacrifice of our lives and consider it a small thing in order to lay hold of the Lamb slain from the foundation of the earth.

The mark of a reprobate is that he has spiritual encounters with God while his walk is unchanged! That was the case with

King Saul. The Spirit of the Lord came upon him. Indeed, the Spirit overcame him so that he prophesied with the prophets. But he remained unchanged in his character and his behavior (1 Samuel 19:17-24). Worship must change us.

WHY STUDY THE TABERNACLE OF MOSES?

There is an old saying that testifies to the relationship between the Testaments: "The New is in the Old concealed; and the Old is in the New revealed." When the New Testament writers penned their histories and letters, they referenced the Law, the Prophets, and the Wisdom Literature of the Old Testament. The New Testament is rooted in the Old Testament. It is hardly understood without it. Paul says to the Romans that the things *"written before were written for our learning"* (Romans 15:4, NKJV). In the first letter to Corinth, he calls the events of the Old Testament *"examples ... written for our admonition"* (10:6, 11). The Law and the Tabernacle, both given at the same time and on the same mountain, are a "schoolmaster" to bring us to Christ (Galatians 3:24). Jesus reminds us, *"Think not that I am come to destroy the law, or the prophets: I am not come to destroy, but to fulfill it"* (Matthew 5:17). The Old was a shadow of the things to come. It is in the New revealed.

The writer of Hebrews gives us great insight into the New Testament relevance of the Old Testament Tabernacle. *"The first tabernacle standing was a figure for the time then present"* (see 9:9). It was an *"example and shadow of heavenly things"* (8:5). More precisely, the Old Testament Tabernacle was a copy of the heavenly, unseen tabernacle (9:23). It was into this heavenly tabernacle, not the earthly copy, that Christ entered with His own blood (v. 24). The earthly tabernacle required the blood of purification (v. 23), but that only pointed to the means by which heaven's tabernacle would be opened so that sinful man could enjoy fellowship with God. As Paul said, *"First the natural, afterward that which is spiritual"* (see 1 Corinthians 15:46, 47). In Romans

1:20, Paul gave us another principle: "The invisible things ... are clearly seen, being understood by the things that are made." So in the Old Testament, symbols and ceremonies are the New Testament plan of redemption concealed.

Some people think the Tabernacle existed for only a few short years in Old Testament history. In fact, it may have been used for as many as 647 years, depending on how one reckons the years between the Exodus and the construction of the temple of Solomon. Let's note the years of Tabernacle usage:

- 40 years in the wilderness (including the year of construction)
- 25 years in Joshua's lifetime, from age 85 (the estimate of Josephus) until his death at 110 (Joshua 14:7, 10; 24:29)
- 450 years under the judges (Acts 13:20)
- 40 years under the ministry of Samuel (v. 20)
- 40 years under the reign of Saul (v. 21)
- 40 years under the reign of David (v. 22; 2 Samuel 5:4)
- 12 years under the early reign of Solomon until the construction of the Temple (1 Kings 6:37, 38).

There is some question as to whether or not the account of the Judges in Israelite history is chronological or a summary of overlapping periods. If time periods are not chronological, then the time that the Tabernacle was used would be less than the 647 years noted here. Conservatively, it was used for well over 400 years.[10]

Temple worship and construction were patterned on the earlier Tabernacle. Israel used essentially the same pattern of worship from its birth as a nation fresh out of Egypt to the time of Christ and the destruction of the Temple in A.D. 70. It is impossible to understand Israel or the Old Testament without understanding the Tabernacle. And, it is virtually impossible to fully understand worship without understanding the tabernacle.

---

[10] DeWitt, 20.

Image courtesy of Melvin Poe

CHAPTER TWO

HOW MANY TABERNACLES
WERE THERE?

Scripture records two earthly tabernacles and two earthly temples that have been both built and subsequently destroyed or dismantled. The first tabernacle was built by Moses. During the period in which the Tabernacle of Moses was being constructed, Israel had a temporary Tent of Meeting.

The second tabernacle was built by David and he sat it upon Mount Zion. It contained only the ark of the covenant, which was taken into captivity by the Philistines during the time of Eli (1 Samuel 4). When Israel took the ark out of the Most Holy Place, they violated 28 different laws.[11] And they lost the ark in the battle. But after seven months of plagues, the Philistines returned the ark to Israel with gifts on a cart pulled by milk cows (1 Samuel 6).

---

[11] David Blombren, *Restoring God's Glory* (Brandon, FL: Trumpet, 1985) 39.

At Beth Shemesh, the men of the city became curious and looked into the ark. Lifting mercy from the Law, they exposed themselves to the sentence of the Law on disobedience. The ark was a symbol of covenant. The tablets spelled out covenant values. And yet, who could keep the law? So God sustained the covenant by mercy. The mercy seat completed the covenant. It "covered" the demands of the law. Yet, the mercy seat without the law is meaningless. Grace is not mercy without the backdrop of righteous requirements. And the ark of the covenant without the mercy seat is incomplete. God's commandments do not tell the whole story of who He is—that's told only by His love. The two belong together.

When the moment of disobedience was over, some 50,070 men had died (v. 19). Like the Philistines, they now wanted the ark out of their territory. They sent men to Kirjath Jearim (7:1, 2) with the request that they come and retrieve the ark. For 20 years, the ark remained there with Eleazar, the son of Abinadad, serving as priest. The house of Abinadad was abundantly blessed during this season. The ark was never returned to Shiloh or to the Tabernacle of Moses (Psalm 78:60, 61; Jeremiah 7:12; 26:6). Rather, it was later brought to Jerusalem and placed in the special Tabernacle, which God allowed David to set up.

Upon entering the land after the conquest of Jericho under Joshua, the Tabernacle of Moses had been set up at Gilgal (Joshua 4:19). Speculation is that it remained there for five years or so while Israel waged war to conquer Canaan. The worship center was then established at Shiloh (18:1) and the Tabernacle of Moses was moved there. The Talmud indicates that the structure was altered there, replaced by a permanent stone structure, traces of which are still there. Some of the enclosures may have served as permanent structures for the priests.[12]

---

[12] James Strong, *The Tabernacle of Israel* (Grand Rapids: Kregel, 1987) 12.

After the judgment of God upon Shiloh years later, there is some indication that worship was relocated to Mizpeh under Samuel (1 Samuel 7:6) and may have been moved again (see 9:12; 10:3). That the Tabernacle of Moses survived is clear from its appearance at Nob (21:1-6). This is where David entered the Holy Place and ate the shewbread (Matthew 12:2-6; see also Mark 2:26). At Nob, due to Saul's jealous rage, 85 priests were slaughtered and the city was destroyed. From Nob, the Tabernacle of Moses was moved to Gibeon (1 Chronicles 16:39).

Whatever shape the Tabernacle had taken by that point is unclear. At least some of the furniture and utensils were there, and the priests lived there (1 Samuel 22:11). At the close of David's reign, Gibeon was the site of a high place that possessed at least some fragments of the original Tabernacle. Burnt offerings were offered there (1 Kings 3:4; 1 Chronicles 16:39; 21:29; 2 Chronicles 1:3-6). Gibeon is the last mention of the structure.[13] Much of the original material was burned, but the articles of furniture were not destroyed, being made of copper, silver, and gold. Some say the furniture of the Tabernacle of Moses was placed in storage and is preserved to this day.

When David became king, one of his first acts as the national leader of Israel was the recovery of the ark and the establishment of a worship center in Jerusalem called the tabernacle of David. His first attempt to recover the ark failed. He had gathered 30,000 men to bring the ark to Jerusalem—but he did not bring it home properly. He placed it on a cart (2 Samuel 6:1–3). The ark of God's Presence was never to be carried on a cart. It was to be borne on the shoulders of priestly men, then and now. Reaching the uneven surface of Nachon's threshing floor, Uzzah put forth his hand to steady the ark. Touching it, he dropped dead (vv. 6, 7). God had allowed the Philistines to

---

[13] Strong, 13.

put His ark on a cart. They were ignorant and unaware of His demands. They were not His covenant people and had not been taught to reverence and obey Him. They were not sanctified to bear His glory. For them, there was a lesser standard, but He would not allow His people to allocate His Glory to a cart. They had a higher standard to observe. So do we!

David was confused and angry with the abrupt manifestation of God's disapproval. The parade came to a dead stop. Uzzah was one of the sons of Abinadad. He had lived in the house with the ark. It may have become so familiar to him that he had lost respect for its significance. His lapse of reverence for God's presence was deadly. He touched it and died. So the dreaded ark was taken to the house of Obed-Edom (v. 10). But no death came there. Instead, he was blessed, favored of God. David recovered from the tragic death of Uzzah and approached the ark in the appropriate and reverent way, bringing it to Jerusalem (2 Samuel 6:12–19). After he properly retrieved the ark of the covenant, he placed it in a simple tent on Mount Zion. The city rejoiced. Burnt offerings and peace offerings were sacrificed by David when it was dedicated, but not regularly afterwards as had been the standard at the Tabernacle of Moses.

The blood sacrificial ceremonies were not a typical component of the worship at the tabernacle of David. After the installation of the ark of the covenant, David instead introduced the sacrifice of praise and the practice of singing and dancing unto the Lord. For the first time, priests and Levites both had access to the ark of the covenant. This brief period of worship was a foreshadowing of New Testament worship. Priests and Levites could now come directly to the mercy seat. This privilege existed only during the reign of David, and only at Mount Zion. This was a radical shift from the restrictive and ritualistic liturgy of the Tabernacle of Moses. And yet, the sacrifices of praise were not meant to replace the blood sacrifices, but to give them new meaning. The absence of the laver did not de-emphasize purity, but redirected it as inner purity (clean hands and a pure heart). The absence of the table with its shewbread was replaced by meditation on the Word. The absence of the lampstand was replaced by the concept of anointing. Prayer and personal communion with God stood in the place of incense.

David's arrangement was to have two high priests. One high priest presided over the blood sacrifices at the Tabernacle of Moses in Gibeon (1 Chronicles 16:37-40). Another high priest presided over the sacrifices of praise at the Tabernacle of David (2 Samuel 8:17) in Jerusalem. The Tabernacle of Moses and the Tabernacle of David coexisted until the time of the Temple of Solomon (1 Kings 8:4; 1 Chronicles 16:37-40; 21:29; 2 Chronicles 1:3-5; 5:5). The sacrifices of praise did not replace the meaning and symbolism found in the Tabernacle of Moses. They completed them. The worship at the Tabernacle of Moses was foundational for worship at the Tabernacle of David. The Tabernacle of Moses was a tutor for understanding the Tabernacle of David. The two stand together. One doesn't exist legitimately without the other. The former is anchored in the Old Testament and the latter is prophetic of the New Testament. And yet, the new is in the old, and the old is in the new.

When the Tabernacle of David was folded, the ark of the covenant was placed in the Temple of Solomon. It was the only original piece of furniture from the Tabernacle of Moses that was utilized in the Temple of Solomon. It had a place in the Tabernacle of Moses, then the Tabernacle of David, and finally the Temple of Solomon. It was the central-most important feature of all those structures. No other piece of furniture was so honored.

The history of the Tabernacle of Moses and our information about all the furnishings, with the exception of the ark of the covenant, end with the establishment of the Temple of Solomon. No reliable record of the disposition of the furniture or the component parts of the Tabernacle is available.

The Temple of Solomon stood until the Babylonian invasion in 586 B.C. when it was destroyed along with the city of Jerusalem. The tribe of Judah was carried into captivity. A restoration Temple was completed in approximately 516 B.C. That Temple, built by Zerubbabel, was the Temple that was enlarged and expanded by Herod the Great. This is the Temple that existed during the time of Christ. It was destroyed in the Roman invasion of Jerusalem in A.D. 70. The last mention of the ark in the Old Testament is in Jeremiah 3:14, 16. Around the time of the Babylonian Captivity, it disappears from the Biblical record.

There are a number of names for the tabernacle, which is first mentioned in Exodus 25:9. It is called the "tent of the congregation" (40:34, 35), not to be confused with its predecessor, the temporary "tent of meeting" (39:32, 40, NKJV). In 38:21, it is called the "tabernacle of testimony." That may be a reference to the ark of the testimony, which characterized the Tabernacle, being the premier article of furniture. It is also called the "tabernacle of witness" (Numbers 17:7, 8). It is called the "sanctuary" (Exodus 25:8). Besides "the tabernacle," it is sometimes called "the tabernacle of the congregation" (27:21; Leviticus 1:1; Numbers 1:1; Deuteronomy 31:14).

A REVELATION OF ECCLESIASTICAL RESTORATION

The physical Tabernacle of Moses is intended as a reflection of unseen spiritual realities, the principles that govern worship in heaven itself. It is a projection from another world into the realm of this natural world that allows us to see things supernatural. It is a special accommodation given by God in order for man to understand prayer and how we approach Him in worship. It is a revelation by God and of God. It is a road map into the presence of God! And it is a bridge built by God across the chasm of sin and death to allow us to be reconciled to the Creator and the Redeemer, and then to fellowship with Him. *"And let them make Me a sanctuary; that I may dwell among them"* (Exodus 25:8).

God instructs Moses to allow the people to create a tent so that He can dwell among them, His tent in the center of all their tents. This was the pattern of the ancient patriarch whose tent was raised with all the tents of his company around him. This special house would be the people's gift to God. Still, in the building of the tent for God, special instructions had to be heeded. There was a pattern they had to follow. Without this pattern, their efforts would be meaningless. *"According to all that I show you, that is, the pattern of the tabernacle and the pattern of all its furnishings, just so you shall make it."* (v. 9).

Note the phrase "according to the pattern." Here we learn that the tabernacle of Moses is a copy of another tabernacle, the one that is in heaven. Since man cannot see into heaven, God gives us a model in the tabernacle, a mirror image that reflects principles that govern heaven's worship. The writer of Hebrews declares, *"[Jesus is] a minister of the sanctuary, and of the true tabernacle, which the Lord pitched, and not man"* (8:2).

To which tabernacle is the writer of Hebrews referring? The Tabernacle of Moses or of David? The answer: neither! Here is the first tabernacle, *"the true tabernacle."* It is the tabernacle that "the Lord pitched, and not man." Moses and David both built tabernacles, but they were mortals. Yahweh also built a tabernacle. His tabernacle is the true tabernacle.

Hebrews declares that Jesus is the High Priest, not of the

earthly tabernacle, but of the heavenly *"true* tabernacle." He is a priest, not after the order of Aaron, but of Melchizedek. We have mentioned the existence of the Tabernacle of Moses and of David, the Temple of Solomon and of Zerubbabel. Of those four structures, only the Tabernacle of Moses is specifically commissioned by God with the details of construction so explicitly given. Although David, in 1 Chronicles 28:11, 12, was given instructions by the Spirit regarding the details of the Temple, the revelation regards permission to expand and establish new peripheral areas—the porch, the houses of the priests, the treasuries, upper chambers and inner parlors, which were around the place of the mercy seat. It was only permission to expand but not to alter the design. He was allowed to multiply the original pieces of furniture (vv. 11-19) of the Tabernacle to match the grander scale of the Temple, but they retained the configuration of the tabernacle.

Basically, the Temple is an expansion of the Tabernacle. But here we have the *true* tabernacle. This is the original after which the Tabernacle of Moses and the Temple of Solomon were patterned. God allowed Moses to see a pattern of worship in heaven, and the Tabernacle of Moses was designed as a mirror reflecting the principles that govern heavenly worship. As we come to understand this Tabernacle of Moses, we begin to understand how to respectfully come into God's presence in heavenly places.

> *For every high priest is appointed to offer both gifts and sacrifices. Therefore it is necessary that this One also have something to offer. For if He were on earth, He would not be a priest, since there are priests who offer the gifts according to the law; who serve the copy and shadow of the heavenly things, as Moses was divinely instructed when he was about to make the tabernacle. For He said, "See that you make all things according to the pattern shown you on the mountain* (Hebrews 8:3-5).

Note the phrase "the example and shadow of heavenly things." The priests on the earth offer natural gifts and sacrifices. They serve "the example." They minister in "the shadow." Jesus ministers in the "real" tabernacle. His sacrifice was more than symbolic; it had spiritual substance. The earthly priests serve to fulfill the Law. Jesus did not offer lambs according to the Law. They were shadows. He offered Himself and entered into the Most Holy Place in heaven! Christ's sacrifice fulfilled the demands of the Law. It finished guilt's terrible reign. The Tabernacle of Moses is really an *example* of the heavenly tabernacle. It is a *shadow* of heaven's tabernacle and the principles of worship in that heavenly place.

As a shadow of the true tabernacle, it is a model for imitation and illustration. It is designed to show us principles for coming into the presence of God! The *real* altar and laver are in heaven as John would see from Patmos. Along with the candlestick and the table, he saw the altar of incense and the ark of the covenant. These are spiritual realities only symbolized by the tabernacle of Moses. Only the tabernacle of Moses was built directly on this divine pattern.

Here in the wilderness with its burning sands, its thorny plants, its colorless surroundings is a bit of heaven on the earth. What a gift! And so it is with us. In our wilderness pilgrimage with its dry places, wasteland and barren promises, God gives us a heavenly tabernacle. He offers us a place of rest under His shadow. An hour here will give us a perspective from heaven. Here we are refreshed by His presence. *"Come in ... rest ... warm yourself by the fire ... refresh yourself at the laver ... taste the bread from the table ... be anointed with oil ...smell the fragrance of communion with God in the Holy Place ... see His glory."* It is the only thing that makes life in the desert bearable. Times of prayer refresh the soul. They borrow from heaven. They pull down the beauty and promise of another world.

This tabernacle of Moses is a special revelation of God, given to us through Moses to understand how to come into the presence of God. *"The Holy Spirit indicating this, that the way into the Holiest of All was not yet made manifest while the first tabernacle was still standing"* (Hebrews 9:8).

It was only after the tabernacle of Moses was folded that the ultimate understanding of what it meant came to us through the ministry of Christ. Actually, it was not until after His ascension that the true tabernacle in heaven was open to us. It had never been sanctified and could not be consecrated with the blood of bulls and goats. Thus, men could only come to the shadow, the tabernacle of Moses or the Temple, for worship. The gap between heaven and earth remained. But Christ established a new way into the holiest in heaven itself. We now can go into heaven's throne room.

The tabernacle of Moses "was a figure for the time then present" (v. 9). In this tabernacle, "both gifts and sacrifices" were offered. Yet, even the priest who offered these gifts could not clear his conscience by the rituals of Tabernacle worship. They "could not make him that did the service perfect, as pertaining to the conscience." But then God sent Christ. He was the High Priest of a perfect tabernacle not made with hands. He entered into heaven's tabernacle with His own blood, not with the blood of an earthly lamb. With His own blood, He sprinkled heaven's tabernacle and its furnishings. Now for the first time, heaven's tabernacle was opened to prayer and worship for man on the earth.

But Christ came as High Priest of the good things to come, with the greater and more perfect tabernacle not made with hands, that is, not of this creation. Not with the blood of goats and calves, but with His own blood He entered the Most Holy

Place once for all, having obtained eternal redemption. ....
And for this reason He is the Mediator of the new covenant,
by means of death, for the redemption of the transgressions
under the first covenant, that those who are called may re-
ceive the promise of the eternal inheritance. .... Then likewise
he (Moses) sprinkled with blood both the tabernacle and all
the vessels of the ministry. (vv. 11, 12, 15, 21).

In order to use the tabernacle of Moses, the structure, furniture and vessels had to be sanctified by blood. Only then could
the tabernacle be a temporary connection point between a
holy God and sinful men. *"Therefore it was necessary that the*
copies of the things in the heavens should be purified with
these, but the heavenly things themselves with better sacri-
fices than these. " (v. 23).

The redemption of the earthly tabernacle of Moses and its
furnishings by the blood of sacrifices was a prophetic type of
the redemptive power of Christ's blood. The heavenly tabernacle was also sanctified for our use, not with the blood of
bulls and goats, but by the blood of the Lamb, Christ. The
blood of Jesus streams from the cross to heaven's mercy seat,
right into the throne room itself. This trail of blood is a redemptive path. It is the blood of the perfect Lamb, spilled by the hands
of sinful man. In heaven's reception of this Lamb, this perfect
Man, all men have found a means of acceptance. He has bridged
the gap back to God. He has created a pathway to heaven. A
"Man" is now in heaven. A *"Man"* lives immortally in the presence of the eternal and holy God. His name is "Jesus." *"For Christ*
has not entered the holy places made with hands, which are cop-
ies of the true, but into heaven itself, now to appear in the pres-
ence of God for us." (v. 24).

The mention of the Kingdom by Jesus is not a reference to
heaven. He is not saying, "In order to go to heaven when you
die, you must be born again." Even though that is a true

statement, it is not His point here. Rather, He is saying, *"There is another world on top of this world. It is a world full of the power and the glory of God, of righteousness, peace and joy in the Holy Spirit"* (see Romans 14:17). When you are born again, another set of eyes open on the inside of you, and you begin to see the spiritual dimension—angels and demons, conviction and celebration, the glory of God. The world you cannot touch becomes as real to you as the tangible world in which you live. This is another dimension that one can move into and operate in only if God, by His Holy Spirit, quickens the dead spirit within to new life. This spiritual world is invisible to the natural, unregenerate man. No, the kingdom of God is not heaven.

What happens on the earth is a mere reflection of what is happening in the heavens. The rise and fall of nations is connected to the changing of the guards or princes in the middle heaven. The collapse of national walls are merely shadows the collapse of some spiritual wall in the heavens. And as the church enters into worship, it experiences not merely the presence of God on the earth, but somehow the church experiences heaven! And in that moment, the power of God is released into the earth, breaking the strongholds of the Enemy. Righteousness is showered on the repentant. Joy is dispensed to the despairing. Peace is passed out to the restless. The Kingdom—the reign of God—is established. Suddenly, we are over, not under. We are above, not beneath. We are ahead, not behind. We are up, not down. We are victorious, not depressed! It is heaven's energy that has been transmitted to the soul that makes these things so.

SEVEN TABERNACLE TRUTHS

The Old Testament is loaded with information on the Tabernacle. Given the way the subject has been ignored, one would think there are a few obscure and hard-to-locate passages and no more. More than 50 chapters are given to the details of the Tabernacle: its pattern, construction, and ministry function.

Exodus 25—40: almost half the book, is absorbed by the details of the construction of the Tabernacle. This is the story of the Exodus of Israel from Egypt and of their finding their true destination—the Tabernacle, representative of the presence of God. Their hope and home was not in a new location, but a new relationship.

Eighteen chapters in Leviticus are about various aspects of Tabernacle function. Numbers contains 13 chapters of Tabernacle data. Deuteronomy has two Tabernacle chapters. Many of the Psalms are tied to worship at the Tabernacle of David or the Temple. Four chapters in the Book of Hebrews provide a New Testament commentary on the Tabernacle. Images of the Tabernacle dance through the Book of the Revelation. The Book of Romans finds its outline in the five offerings of Leviticus 1-5.[14]

There are seven different areas of truth wrapped up in the tabernacle and the subsequent temple, all revealing aspects of God's revelation.

1. The Tabernacle and its history
2. The furnishings of the Tabernacle
3. The sacrifices and offerings
4. The priesthood
5. The feast days, the cycle of Israel's holy days
6. The history of the ark
7. The Tabernacle of David and the theme of restoration

We will focus our study only on the furnishings and the offerings (items 2 and 3).

MOSES AND JOHN—A SIMILAR VISION

The tabernacle of God in heaven, which Moses saw from Mount Sinai, John the Revelator also saw from the island of Patmos about 1,500 years later. This is significant, since it reflects

---

[14] C. W. Slemming, *Made According to Pattern* (London: Marshall, Morgan and Scott, 1938) 10.

a parallel perspective of heaven found in both Testaments. The Tabernacle is often viewed as the property of the Old Testament. The writer of Hebrews has challenged that notion, showing us the ministry of Christ in heaven's tabernacle after His ascension. And in the last vision of heaven recorded in Scripture, located in the last book of the New Testament and written just prior to the end of the first century, we catch a glimpse of heaven and another view of the Tabernacle. It is in use, prominent in heaven. *"Then the temple of God was opened in heaven ..."* (Revelation 11:19).

There is coming a time when heaven's tabernacle will be opened and visible from the earth. The inhabitants of the earth will see the world on top of this world. This heavenly temple is seen here as full of smoke—the effect of God's glory. The invisible was now visible. *"After these things I looked, and behold, the temple of the tabernacle of the testimony in heaven was opened. .... The temple was filled with smoke from the glory of God and from His power ..."* (15:5, 8).

At the end of the age is the declaration that heals the alienation of man from God that occurred at Eden. God will again "tabernacle" (dwell) with men. They will belong to Him; He will belong to them. Redemption's reconciliation will then be complete. It will break from the realm of the spiritual into the natural, from the intangible to the tangible. *"And I heard a loud voice from heaven saying, "Behold, the tabernacle of God is with men, and He will dwell with them, and they shall be His people. God Himself will be with them and be their God. "* (21:3).

What Moses saw, John also saw. The revelation insights rooted in the tabernacle are still relevant today.

THE BRAZEN ALTAR IN THE REVELATION

In his vision, the prophet Isaiah records the angel taking a coal off the altar in heaven and purging his lips (6:7). That fiery coal was so hot and pure that it had to be handled by tongs. This altar of fire in heaven is seen again in the Revelation, when an angel takes live coals off the altar of God's judgment and casts them into the earth:

> *Then another angel, having a golden censer, came and stood at the altar.... Then the angel took the censer, filled it with fire from the altar, and threw it to the earth. And there were noises, thunderings, lightnings, and an earthquake. (8:3, 5).*

There are two altars here. The angel stands at the golden altar. This would have been in the Holy Place, before the veil, before the ark of the covenant. The "fire of the altar" would have been from the brass altar. This is the altar of God's judgment upon sin, of His consuming righteousness, of His commitment to purity. Twice daily, the two altars came together. The fire that quenches sin is taken in the form of live coals and blended with sweet incense (prayer) at the golden altar. Incense demands fire. There is no sweetness without it. The smoke of the incense fills the Holy Place. This represents the prayers of the saints, the sweetness of their prayerful dependence upon God, and the purity of their repentance and redemption. In this climactic moment, God is taking the incense of prayer and releasing its power back into the earth.

The earth has rarely been touched with the fire of judgment from off this altar, but that day is coming. And when it comes, it will be as if the whole earth were standing at the foot of Sinai with the mountain on fire, hearing the blaring voice of the trumpet, smelling the smoke and feeling the mountain quake. This encounter with the awesome God is to remind the people of the earth with whom they are dealing. This final Judgment is a result of the prayer of the church— *"Thy kingdom come, thy will be done in earth, as it is in heaven!"* (Matthew 6:10).

Only those who have made peace with God at that heavenly altar, by the gracious saving work of Christ the Lamb, will be exempt from the fiery judgment of this altar.

THE LAVER IN THE REVELATION

Before the throne there was a sea of glass, like crystal. ... And I saw something like a sea of glass mingled with fire, and those who have the victory over the beast, over his image and over his mark and over the number of his name, standing on the sea of glass, having harps of God. (Revelation 4:6; 15:2).

Before God's throne is "a sea of glass." Notice the idea of reflective, translucent surface; mirror-like and mingled with fire. The highly reflective copper laver filled with water would have captured the image of the dancing flame on the altar, a fire kept away from the mercy flame on the altar, only a few feet away. Fire and water—both agents of purification—met at the altar. Here love bathed in fire and water. In the Revelation, we find an illusion to the laver. It is placed before God's throne just as the laver stood before the Holy and Most Holy Place where the mercy seat, His earthly throne, was located. The laver demanded self-examination and called for purity. Here, before the Holy Place around His throne, we stand in a sea of transparency. There is no place to hide. We are in a see-through environment. Everything is exposed; nothing can be hidden. The presence of God forces self-examination again. No impurity can stand in His presence.

We are back in the Garden, naked before Him. But this time, there is no need to hide beneath the fig leaves. So in the Revelation, the pure and victorious over sin stand on the image of the laver now transformed into a platform. Purity, made possible by the peace we make with God at the cross, is the surefootedness needed in standing before God's holy throne. Unlike the laver of the tabernacle, where ceaseless cleansing was needed, those who stand here will never again need the water of regeneration.

THE CANDLESTICK

> *Then I turned to see the voice that spoke with me. And having turned I saw seven golden lampstands, and in the midst of the seven lampstands One like the Son of Man, clothed with a garment down to the feet and girded about the chest with a golden band. .... The seven stars are the angels of the seven churches, and the seven lampstands which you saw are the seven churches* (1:12, 13, 20).

The candelabra is the church. He is in the midst of it. In truth, He is the central candle—the shaft. Out of His sides come the branches. It is not a thing; it is organic—alive, human and divine. The candlestick was a whole work. So the church is a whole, with Christ, the head, in the midst.

> *To the angel of the church of Ephesus write, 'These things says He who holds the seven stars in His right hand, who walks in the midst of the seven golden lampstands: .... Nevertheless I have this against you, that you have left your first love'* (2:1, 4).

He is the first love of the church! No work for Him can replace worship of Him. No enterprise in His name can replace entertaining His presence. A passion for the gospel's proclamation cannot replace the need for a passion for the Christ of the gospel. The shift from Him to the church, from Him to His work, from Him to His rewards and blessings is so slight and yet, so deadly.

> *Remember therefore from where you have fallen; repent and do the first works, or else I will come to you quickly and remove your lampstand from its place--unless you repent.* (2:5).

The first work of the disciples was to be with Him! The first work of every believer is prayer—not focused on acquisition or even the noble task of intercession, but on communion with Him for the sheer pleasure of His presence. The first duty of the believer is to love God with all our heart, soul and might—and out of the overflow of that love relationship, to love our neighbor. We are, as Jude said, to keep ourselves in the love of God (v. 21). Without this central love relationship, everything about our Christian faith becomes distorted.

The Ephesian church, unfortunately, was not ablaze with the Holy Spirit. The light had gone out. The fire of passionate love for Jesus no longer burned. Now, He threatened to remove even the candlestick itself. The point is clear: either we burn with the light of His glory or we lose our place as His agents in the earth. Christ, the Candle, will give birth to another fruit-bearing branch, but He will not have about Him dead branches. In the coming city of God, there will be no need of sun or moon, for *"the Lamb is its lamp"* (Revelation 21:23, NKJV).

THE TABLE

> Let us be glad and rejoice and give Him glory, for the marriage of the Lamb has come, and His wife has made herself ready ... Then He said to me, "Write: 'Blessed are those who are called to the marriage supper of the Lamb' " (19:7, 9).

Here is the marvelous image of the table, rich with eschatological meaning. It is the place of the family at heaven's own wedding feast, the Marriage Supper of the Lamb. This table unites the multicultural and diverse group called the Church. It is broken bread that symbolizes their fellowship and shared faith. Here is a meal with God. All of His children are home, safe! Here is celebration. The triumph of righteousness is certain. The Lamb has defeated His foe. The beleaguered and persecuted church has prevailed. Love has triumphed over hate, truth over untruth.

Light has conquered the darkness. Hope has defeated despair. Joy has triumphed over sadness. The song and the sound of joy have survived the nightmare of Lucifer's lunacy.

THE GOLDEN ALTAR

Then another angel, having a golden censer, came and stood at the altar. He was given much incense, that he should offer it ... (8:3).

Now we are again at the golden altar. We saw it earlier in connection with the brass altar. It is the golden altar in heaven upon which incense is burned, as it was upon the golden altar in the Tabernacle of Moses. Here, incense is a symbol of the prayers of the saints—sweet communion between the believer and the Father. Here is high praise. Here is the power of fellowship and prayer. Here we discover that when we prayerfully worship, God works.

How angels are involved in the administration of our prayers is a mystery. We do not pray to them, nor should we. But here, an angel is seen offering incense. Neither the Tabernacle on earth or in heaven was provided for angelic worship. They needed no blood for redemption, no water for sanctification. They needed no bread to sustain them or fire to illuminate them. They needed no redemptive bridge to allow them to reconnect with heaven. Our relationship with God is altogether different than that of the angels. The Tabernacle is for men, not angels. And yet, they appear to minister in it in behalf of God's purposes. The accumulated incense, however, is not a symbol of something angelic. It is a symbol of our prayers— our unanswered prayers. Heaven is about to "burn incense" big time. God is about to answer prayers to which He has said, "Yes, but not yet!" The angel is given much incense, a stored-up amount. And the power of that sealed fragrance is to be unlocked as it is mixed with the fire from the brass altar. The earth is about to experience the power of answered prayer!

THE ARK OF THE COVENANT

> *Then the temple of God was opened in heaven, and the ark of His covenant was seen in His temple. And there were lightnings, noises, thunderings, an earthquake, and great hail* (11:19).

Finally, we see in heaven the ark of the covenant. The mystery of what happened to the ark is not answered, but this is the original of which the earthly one was only a copy. This ark, unlike its earthly counterpart, was never captive or lost. This is not an ark made with hands, but the spiritual reality of which the earthly ark was only a shadow. The ark is His throne, the place of His Presence. It is designed to offer a revelation of His glory. It represents the "fullness of the Godhead bodily" revealed in Christ (Colossians 1:19; 2:9). From this place comes the voice of God.

Here in the Revelation, in John's final vision, in the last word we have from an apostle who walked with Christ, we discover in heaven what the writer of Hebrews called *"the true tabernacle, which the Lord pitched, and not man"* (Hebrews 8:2). It is not some ancient relic in heaven's museum preserved for us to see on a slow day. It is alive with fire and incense, fresh bread and oil, the presence of the resurrected Christ and the glory of God. It represents the very essence of heaven's worship. Long after the tabernacle of Moses has been folded, the principles it represented live on. The pattern given to us long ago in that tabernacle—a pathway for coming into His presence—is still valid.

The ark of the covenant, the golden altar and the table have unique features. They are the only pieces of furniture that have crowns. The crowns represent the kingly status bestowed upon us by God, in Christ. They represent the kingly and authoritative function of worship, prayer and the ministry of the Word. We are invited to a royal table. We are the royal sons and daughters of God, having been adopted into His family. We have the royal privilege of prayer. We have access to the royal court of heaven. Our prayers are heard by the King of the earth. We have the extraordinary pleasure of intimacy with God. And as a royal people, we have a royal covenant.

The hidden manna also shows up in Revelation 2:17, offered to the church that overcomes.

The Tabernacle in The New Testament

The New Testament is filled with terms we use rather generously, all finding their meaning in the Tabernacle. The terms include the following:

- *The veil*, rent on the day of Christ's crucifixion
- *The mercy seat*, found on the ark of the covenant, the Most Holy Place
- *Propitiation*, which references the mercy seat
- *Regeneration*, which finds its meaning in the laver—literally, "the laver of regeneration"
- *The Lamb of God*, who takes the sins of the world away
- *Washed*, in the blood of the Lamb
- *Cleansed*, by the washing of the water (the laver)
- *Reconciled*, a word rooted in the offerings
- *Sacrifice*, which is the heart of the ministry at the altar
- *Purged*, at the laver
- *Offering*, of the sacrifices
- *Atonement*, by the blood of the Lamb
- "Without the *shedding of blood* there is no remission."

These concepts, used so often, have their roots in the worship introduced at the Tabernacle. There is no understanding of the New Testament and these most basic terms without the tabernacle. It is the root system of our redemptive story. The Book of Exodus is loaded with word pictures of these deep and theologically rich concepts.[15]

---

[15] William Brown, *The Tabernacle—Its Priests and Its Services* (Peabody, MA: Hendrickson, 1996) 3.

Image courtesy of Melvin Poe

CHAPTER THREE

INTRODUCING THE TABERNACLE OF MOSES

The Tabernacle was constructed out of the proceeds of a freewill offering. God said to Moses, *"Speak to the children of Israel, that they bring Me an offering. From everyone who gives it willingly with his heart you shall take My offering"* (Exodus 25:2).

AN OFFERING

The offering is the high point of worship! God is present among us because of an offering—the offering of His own Son. And the continuity of His presence in our midst is facilitated by a giving people. A grudging spirit destroys true worship. Tight fists and closed hands don't receive blessings. Only when we come into divine presence, dropping the things of this world in order to load ourselves down with His *chabod* ("weighty glory") do we know true worship.

The offering that is to be taken is *"gold, and silver, and brass"* (v. 3). It is not our throwaways that please God. If we are to experience His best, we must give Him our best! The gold would be used for the furniture of the Holy Place and Most Holy Place. The walls would be covered in gold as well as the four pillars that held the veil. There would be no stranger's or alien's gold in this Tabernacle.[16] It was a gift to God from His newly ransomed bride, Israel. Silver would be used as foundation stones for the walls of the Holy and Most Holy Place and as caps for the 60 posts that would support the separating curtain surrounding the courtyard. Brass or copper was used for the furniture of the courtyard.

In addition, offerings of *"blue, and purple, and scarlet, and fine linen, and goats' hair, and rams' skins dyed red, and badgers' skins"* (vv. 4, 5) were accepted. This was a colorful offering. The various colored threads, probably wool, were woven into the fine linen. With these, the workmen created artful tapestries that were used decoratively. No one is certain of the ancient designs in the veil, the drawing with the visible ceilings of the Holy Place and Most Holy Place. The veil separating the Holy Place and the Most Holy Place, as well as the screen separating the Holy Place and courtyard, were fine-linen colorfully designed tapestries. The multicolored gate at the entrance was the same type of composition—colored threads woven into linen.

"Shittim wood" (v. 5), also called *acacia,* was used uncovered for the 60 posts of the courtyard. The five pillars of the Holy Place and four pillars of the Most Holy Place were also made of this wood and then overlaid. The wood was used in the construction of both altars, the table and the ark.

This is a diverse and practical offering. Additional materials

---

[16] John Ritchie, *The Tabernacle in the Wilderness* (Grand Rapids: Kregel, 1982) 14.

brought were "oil for the light" of the candlesticks, "spices for anointing oil" furnished by the people, sweet incense offered on the altar of incense, onyx stones for the shoulders of the high-priestly ephod, and the various stones to be set in the breastplate of the high priest (vv. 6, 7). *"And let them make Me a sanctuary, that I may dwell among them"* (v. 8).

The commandment regarding the offering was in verses 1-9, but the record of the offering is in 35:4-29. Here we gain more insight about this recorded offering.

> And Moses spoke to all the congregation of the children of Israel, saying, "This is the thing which the Lord commanded, saying: 'Take from among you an offering to the Lord. Whoever is of a willing heart, let him bring it as an offering to the Lord: gold, silver, and bronze... All who are gifted artisans among you shall come and make all that the Lord has commanded (vv. 4, 5, 10).

First, the materials were offered. Then, talented people were called to take the donated materials and create a work of art. God's dwelling place would not be cheap, nor would it be dull. It was meant to inspire worship. It was to be built by the pattern revealed, and yet with room for creativity. And yet, this was not a freelance design. Isn't that the way of God? He wants no robots. He allows for our imaginative inventiveness. Bezaleel would serve as the chief artisan. His name means "in the shadow of God."[17] He was a man filled with wisdom, understanding and knowledge. In addition to his nature skills and his training, he was filled with the Spirit (31:1-5; 35:30-35).

Money is never enough. Godly men, wise and skillfully

---

[17] W. S. Hottel, *Typical Truth in the Tabernacle* (Cleveland, OH: Union Gospel, 1943) 33.

trained men are needed for the task. And they almost never serve alone. God has a way of pairing men—Moses and Aaron; Joshua and Caleb; David and Jonathan; Jeshua and Zerubbabel; Ruth and Naomi; Peter and John; Paul and Silas; Barnabas and John Mark. Here, Bezaleel of the tribe of Judah was partnered with Aholiab of the tribe of Dan (31:6; 35:34, 35). Judah was the first tribe, the one that led the way in the march and camped nearest the gate. Dan was the last, bringing up the rear. God uses the first and the last.

Later, in the same chapter, the narrative continues. The whole camp was caught up in a spirit of resourcefulness and vision. Everyone wanted to give perhaps to be able to point to the purple thread and say, "I gave some of that!" or to imagine that their gold was now a part of the ark of the covenant. In giving, they became a part of the Tabernacle. They were invested. In New Testament terms, we are the tabernacle. We do not give mere things, but ourselves as a dwelling place of God. Notice the willingness of the people and their spirit of sacrificial giving (35:21-29):

- It is a **heart** thing, an inner stirring—"*every one whose heart stirred him up.*"
- It was a **voluntary** thing—"*every one whom his spirit made willing.*"
- The offering was **brought** not collected—"*They brought the Lord's offering to the work of the tabernacle of the congregation.*"
- It was an **individual** matter. Men and women each gave and then labored together—"*They came, both men and women, as many as were willing hearted.*"
- Their offerings were **personal**, not disposable things, not items from storage. These were personal gifts—"*bracelets, and earrings, and rings, and tablets, all jewels of gold: and every man that offered an offering of gold unto the Lord.*"
- Their offerings were **diverse** in nature—"*blue, and purple, and*

scarlet, and fine linen, and goats' hair, and red skins of rams, and badgers' skins, brought them."

- It was no longer **their stuff**; the Lord needed it. It belonged to Him—*"Every one... brought the Lord's offering."*
- They gave **themselves**, not merely their things—*"And all the women that were wise hearted did spin with their hands, and brought that which they had spun, both of blue, and of purple, and of scarlet, and of linen."*
- They contributed in a **passionate** way—"And all the women whose heart stirred them up in wisdom spun goats' hair."
- Rulers and leaders, those with more wealth and means, position and power gave, but they did not give everything—*"And the rulers brought onyx stones, and stones to be set, for the ephod, and for the breastplate; and spice, and oil for the light, and for the anointing oil, and for the sweet incense. The children of Israel brought a willing offering unto the Lord, every man and woman, whose heart made them willing to bring for all manner of work, which the Lord had commanded to be made by the hand of Moses."*

The whole camp was caught up in this spirit of sacrificial giving—to build a tabernacle for God. *"So they continued bringing to him freewill offerings every morning"* (36:3).

Every morning there was a new line, every morning a fresh pile of new items of gold, colorful threads, precious jewels. Many were laboring to bring fresh items. Not all of the offerings were ready-made and at hand. They feverishly released their work and wealth to make a place for God among them. So pervasive was the giving, so generous the contributions, that there was more than enough!

> Then all the craftsmen who were doing all the work of the sanctuary came, each from the work he was doing, and they spoke to Moses, saying, "The people bring much more than enough for the service of the work which the Lord commanded us to do (vv. 4, 5).

An incredible thing happened. They were told not to "make

any more work" for the sanctuary because Moses commanded the end of the offering! No more gifts would be received. There were some who came to give too late. Their gold would be their own. Their woolen and colorful threads could be woven into a garment for their own keeping, but they would forever know that their gifts were not a part of the Tabernacle. They had waited too late to give! Such gold diminished in value.

> So Moses gave a commandment, and they caused it to be proclaimed throughout the camp, saying, "Let neither man nor woman do any more work for the offering of the sanctuary." And the people were restrained from bringing, 7 for the material they had was sufficient for all the work to be done--indeed too much (36: 6, 7).

"Restrained from bringing!" The giving was not easily brought to an end. "Please take this," you might have heard one say. "This belonged to my father. I want it in the Tabernacle, please." But the command to cease the giving had come. And oh, what a spirit of giving. There had never been another offering like it. By this offering, the nation accommodated the presence of God among them. By the offering of Jesus, we have now received the greater gift of His presence dwelling in us. And the Father has said again, "It is enough!" To gain His presence, there is no need for a further offering than His precious blood. It is enough.

TYPES OF MATERIALS

Seven different types of materials were used in the Tabernacle (Exodus 25:3-7; 35:4-9). These materials, now in the possession of renegade slaves, had been gathered from the Egyptian taskmasters immediately prior to the Exodus. The children of Israel had asked of the Egyptians jewelry with precious stones, gold and silver, and fine clothing.

> And I will give this people favor in the sight of the Egyptians; and it shall be, when you go, that you shall not go

empty-handed. But every woman shall ask of her neighbor, namely, of her who dwells near her house, articles of silver, articles of gold, and clothing; and you shall put them on your sons and on your daughters. So you shall plunder the Egyptians (3:21, 22).

This payment was the reparation for centuries of slavery and ill-treatment under the Egyptians (36:3-7). And now it was to be given to God. Much had been squandered on the golden calf.

1. **Fabric.** Two kinds of fabric were used.

- *Fine linen.* This was linen (*shesh*) from Egypt. It was the finest pure-white linen.[18] From the tombs of the pharaohs, thanks to the dry climate of Egypt, we have some of the *shesh* linen of ancient Egypt preserved even today. The number of threads per square inch are 152 to the warp (lengthwise) and 71 to the woof (filling). The finest linen available today is about 86 threads per square inch. Each slender thread was composed of 360 distinct threads.[19] The linen used in the Tabernacle is of unequaled fineness. The typical word for unbleached linen was *bad* as distinguished from *shesh*. The Hebrew *shesh moshzar* means "white, twisted cloth."[20]

  Linen was used throughout the Tabernacle. The fence around the perimeter was made of linen. Multicolored fabric was used for the outer gate, the doorway into the Holy Place, the veil and the linen ceiling in both the Holy and Most Holy Place. The garments of the priests were made of linen with the colored woolen threads woven into it for texture and design. Only the white linen fence was left unadorned.[21]

---

[18] William Brown, *The Tabernacle—Its Priests and Its Services* (Peabody, MA: Hendrickson, 1996) 24.

[19] Eugene Muntz and Louisa J. Davis, *A Short Story History of Tapestry* (Whitefish, MT: Kessinger, 2006) 5-6. Quoted by Brown, 23.

[20] James Strong, *The Tabernacle of Israel* (Grand Rapids: Kregel, 1987) 21.

[21] C. W. Slemming, *Made According to Pattern* (London: Marshall, Morgan and Scott, 1938) 43.

- *Goat's hair.* The 11-section covering used over the Holy Place and the Most Holy Place was made of goat's hair. This fabric was laid on top of the multicolored fine linen and used both the ram-skins and outer covering. Therefore, it was not visible from inside or outside of the structure. It consisted of woven goat-hair fabric. Eastern goats are black.[22] So this covering was probably black, not white as often portrayed by illustrators. This was a common tent material used by the nomadic peoples in that area. When goat's hair is exposed to water, its fibers swell, becoming virtually waterproof. So, the goat's hair has a practical usefulness—additional protection for the holy structure and its contents from rain.

2. **Animal skins.** Two kinds of skins were used (26:14; 36:19).

- *Ram's skins.* This animal was used in sacrifice. The skins were taken from the male sheep and dyed red. They were symbols of blood and death. Everything in the Holy Place and Most Holy Place were then "under the blood!"

- *Badger's skins.* Various translations say "sealskins" (ASV), "sea cows" (NIV), "goatskins" (RSV) and "porpoise hides" (NEB).[23] We are not sure what animal was used here. Several varieties of badgers exist in various parts of the world. None are currently adapted to Egypt or the Sinai. The animal referred to here was probably a marine creature. Seals and porpoises were prevalent along the Nile and Mediterranean, hence the speculation. The purpose of this rugged covering was to protect the structure against the elements of sand and sun, wind and rain. The dugong is an aquatic mammal, simi-

---

[22] Paul Zehr, *God Dwells With His People* (Scottdale, PA: Herald, 1981) 74.

[23] Roy Lee DeWitt, *The History of the Tabernacle* (Chatham, IL: Revival Teaching, 1986) 38.

lar to our manatee. It is still used for shoe leather by the bedouins. This may be the material referred to.[24]

The same term was used for footwear. However, the reference is not to ugly and unadorned footwear for men, but fashionable footwear for women (see Ezekiel 16:9–15).[25] So, we are still uncertain as to what material was used, or what its appearance might have been like.

James Strong says that the articles of the Holy Place may have had furs as coverings to protect the gold finish.[26]

3. **Wood.** The only wood used was acacia, which came from the *shittah* tree. This tree has a pleasant scent. Some of its species have flowers from which nectar is drawn for perfume. Our English word acacia is a Greek derivative, which means *"thorn,"* probably in reference to the sharp, prickly features of some plants in the acacia species. The acacia is a member of the *leguminosan* or *mimosa* family. It is a fine-grain wood that darkens with age, and it is harder than oak. In the spring it is covered with round tufts of yellow blossom so much so that it is called "the yellow-haired acacia."[27] The Egyptians used this wood in the construction of the coffins for the pharaohs. The 450 species of plants in this family range in size from shrubs to trees 25 to 35 feet high.[28]

From this wood, 60 posts or pillars were constructed to support the linen fence surrounding the court of the Tabernacle. Strong says they were about 5 inches in diameter and were probably round, the same size from top to bottom.[29] The brazen altar was made from this wood and overlaid with brass. The table, the golden altar and

---

[24] www.hisemissary.com/tab2.html.
[25] Brown, 33.
[26] Strong, 26.
[27] Strong, 147.
[28] Zehr, 185.
[29] Strong, 17.

the ark were all made from this wood and overlaid with gold, as were the boards that comprised the walls of the Holy and Most Holy Place. The five pillars for the door to the Holy Place and the four pillars for the veil to the Most Holy Place were also made of this wood. Finally, the staves used for lifting and carrying all the pieces of furniture were made of this wood. Staves used to carry the brass altar and laver were overlaid with brass. All other staves were overlaid with gold.

4-6. ***Three auxiliary materials.*** Three materials were used in the Tabernacle, though they were not a part of the structure.

- *Oil.* This oil was made of the purest olive extract. It was utilized as fuel for the lampstand and for anointing (Exodus 25:6; 27:20; 30:22-33).

- *Spices.* These were utilized as fuel for the golden altar. The spices that were used included myrrh, an aromatic gum resin from the balsam bush that was so prevalent in Arabia and Africa. Only pure myrrh that flowed spontaneously from the bark was used. Cinnamon oil was also used, taken from the inner bark of the cinnamon tree. Calamus, another spice, came out of the root of sweet cane. Cassia came from a shrub similar in appearance to the cinnamon tree. The holy anointing oil was a combination of myrrh, cinnamon, calamus, cassia and olive oil (vv. 23-25). No estimate for the value of the spices can be found.

- *Stones.* Twelve different stones were utilized in the priestly garments:

And thou shalt make holy garments for Aaron thy brother for glory and beauty.... Make Aaron's garments to consecrate him, that he may minister unto me in the priest's office (28:2, 3).

Thou shalt take two onyx stones, and grave on them the names of the children of Israel: Six of their names on one stone, and the other six names of the rest on the other stone, according to their birth (vv. 9, 10).

And thou shalt put the two stones upon the shoulders of the ephod for stones of memorial unto the children of Israel: and Aaron shall bear their names before the Lord upon his two shoulders for a memorial (v. 12).

And thou shalt make the breastplate of judgment with cunning work; after the work of the ephod thou shalt make it; of gold, of blue, and of purple, and of scarlet, and of fine twined linen, shalt thou make it. Foursquare it shall be being doubled; a span shall be the length thereof, and a span shall be the breadth thereof. And thou shalt set in it settings of stones, even four rows of stones: the first row shall be a sardius, a topaz, and a carbuncle: this shall be the first row. And the second row shall be an emerald, a sapphire, and a diamond. And the third row a ligure, an agate, and an amethyst. And the fourth row a beryl, and an onyx, and a jasper: they shall be set in gold in their inclosings. And the stones shall be with the names of the children of Israel, twelve, according to their names, like the engravings of a signet; every one with his name shall they be according to the twelve tribes (vv. 15-21).

In the first row, the stone sardius represented Reuben (Genesis 29:32). It was a red stone. The topaz represented Simeon (v. 33), being pale greenish-yellow in color. Carbuncle represented Levi (v. 34) and was also reddish in color, a scarlet-like shade.

The second row contained an emerald representing Judah (v. 35). This was a bright-green color. Dan (30:6) was represented by a sapphire stone. The sapphire was a clear-blue color, almost as hard as a diamond. Naphtali (v. 8) was represented by the diamond.

The third row consisted of a ligure, a dull-red or cinnamon color with a yellow hew, representing Gad (v. 11). The agate stone represented Asher (v. 13). It was multicolored—white, reddish, greenish and yellow. Of the flint family, it was the cheapest of all the precious stones. Amethyst represented Issachar (v. 18). It was red and blue, creating a purple hew.

In the fourth row, beryl represented Zebulun (v. 20). There is some question about the identity of this stone. Some believe that this is chrysolite, thus it would be yellowish-green. Others suggest it was bluish-green. Joseph (v. 24) is represented as onyx, which was in a variety of colors. Jasper represents Benjamin (35:16-19). It is typically a gem of a bright-green color, although at least 15 varieties of jasper exist. The estimated value of the precious stones used is $175,000.[30]

Notice all of the colors—red, greenish-yellow, scarlet, bright green, blue, translucent, cinnabar, yellow, and purple.

7. **Metal.** Three metals were used in the construction of the Tabernacle.

---

[30] DeWitt, 40.

- *Gold.* It weighed 29 talents and 730 shekels (Exodus 38:24). A talent was 60 minas, and a mina was 50 shekels. Thus, a talent was 3,000 shekels.[31] There is incredible variation in both the calculation of the weight of gold and its value. Remember, coins were not minted until about the seventh century B.C. That would have standardized size and weight.[32] So how much gold is this, and what is it worth? The answer ranges from about 2,200 pounds of gold[33] to 1.65 tons.[34] One source suggests that each talent was 1,320,000 grains or 230 pounds troy.[35] At 29 talents, that is a whopping amount of gold. With today's gold price, the value would be well in excess of $20 million, perhaps three times that amount. Gold never tarnishes. It means "to shimmer." It is soft metal, too soft for instruments and weapons.

- *Silver.* It weighed 100 talents and 1,775 shekels (vv. 25-28). This equals about 7,550 pounds of silver. DeWitt says approximately 5 to 6 tons[36] of silver were used. Conservatively, the value of that silver on today's market would be in excess of a million dollars. The silver was conscripted.

Every male, regardless of status or economic means, was required to bring a half shekel of silver as a token of redemption.[37] The word means "pale," probably in reference to its silver-white appearance. It has always been

---

[31] David and Pat Alexander, *Eerdman's Handbook to the Bible* (Grand Rapids: Eerdmans, 1973) 108.

[32] Alexander, 108.

[33] www.sundayschoolresources.com/biblestoryactivities2.htm.

[34] Calculated at $500 per ounce. Today's value has soared to three times that price.

[35] Alexander, 108.

[36] DeWitt, 78.

[37] At a value of $12 per once, the silver in the Tabernacle would be worth over a million dollars.

highly valued as a metal, next to gold. It is harder than gold, and not as hard as copper, but still unsuitable for weapons.

- *Brass (our copper).* It weighed 70 talents and 2,400 shekels—3.3 tons (v. 29). The value today would be $66,528. Modern brass is an alloy and was unknown in ancient times. Most archaeologists and historians agree that the brass referred to here is our copper.[38] It may have been a mixture of copper and tin, widely used in ancient times, not a mixture of copper and zinc, which is classically understood as brass and was developed later.[39]

These are durable metals. The melting point of brass (our copper), which was used for the brazen altar and contained the fire of sacrifice, is 1,985 degrees Fahrenheit. The melting point of gold, out of which the candlesticks and the golden altar were made, is 1,949 degrees Fahrenheit.

VALUES

The estimated value of the fabric, animal skins and wood, excluding the auxiliary materials used in the Tabernacle, would total on today's market about $442,000. DeWitt estimated that the cost of the materials alone to replace the Tabernacle would be $16.5 million plus labor, skilled specialists and consultants.[40] His estimate is dated. The gold alone is now worth more than that amount. We estimate that the value of the materials alone would be in the range of $20-$25 million. Assume that the labor investment was at least equal to the materials, and the value escalates to between $40 million and $50 million. And that is probably a conservative estimate.

---

[38] DeWitt, 37.

[39] Theodore H. Epp, *Portraits of Christ in the Tabernacle* (Lincoln, NB: Back to the Bible, 1976) 72.

[40] DeWitt, 41.

AERIAL VIEW

The Tabernacle was in the center of the camp. Even in marches, the Tabernacle was central in the march. When Israel conquered Canaan, the Tabernacle was set up temporarily at Gilgal, the headquarters for Israel during the conquest era. Later, the Tabernacle was moved to Shiloh, the geographic center of the new nation. No other place was an acceptable location for sacrifice. Only at the Tabernacle could a lamb be slain to defer the penalty of sin. The Tabernacle was the central unifying symbol of God's presence for the tribes. Prayer and worship are still the unifying principles in the life of the church.

Each tribe had a designated camping location—east, west, north or south of the Tabernacle. So, daily life centered around God's Tent! An exact description of the encampment is found in Numbers 2. In summary

ENCAMPMENT OF THE TRIBES

- Judah, Issachar and Zebulun were to the east, a total of 186,400 men (vv. 3-9). These tribes camped under the banner of the lion.
- Reuben, Simeon and Gad were to the south, a total of 151,450 men (vv. 10-16). These tribes camped under the banner of the eagle.
- Ephraim, Manasseh and Benjamin were to the west, a total of 108,100 men (vv. 18-24). These tribes camped under the banner of the ox.
- Dan, Asher and Naphtali were to the north, a total of 157,600

men (vv. 25-31). These tribes camped under the banner of man.

The total number of men was 603,500, besides women and children, and the priestly community. The tribal population would have been in the range of two to three million.

Some believe that the camping arrangement itself—to the north and south, the east and the west—was in the form of a cross with the diagonal areas left open.[41] As we will see later, the cross is also seen in the arrangement of the furniture.

In the ancient Near East, every nomadic community had a sheikh, or ruler. Often, he was the head of an extended family along with servants. He always led the way when the community was in transition. When he found a suitable camp, he signified the place of his tent by planting his spear in the earth. That spear might have been 15 to 20 feet long. Servants responded by hastily erecting his tent, and then their own in a circle around the master's tent. The sheikh dwelt in the midst of his family. His decision to break camp and move on was indicated by the removal of his spear. As he drew it out of the ground and rode forth, it was a signal for all to follow.[42]

Israel was a community of slaves—a fatherless family whom God had adopted. He was their leader. Israel followed Him through the wilderness in dependence upon Him. Wherever His cloud stopped, the people erected His Tent. Then each tribe, and within it each family, pitched their tents in reference to the Tabernacle.

Our "tent" is always ordered by God's tent. When He moves, we move. When He sets up camp, we set up camp. We know our place in relationship to His place. When we lose our

---

[41] Kevin Conner, *The Tabernacle of Moses* (Portland: Bible, 1975) 12-3.
[42] Slemming, 16.

perspective of God, we become lost. To forget who He is leads to a loss of self-identity and direction. We attempt to get God to go with us throughout our journey. We need to learn to follow His cloud, to live under His glory. As the psalmist declared, "God is in the midst of her; she shall not be moved: God shall help her, and that right early" (46:5). Deuteronomy records, (23:14).

They were a pilgrim people, living in tents. And so are we. We must not sink our roots too deeply into this world. We live ready to move, eager to serve, anxious to follow, anticipating God's guidance. Israel was in the camp of the Lord. That is a military concept. They were the "armies of the Lord" under His leadership. The church is the "camp of the saints" (Revelation 20:9) under the command of Jesus (Hebrews 2:10; 2 Corinthians 10:3, 4). We, too, are soldiers (2 Timothy 2:3, 4; Ephesians 6:12).

Between the common people and the Tabernacle, the company of priests and Levites camped, along with their families. The Levites were the tribe from which Aaron descended. Aaron's line would be the priests. The Levites usually served for 25 years from the age of 20 onward (Numbers 8:24).[43] In the first numbering, there were 38,000-24,000 were workers, 6,000 officers and judges, 4,000 porters, and 4,000 musicians. They served in 24 courses of one-week duty.[44] In order to serve, they were to be cleansed and separated. It was not ordination or training that qualified them to serve the priestly community, it was purity and sanctification. They were to shave, wash themselves and put on clean clothes. Paul seems to pick up this idea when he says, *"Therefore, having these promises, beloved, let us cleanse ourselves from all filthiness*

---

[43] DeWitt, 78.
[44] Ritchie, 114.

of the flesh and spirit, perfecting holiness in the fear of God" (2 Corinthians 7:1).[45]

Beyond the priests and the Levites, the Merarites numbering 6,200 men camped to the north. The Gershonites numbering 7,000 camped to the west. The Kohathites numbering 8,600 camped to the south. The families of Moses and Aaron placed their tents to the east, nearest the gate (Numbers 1:47-54). The span of 30-50 years was first established (Numbers 4:3) for the census of Levi. It was lowered to 25 in 8:24, 25. At the beginning of Solomon's reign, they were again numbered from 30 upward, and then lowered to age 20 (1 Chronicles 23:24, 27). The age appears to be lowered or raised depending on the need.

W. G. Rhind says the tents of the common people were set back from the linen curtain a distance of 2,000 cubits, which would be the length of 10 NFL football fields—1,000 yards or 3,000 feet. This is the same distance Israel was commanded to keep from themselves and the ark when later crossing the Jordan[46] (Joshua 3:4). This was enough room to gather the 2 million around the Tabernacle for assembly. They would have needed 30 boxcars of food daily, along with 300 tank cars of water. Traveling 50 abreast, if that is imaginable, the procession would have stretched out for 40 miles.[47] Between Mount Sinai and the Promised Land, they would camp at some 30 different places.[48]

In transit, the order of the march varied according to Numbers 4:4-33; 10:14-28, 33, 34.

---

[45] W.G. Rhind, *The Tabernacle in the Wilderness: The Shadow of Heavenly Things* (London: Samuel Bagster and Sons, Paternoster Row, 1845) 11.

[46] David M. Levy, *The Tabernacle: Shadows of the Messiah* (Bellmawr, NJ: Friends of Israel Gospel Ministry, 1993) 19.

[47] Zehr, 137.

[48] Slemming, 19.

- The Cloud (God)
- The tribes of Judah, Issachar and Zebulun
- The Gershonites with two wagons carrying the curtains, coverings, hangings, gate and door
- The Merarites with four wagons carrying the boards, bars, pillars, sockets, court pillars, court sockets, pins and cords
- The tribes of Reuben, Simeon and Gad
- The Kohathites bearing the ark (God in the midst)
- The table of shewbread
- The candlestick
- The golden altar
- The brazen altar
- The laver (We do not know where the laver appeared in the march. It is not mentioned. It is logical to speculate that it followed the brazen altar, since it was located adjacent to the altar.)
- The tribes of Ephraim, Manasseh, Benjamin, Dan, Asher and Naphtali. [49]

The Gershonites packed and loaded the fabrics including curtains, coverings, hangings of the court, the gate and the door, but not the veil (4:25, 26). The Merarites disassembled the structural part of the Tabernacle including the boards, bars, pillars, silver and brass sockets, pins, and cords (vv. 31-33). The family of the Kohathites carried the sacred furniture including the ark. The ark was covered by the veil and then badgers's hides, with an outer covering of blue (vv. 5-15), perhaps symbolizing the glory of God.

The preparation and covering of the ark for transport was done by Aaron and his sons (vv. 5-15). It is thought that Aaron and his sons entered the Holy Place and removed the veil from its hooks, holding it in such a way that the veil remained between them and the ark. Then they walked westward, into the space of the Most Holy Place, and covered the ark with the

---

[49] Conner, 35.

veil. The veil symbolized the flesh of Christ. So the ark of glory was wrapped in the veil of flesh. What a picture of Christ! Additional coverings were packed.

The table of shewbread was covered with a blue cloth (glory). On it were places for the transit, dishes, spoons, bowls and covers, and also the bread. Over all this was a cloth of scarlet, a symbol of the blood, and then badgers' skins.

The candlestick came next, along with the golden altar, both of which were covered in blue and then in badgers' hides. The vessels of the Holy Place were packed in the same manner.

Finally, the brass altar was covered in purple, symbolizing royalty and the royal Lamb who would bring salvation. Packed along with it were the censers, fleshhooks, shovels and basins. All of these were then covered with badgers' hides.

Eleazar, the son of Aaron, was responsible for the lighting oil, anointing oil, incense and meal. During this time period, the wagons of the Egyptians were single-axle carts, not two-axle wagons as we might think. The term *agalah* means "a rolling thing." The silver sockets alone would have weighed 6 gross tons; all the metallic parts more than 9 tons.[50]

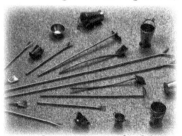

Image courtesy of Melvin Poe

It is difficult to imagine these carts alone carrying such a load. Strong suggests that each silver socket, weighing about 136 pounds, might have been carried between two men on a pole. The 60 posts each weighed about 50 pounds, the wall planks about 600 pounds, apart from the weight of the gold plating.[51]

---

[50] DeWitt, 78.
[51] Strong, 75, 76.

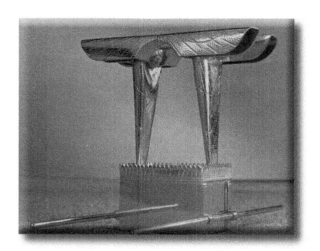

Images courtesy of Melvin Poe

CHAPTER FOUR

TAKING A TOUR
OF THE TABERNACLE

The Tabernacle was divided into three sections—the outer court, the Holy Place and the Most Holy Place.[52] Notice the states of light in each. The outer court used only natural light! The Holy Place had only the light of the lampstand. The Most Holy Place had the light of the glory of God—by the presence of God—who is Light. So it is, some dwell in the court and know only natural light. They have come to the altar of redemption, but have gone no further. They read the Bible, but it rarely makes sense to them. Their attempt to understand

---

[52] James Strong, *The Tabernacle of Israel in the Desert* (Grand Rapids: Baker, 1952) 8-9. The triple arrangement of a shrine within a shrine was a feature that Moses might have become familiar with from his exposure to the Egyptian temples. Beyond that, there is little information in rabbinical sources or other antiquities that helps us understand the Tabernacle. Additionally, the Egyptians used an ephod as the sacerdotal regalia of their priests. And the hieratic boat, typically stored in the *adytum* [meaning "secret entrance; often, 'do not enter'; the inner or secretive chamber; considered the place of oracles"] of the Temple and sketched on sculptures bearing processions by Egyptian priests looked similar to the ark.

and interpret it is by the standards of the world, by natural light. They do not understand the things of the Spirit. They are often bored with the spiritual. They are good, moral people, even religious. They consider themselves Christians, yet they try to understand spiritual things with natural reason. That is the level of light in the court.

Some have pressed into God and have gone beyond the natural light of the court. They have learned to listen to the Holy Spirit and experience the illumination of the Word by the Spirit. They understand at a deeper level the light of the Holy Place. They have experienced the light of the Spirit from the lampstand, illuminating the table and the bread. Inside are the beautiful colors, the dazzling gold and silver, the faces of cherubim. This place is so different from the blood and fire of the brass altar.

Still less have pressed further, from the Holy Place into the Most Holy Place, where they have had a life-altering encounter with God and His glory. There, God spoke with them, as He promised He would speak to Moses from the mercy seat. For these believers, there can never be any doubt that God is real.

The Holy Place is also called the sanctuary (Leviticus 4:6; Hebrews 8:2; 9:1, 2; 13:11). The Most Holy Place is popularly called the Holy of Holies, but never in the King James Version of Scripture. Most frequently, it is called the Most Holy Place (Exodus 26:33, 34; 1 Chronicles 6:49). It is also called the Holiest (Hebrews 9:3, 8; 10:19).

DIMENSIONS

The measurements are given in cubits. The outer court measured 50 cubits by 100 cubits. What is a cubit? Originally, it was the measurement from a man's elbow to the wrist.[53] James Strong, a Bible researcher and expositor, defines the cubit as

---

[53] Strong, *The Tabernacle of Israel* (Grand Rapids: Kregel, 1987) 118.

20.625 inches.[54] C. W. Slemming, in his classic book, *Made According to Pattern*, denotes a wooden Egyptian cubit as 20.625 inches, apparently agreeing with Strong.[55] Some scholars distinguish between a royal cubit of 20.6 inches and a common cubit of 16-18 inches. The royal Egyptian cubit, according to some, was 25 inches. A cubit in the Great Pyramid of Egypt is 25 inches.[56] In contrast, tombs in Palestine indicate an average cubit as 17.6 inches.[57] We will not debate which of these measurements is correct. For our purposes, we will calculate the cubit as 18 inches. This would make the dimensions of the Tabernacle 75 feet wide (the north-south measurement) and 150 feet long (the east-west measurement).

The main structure included the Holy and Most Holy Place. This single structure was 10 cubits wide and high and 30 cubits long (15 feet wide and high and 45 feet long). It sat in the western section of the court, beginning at the midpoint. From the west wall of the Most Holy Place to the western fence, there was a space of 20 cubits that stood open. The center of the eastern half of the courtyard would have been marked by the brazen altar. The center of the western half would be marked by the Most Holy Place—a perfect square. In the center of the Most Holy Place was the ark of the covenant. The eastern half of the Tabernacle emphasized preparation for His presence with the altar being central. The western half emphasized the encounter with His presence with the ark, the seat of His glory, being central. These correspond to one another. The sacrificial lamb on the altar invites and sustains the glory of God

[54] Strong, *The Tabernacle of Israel in the Desert*, 12.

[55] C. W. Slemming, *Made According to Pattern* (London: Marshall, Morgan and Scott, 1938) 23.

[56] Roy Lee DeWitt, *The History of the Tabernacle* (Chatham, IL: Revival Teaching, 1986) 42.

[57] "Cubit," *International Standard Bible Encyclopedia, Vol. II* (Grand Rapids: Eerdmans, 1939) 765.

over the ark. The blood unites them—altar and ark. Half of worship is preparation at the altar. Without proper preparation for an encounter with His presence, worship is not whole. It does not heal us. It leaves us broken and hollow.

THE FURNITURE

There were seven pieces of furniture used in the Tabernacle of Moses. Two were in the court, three were in the Holy Place, and two were in the Most Holy Place. The outer court contained the brass altar and the brass laver. The Holy Place contained the candlestick or lampstand, placed on the south side of the room. The table of shewbread was on the north side of the Holy Place, across from the lampstand. Immediately before the veil, centered at the western edge of the Holy Place was the golden altar of incense. In the Most Holy Place, we find the ark of the covenant with its cover, the mercy seat.

THE FENCE

The fence stood 5 cubits high (7.5 feet tall) and was made of fine linen, representing righteousness (Exodus 25—27). The outer court was surrounded by this linen curtain supported by

Image courtesy of Dr. Terry Harman
www.tabernacleman.com

60 pillars—20 to the north and south, 10 to the east and west (see 38:10-20). The pillars were set in movable foundations, or sockets of brass, which were anchored in the desert floor. The pillars were capped with silver!

Cords made of goat's hair, anchored to the posts by silver hooks and the ground by brass stakes or pins, steadied the posts (the same word, *yether*, is used elsewhere for tent pins. They were round and pointed with a head or notch to keep the cord from slipping off[58] (27:19). Rods of silver ran from pillar to pillar upon which the curtains were hung.

THE PASSAGES

There were three passageways in the Tabernacle. The first led from the camp to the courtyard. It was the only way in or out of the Tabernacle. The second was from the court area with the brass altar and laver into the east side of the Holy Place, at the midpoint of the enclosed Tabernacle area. The entrance to the Holy Place was 50 cubits (75 feet) from the entrance into the courtyard. The third passage was between the Holy Place and the Most Holy Place. It was called "the veil" because it hid the Most Holy Place, accessed only by the high priest on the Day of Atonement, from the daily activities in the Holy Place. It was 20 cubits (30 feet) from the doorway into the Holy Place and 70 cubits (105 feet) from the gate into the courtyard.

This is a fascinating idea. Unlike other gods, this enclosure shielded God from His people, not just to accomplish some scheme of mystery. The divide is along the line of man's sin and God's utter holiness. Were man, with his sin, to be exposed to the holiness of God, he would die. God created this protective barrier for man out of mercy. The fence shuts out sinful men, forcing their entry to the altar. These boundaries are to protect man.

OUTER COURT

The only entrance through the linen fence was the gate on the eastern side of the Tabernacle, facing the rising sun. It was

---

[58] Strong, *The Tabernacle of Israel*, 18. Strong says the pins or pegs took the shape of the sixth letter of the Hebrew alphabet, pronounced *vav*. The shape of the letter varies from a Y shape, a T or even a 7.

called "the gate," opening into the court (Exodus 27:16; 38:15). It is called the "door of the court" (35:17). The dimensions were 20 cubits wide. Four pillars supported a linen curtain embroidered with blue, purple and scarlet on a pure-white background (27:16; 38:18).

HOLY PLACE

We will refer to this entrance as the door into the Holy Place. The dimensions were 10 cubits wide and 10 cubits high. The square footage in material used for the door is the same as that for the gate—225 square feet, or 100 square cubits. However, the door was twice as narrow and twice as high as the gate. Things wide and low draw our focus to the earth. With things narrow and high, our gaze turns upward. Coming through the outer (Eastern) gate, entering the courtyard, and viewing the holy place, our vision is drawn heavenward. Leaving the tabernacle, the focus is again earthward. The gate curtain was hung on wooden pillars that were seven-and-a-half feet high. The doorway curtain was hung upon five golden pillars some 15 feet high.

MOST HOLY PLACE

This entrance into the Most Holy Place was called the veil. The dimensions were 10 cubits wide by 10 cubits high. It was hung upon four golden pillars.

THE COLORS (EXODUS 26:1)

Four colors are used in the Tabernacle. They are blue, purple, scarlet and white—all made of fine linen. This order is repeated at least 24 times in Exodus, and it never varies. Would this order be so repetitive and so consistent without meaning?[59]

---

[59] Henry Soltau, *The Tabernacle, the Priesthood, and the Offerings* (Grand Rapids: Kregel, 1972) 17.

The colors have a theological meaning. Blue is the color of heaven; purple is universally the color of royalty; scarlet is the color of redemption; linen (white) is a reminder of righteousness. The colors tell the story of redemption: The Creator God of heaven (blue) became flesh and was revealed in time as the King of kings (purple). Rejected of men, His blood (scarlet) was shed in crucifixion at Calvary that we might be clothed in His righteousness (white linen)!

The warp (lengthwise) of the linen was its foundation. The colors were woven into the weft of the material.[60]

The blue color would have been most likely drawn from a shell found in the Mediterranean—thin, flat and coiled. The animal living in the shell emits a beautiful color when crushed. The purple was from a larger spiral shell also found in the Mediterranean. The liquid from this shell creature turns a brilliant purple after it is exposed to air. The scarlet, or red color, came from a wingless female worm, a parasite that frequented the Tyrian oak. Its color is both brilliant and permanent.[61]

NUMEROLOGY OF THE TABERNACLE

No irregular multiples or fractions are used in the Tabernacle.

The number 12 is common to us—a dozen. But that is a relatively modern notion. The lunar cycle would have included 12 months, occasionally 13. But the number 12 seems to relate to the sons of Jacob, the number of the tribes. It is translated to the number of apostles. It takes on national and ecclesiastical associations. There were 12 cakes of shewbread on the table, and there were 12 stones in the breastplate of the high priest. The structure was composed of 48 upright boards, a multiple

---

[60] William Brown, The Tabernacle—Its Priests and Its Services (Peabody, MA: Hendrickson, 1996) 24.
[61] Strong, *The Tabernacle of Israel*, 22.

of 12. They sat on 96 foundations of silver. The number of pins for the 60 posts was 120, the same as the cords. Sixty caps were created for the 60 posts, along with 60 foundation pieces, the sockets of brass. Sixty rods of silver connected the 60 posts.

The number 10 is often connected to the fingers on the hands. Men counted with their fingers in multiples of 10. It became a number for measurement, addition and subtraction, order, organization and government. There were 10 commandments. The Tabernacle is built on multiples of 10 – 50 by 100 cubits. The structure is 10 cubits wide and high, 30 cubits deep. The Most Holy Place was a 10-cubit cube. The entrance was 20 cubits, two times 10. The total number of curtains was 10. The number of *taches* (clasps) was 50, connected to 100 blue loops. The gate was 20 cubits wide and 5 high. The curtain at the entrance to the Holy Place was 10 cubits high and 10 wide. The 60 posts and their accessories are multiples of 10.

The number 7 is less conspicuous. It is drawn from the number of days in the week of Creation and may reflect the Sabbath. It becomes the sacred number, indicating completion. The curtains were 28 cubits long, a multiple of 7. The candlestick had seven lamps. The number of silver sockets, the foundations for the walls, was a symbol of redemption. There were 98 of them, a multiple of 7. Seven times two 7's (14), equals 98 (7 x 14 = 98).

The number 5 is also found. Five bars are on each side of the Tabernacle, 15 altogether. There were five basic offerings (sacrifices). There were five posts at the opening of the Holy Place. The brass altar was 5 cubits square. The gate and fence were 5 cubits high.

The number 4 is found abundantly in the foursquare nature of the two altars, the four horns on both altars, the rectangular (four-sided) shape of the Tabernacle itself, the Holy Place and the Most Holy Place, the golden table and the ark. There are four pillars that support the hanging of the gate. Four pillars support the veil and stand on four silver foundations. There are four colors throughout—blue, purple, scarlet and white. There were four ingredients in both the incense and the anointing oil.

As Christians, it is easy for us to see the number 3 in connection with the Trinity. It may also reflect the terrestrial universe—land, sea and atmosphere; the elements—water, fire and air; the kingdom divisions of beast, bird, and fish; and, of course, man—body, soul and spirit. That number is noticed with the triple arrangement of the courtyard, the Holy Place and the Most Holy Place; the gate, the doorway to the Holy Place, and the veil; the three states of light—natural in the courtyard, the lampstand in the Holy Place, and the glory of God in the Most Holy Place. Three pieces of furniture are found in the Holy Place. Three objects are found in the ark. Three metals were used. Three liquids were used—blood, oil and water. Each post was copper in foundation, wood in body, with a silver crown. Each post was anchored by a brass stake, goat-hair cord and a silver hook.

The number 2 is found as well. It is revealed in the many contrasts—light and dark, day and night, above and beneath, heat and cold, morning and evening. The duplicate features show up in even numbers too numerous to mention. Beyond those even numbers, consider the two pieces of furniture in the courtyard, the ark in two pieces, and the two tablets. Two of the coverings were skin—badger and ram; two were cloth—goat's hair and linen. The ark, the table, the golden altar and the brass altar were all carried by two staves. Two silver trumpets were attached to the golden table. The bread on the table was in two stacks. The lampstand is thought of as having two vestments— one on each shoulder. Each day was marked by two burnt offerings, one in the morning and the other in the evening. There were two cherubim on the ark and woven into both sides of the fabric of the veil.[62]

APPLICATION OF TRUTH

The Tabernacle is a reflection in the natural of spiritual principles. The Tabernacle is God's accommodation to help us understand His revelation. It is a road map into His presence.

A CHRISTOLOGICAL INTERPRETATION

Much study of the Tabernacle focuses upon Christological interpretations. In the Tabernacle there is a picture of Jesus.

- Jesus, the Sacrifice—the brazen altar
- Jesus, the Sanctifier—the bronze laver
- Jesus, the Light of the World—the golden candlesticks
- Jesus, the Bread of Life—the table of shewbread
- Jesus, our Intercessor—the golden altar
- Jesus, the Covenant Maker—the ark of the covenant
- Jesus, the Covering of our sins—the mercy seat

Christologically, the gate is Jesus—"the way" of salvation. At the door to the Holy Place is Jesus—"the truth." Beyond the veil is Jesus—"the life." He is the way, then the truth, and finally the life, but only as we move more deeply into the relationship. The writer of Hebrews tells us that the rent veil is His flesh: *"Having therefore, brethren, boldness to enter into the holiest by the blood of Jesus, by a new and living way, which he hath consecrated for us, through the veil, that is to say, his flesh"* (10:19, 20).

---

[62] Strong, *The Tabernacle of Israel*, 117-9.

Here is Calvary in the Tabernacle. The only way into the Most Holy Place is through the Cross event, through identification with His torn flesh and His death. Then, in the Most Holy Place, we experience the power of His resurrection.

AN ECCLESIASTICAL INTERPRETATION

In our study, we will focus on the ecclesiastical implications of the Tabernacle, looking beyond the work of Christ as the Tabernacle of God. In this model, we can see the ministries of the church.

- *The altar*: the ministry of the blood sacrifice of Christ and the place of repentance, restitution, the forgiveness of sin, and the consecration of self
- *The laver:* water and cleansing by the Word of God. Here we meet Christ, the mirror, the standard of our lives.
- *The lampstand:* fruit, oil and fire—the ministry of the Spirit out of the office of Christ
- *The table of shewbread:* bread and nourishment, fellowship and feeding. This is the ministry of the Word at the Father's table.
- *The golden altar*: incense and fire, prayer and pure worship
- *The ark:* rod, manna, tablets—security in relationship
- *The mercy seat:* made of solid gold—the place of the glory of God

The direction in Scripture is always from the ark outward. That is God's direction toward us. The record begins in the Most Holy Place with the ark and proceeds to the Holy Place and on to the court. The direction is always from the presence of God outward to man. Good worship begins with God. The Tabernacle, then, is not an instrument of man's search for God. It is the revelation of God's accommodation to sinful men. God is the initiator. Watch the order:

- The Tabernacle proper is set up (Exodus 40:2).
- The ark of the covenant is set in the Most Holy Place (v. 3).

- The table and the candlestick are installed (v. 4).
- The golden altar is placed in the Holy Place (v. 5).
- The brass altar is set up (v. 6).
- The laver is installed (v. 7).
- The hangings of the court are set up (v. 8).

The order of revelation and even the construction of the Tabernacle are also from the Most Holy Place outward (revelation, or direction: 25:8—30:38; construction: 36:1—38:31). The direction is important. We did not establish this pathway. We could not find Him. He hides under our nose. But He will be known by those who will seek Him with all their heart. We begin with and end in the presence of God, represented by the ark of the covenant, and then we proceed eastward (outward)—through the Holy Place and into the court, and back into the world. Here we have a missionary God. We can find Him and know His presence because He has left us clues—a trail of furniture that leads into His secret place.

God takes the initiative in pursuing man. He is not hiding; He wants you and me to know Him. The furnishings are a path into His presence. By following these clues—the gate, the altar, the laver, the lampstand and the table, the golden altar, the veil, the ark and the mercy seat—we end up in His presence. In each article of furniture are embedded principles for finding and facilitating the presence of God in our lives and our world. The revelation of the Tabernacle is a road map given to us by God to find Him. He has pursued us, desiring fellowship with us. Man-ward, from the Most Holy Place outward, is the path of grace. God-ward, from the gate to the Most Holy Place, is the walk of faith.[63] In Christ, and the torn veil, He has left an open door.

He calls to us, just as He did to Adam in Genesis. There, God

---

[63] Kevin Conner, *The Tabernacle of Moses* (Portland: Bible, 1975) 15.

came walking in the cool of the day calling, *"Adam ... Adam ... Where are you?"* (See Genesis 3:8, 9). God knew where Adam was, but He wanted Adam to drop everything he was doing and move into His presence. In the same way, God breaks into our world. He comes in the night or at some point during our day. He calls us by name and He desires that we drop everything and move into His presence! He is pursuing us. Follow the clues—the furniture—and you end up in His presence!

CHAPTER FIVE

THE GATE

The Principle of Praise

W e will use three words to capture the essence of the believer's experience in the court: *praise* at the gate, the *presentation* of offerings at the brazen altar, and *purging* at the bronze laver!

THE DISCIPLINE OF PRAISE

At the gate, we engage in the discipline of praise (Psalm 95:2; 100:4; 107:22; 116:17; Isaiah 61:3; Jonah 2:9; Hebrews 13:15).[64] You recall, the tribes camped around the Tabernacle. Three tribes were on each side. Between the tribes and their camps were the camps of the priests. The tribe camping the closest to the gate was the tribe of Judah. The very term Judah means "praise." So, the tribe of praise camps nearest the gateway into His presence. Or to express it another way, if we

---

[64] Here we admittedly are layering principles from the Tabernacle of David onto the Tabernacle of Moses.

desire to enter into His presence, we have to pass by the territory of the tribe of praise!

PRAISE—A PREREQUISITE TO HIS PRESENCE

The Scriptures emphasize praise as a prerequisite to His presence. It changes our focus. Worship cannot be about us. Our greatest blessings are always attached to some deeper discovery, some greater awareness of who He is!

- "Let us come before his presence with thanksgiving, and make a joyful noise unto him with psalms" (Psalm 95:2).
- "Enter into his gates with thanksgiving, and into his courts with praise: be thankful unto him, and bless his name" (100:4).
- "Sacrifice the sacrifices of thanksgiving" (107:22).
- "Offer the sacrifice of thanksgiving" (116:17).
- "Let us offer the sacrifice of praise to God" (Hebrews 13:15).

PRAISE BREAKS THE SPIRIT OF DEPRESSION

"Give unto them the garment of praise for the spirit of heaviness... that He might be glorified" (Isaiah 61:3). The "spirit of heaviness" is a reference to depression. When we are depressed, we certainly do not feel like dressing up in the bright, colorful garments of praise. When we are depressed, we hardly feel like singing or rejoicing, praising or celebrating. That is precisely the problem that Scripture addresses here. My worship is not to be subordinate to my emotional state. My choice is to live under the weight of depression or to act my way out of emotional captivity by deliberate praise and worship. I choose to act out the victory of God rather than the present pain of my experience. I feel like weeping, but I defy my depression by rejoicing instead. My purposeful act of praise breaks off the "spirit" of depression. Praise is the step stool out of this dungeon of despair. Praise pierces the darkness and breaks open the dawn.

Depression is the low-energy side of the emotional cycle all of us experience. It is normal for all of us to feel down on occasion. The "blues" and "blahs" come and go. But here, more than normal depression is in view. Here, depression takes on a spiritual quality. When the "spirit" of depression grips our life, we are getting help from outside influences that seek to entrench us in a deep trough of despair. Praise—a deliberate act by which I choose to behave in a way that is counter to my emotional state— is required to break out of this cycle of depression.

Biblical worship nudges me toward a positive, faith-oriented perspective and produces positive behavior rooted in faith, not feelings. Living in a negative world, prayer and worship are the context wherein I adjust my emotional thermostat toward the optimistic. This is where I renew personal hope and receive personal help from God Himself. Pressure invites a self-focus; praise invites a divine focus.

Praise in worship is not an act of emotion, but of discipline. Sometimes I must sacrifice to praise. Something in or of me that is resisting worship must die! I may not feel like praising, but I sacrifice. I discipline myself to praise Him. God is always worthy of praise. My gift of worship must not be held hostage by my emotional state.

David asked, *"Why are you cast down, O my soul? And why are you disquieted within me?"* (Psalm 42:5). The soul is the mind, will and emotional part of man. David has lost his inner sense of quiet. There is a restlessness in his soul, a storm raging on the inside. The result? His soul was "cast down." That phrase is peculiar to the work of shepherds with sheep. David often watched over his father's flock. He knew sheep depended on a shepherd because they are not the most intelligent of animals. They leave their young; thus, the term *bum lambs.* They absentmindedly nibble themselves right off the edge of a cliff. They panic near gurgling brooks; hence the beauty of the term *still waters* in Psalm 23. Here David used the term cast down, meaning that the sheep is down and cannot get up. The cast-down condition occurs when the sheep overeat and become bloated, or when their wool becomes too heavy with water or dew and they cannot get back on their feet. When a sheep is cast down and cannot get up, they tend to panic. Fear grips them to the point that they may die on the spot of heart failure! Unless the shepherd gets to them fast and helps them up, he may suffer the loss of one of his fold.[65]

David confesses that there were times when his soul was cast down with fear. His thinking was paralyzed emotionally, without the energy to rise again; his will became immobilized; hope was lost with a storm raging in his head and heart; and he felt like he was going to die. What alternative do we have when we are cast down? *"Hope in God, for I shall yet praise Him For the help of His countenance"* (Psalm 42:5).

David's only alternative was to hope. By hoping, he regulated his thought life. He willed to hope. He willed to believe, even when faith wavered. He sang, even when he really wanted to weep. Hope was expressed in praise. Here is the regulation of his actions: Thinking changes; then actions change. Both change in defiance of his very real feelings.

This is not reactive praise based on some shallow emotional and superficial joy with fleeting feelings. This is decisive, proactive praise. This is deep and settled praise. This praise looks and longs expectantly "for the help of His countenance." Praise is the doorway into the presence of God. Praise brings us face-to-face with God. There is help and hope when I see His face. And it is praise that ushers me into His presence.

---

[65] P. Douglas Small, *The Perils of Sheep and Shepherds* (Largo, FL: Alive Ministries, 1996) 10.

Later, in verse 11, David uses the same phrase, but with a different conclusion: *"Why are you cast down, O my soul? And why are you disquieted within me? Hope in God; For I shall yet praise Him, The help of my countenance and my God. "*

In verse 5, David longed to see God's face. Here in verse 11, we see David's face. Hope and active praise have given "health" to his countenance. Earlier his face reflected depression—he was weeping (v. 9). Now his countenance is healthy; he is smiling. Why? He saw the face of God. As a result, his face is healed. Earlier, he saw his problems, his enemies. Now, in praise, he saw the solution—God, his Advocate and Victor!

PRAISE—BIBLICAL AND RESPONSIBLE ACTION

Worship is choosing to respond Biblically and responsibly despite the environment or circumstances. Somehow, we have come to accept an emotion-centered approach to worship that says, "If I do not feel like expressing worship to God, it is hypocritical to do it!" In no other area of life do we accept this philosophy. Because it is the responsible thing to do, we go to work, drive on the right side of the road (most of us), pay our bills, restrain ourselves from saying certain things at certain times to certain people—although we feel differently inside! We say, "I'm sorry" and "I forgive." Do we always feel like being nice? Or forgiving? No! God never said, "If you feel like it, forgive. Or, if you are having a good day, love your enemies! And in leap years, on nights when there is a full moon, bless them that persecute you, and do good to them that spitefully use you!"

In the natural, when are you going to feel like loving a drunk driver who takes the life of a loved one? Or forgiving a rapist who brutalized your wife? Or being kind to a trusted relative who forced you or your child into a life-scarring act of incest?

When will you feel like responding positively to someone who injures your reputation and appears to have no remorse? For any or all of these, an act of discipline is required. Our choice is to live in the grip of bitterness or be set free by the healing power of God's love. As I come into worship, I can remain under the worldly bondage of fear, anxiety, depression and more. Or, I can discipline myself to praise and experience a freeing encounter with Jesus Christ.

Sometimes our emotions have been taken captive by the hostile environment of our world. We live in a climate that is antagonistic to the spiritual world. Breathing the spiritually polluted air of this planet, taking in the fragrances of this world, we poison ourselves spiritually. We were not made to thrive in an atmosphere so choked by sin and self. Our emotions fail us. The only way to revive the soul is for the inner man to rise up and drink in heaven's air—the wind of the Holy Spirit. Praise invites the breath of God. And the breath of God renews us.

The problem is, most of us have been Spirit-energized but we have remained body-dominated! The flesh rules and controls us. Our flesh dominates our will, our mind and our emotions. We come into a worship context, but we are slaves to some fleshly dynamic. There is some area of our life still under the influence of sin's impact. We sing of redemption, but we have experienced it only in part. We have yet to be totally set free so that our mind is the mind of Christ, our desire is to do the will of God, and our emotions are being changed to reflect the joy and peace of God!

Our faith embraces the emotive and the cognitive, but it centers in the volitional—the will. Christians are people who are called to act, not merely react. They are not under the bondage of their emotions.

If I come to church happy and I rejoice, my worship may be

a mere expression of my emotional state. If I come to church depressed and I cry, again I am merely projecting in the worship context an expression of my current emotional condition. And, it is probably very healthy and often proper to express those emotions to God. But, ultimately, worship must not center on my emotional state, but upon who God is and what my appropriate response to Him should be, regardless of my emotional state.

THE FOCUS OF PRAISE

The character and content of the praise we offer God must also be reflective of who He is. Whatever my plight or circumstances, He is worthy of my praise, for He is God. Praise and worship is the experience of lifting up my eyes above the world and encountering God—seeing Him, the transcendent One! His name is...

- *Jehovah-Elohim*—the Eternal Creator
- *Jehovah-Elyon*—the Lord Most High
- *Jehovah-Hoseenu*—the Lord our Maker
- *Jehovah-Jireh*—the Lord our Provider
- *Jehovah-Mekaddishkem*—the Lord our Sanctifier
- *Jehovah-Nissi*—the Lord our Banner
- *Jehovah-Rohi*—the Lord our Shepherd
- *Jehovah-Rapha*—the Lord our Healer
- Jehovah-Sabaoth—the Lord of Hosts
- *Jehovah-Shalom*—the Lord our Peace
- *Jehovah-Shammah*— "The Lord Is There"
- *Jehovah-Tsidkenu*—the Lord our Righteousness.

He is worthy to be praised for who He is! Worship is seeing the exalted Lord of Glory! He is the unchangeable Yahweh—the only sure Anchor in a transient age. He is the Ancient of Days, who presided over the birth of the universe, yet sits outside the realm of time and space. He is the God of love and light. Some folks come to church Sunday after Sunday, yet they never see Him.

Elizabeth Barrett Browning says it so well:

> *Earth is crammed with heaven*
> *And every common bush is fire.*
> *But only he who sees takes off his shoes.*
> *The rest sit around and pluck blackberries,*
> *And dab their faces unaware.*

Isn't it strange that the same two people can share the same worship moment and draw different conclusions? One leaves bored, the other blessed. One says, "Powerful word!" The other, "Marvelous blackberries." One sees the fire on the bush, the other only the berries. One stands on holy ground, the other feels only the heat of the desert. Why? It is a matter of perspective.

He is all around us, but some rarely see Him!

PRAISE—FOR WHAT HE HAS DONE

It is helpful to remember God's mighty deeds by rehearsing history. He is...

- The Angel of Yahweh that cooled the furnace in Babylon
- The Beginning and the End, the Author of time and space
- The Creator, who has endowed us with life
- The Deliverer, who freed us from bondage
- Elijah's Source of power
- Fire of the burning bush
- Gideon's angelic Companion, who gives victory, and Haggai's "glory" upon the restored Temple
- The Intercessor of heaven's tabernacle, who ever lives to pray for us
- Jacob's Angel, who offers us a new name
- The Seed of King David, who will reign forever
- Light, breaking into our darkness, and Manna falling in our wilderness
- The newborn Babe in the manger, the origin of all life
- Purity and Power together
- The Quickener of dead
- The Resurrection, who keeps raising us from the dead
- Our Savior, the same yesterday, today and forever
- The timeless One, the Ancient of Days
- Unequaled and incomparable

- Wonderful Counselor, Mighty God
- The exceedingly glorious One
- Yahweh, the "I Am That I Am"
- Zion's Song, her Redeemer, her Light and her Joy.

PRAISE—FOR HIS SPECIFIC ACTS

Rehearse your personal spiritual history during a time of prayer. Thank God for His specific acts of kindness toward you! Thank Him for...

- Amazing grace
- Bountiful blessings
- Comfort in the Spirit
- Delightful daily encounters
- Encouraging promises in Scripture
- Food from His table
- Goodness
- Happiness that comes from His gift of fullness
- Inviting us to walk with Him
- Joy, and a light load that comes from a life set free from sin
- Kindness
- Love
- Ministries
- Nearness of His presence
- Open doors
- Privileges of salvation
- Quickening by the Spirit
- Rest in Him
- Sovereign designs
- Triumph through the crucified One
- Undergirding strength
- Valuing you
- Watching over you his excellence
- Youthful energy that allows old men to be renewed
- Zeal of the Holy Spirit

Praise Him for His hand in history. He is...

- Augustine's (insights)
- Booth's Salvation Army
- Calvin's certainty
- David Brainerd's prayer example
- Eusebius' insights
- Father Nash's reason for praying
- Graham's (Billy) reason for preaching
- Hus' motivation in martyrdom
- Isaac Newton's greatness
- John Wesley's energy
- Knox's courage
- Luther's mighty fortress
- Moody's passion
- Nightingale's caregiver
- Origen's teacher
- Polycarp's resolve
- Quakers' quietness
- Roger Williams' steadfastness
- Spurgeon's silver tongue
- Tyndale's looming light of liberation
- Unger's inspiration for the Bible handbook
- William Carey's missionary zeal
- Yonggi (David) Cho's drive for prayer and church growth
- Zwingli's simplicity

Image courtesy of www.tabernacleman.com

CHAPTER SIX

THE BRAZEN ALTAR

The Principle of Sacrifice

After entering the gate, the first stop on the journey westward toward an encounter with God is the brazen altar. We have often made the altar the climax event of evangelical worship, the last stop on our worship agenda. But, tabernacle worship gives priority to the brass altar. In many liturgical churches, repentance is the first action in worship. The altar is the only place where we can be prepared for worship. Here we are made ready for His presence. Pentecostal worship in earlier years began after a season of prayer in the prayer rooms. In many nations today, it is not uncommon for the people to enter the church and immediately find a place to kneel in prayer. Catholics are taught to never sit before going to their knees and focusing their eyes toward the cross. So much worship is shallow today because people do not stop at the altar, to pause there and prepare themselves for worship. And yet, symbolism is never enough. Nor is tradition, whether it is formal or informal. Genuine encounters at the altar, those that change hearts, are necessary.

PRESENTATION—AT THE ALTAR

> *You shall make an altar of acacia wood, five cubits long and five cubits wide--the altar shall be square--and its height shall be three cubits. You shall make its horns on its four corners; its horns shall be of one piece with it. And you shall overlay it with bronze. Also you shall make its pans to receive its ashes, and its shovels and its basins and its forks and its firepans; you shall make all its utensils of bronze. You shall make a grate for it, a network of bronze; and on the network you shall make four bronze rings at its four corners. You shall put it under the rim of the altar beneath, that the network may be midway up the altar. And you shall make poles for the altar, poles of acacia wood, and overlay them with bronze. The poles shall be put in the rings, and the poles shall be on the two sides of the altar to bear it. You shall make it hollow with boards; as it was shown you on the mountain, so shall they make it.* (Exodus 27:1-8).

The brass altar is called "an altar of shittim wood" in the text above. It is sometimes simply called "the altar" (29:36-44; Leviticus 1:5; 8:11), the "altar of the burnt offering" (Exodus 30:28; 31:9, 35:16; 38:1; 40:6) and the "altar that is by the door of the tabernacle" (Leviticus 1:5). It is identified as the brass or brazen altar (Exodus 38:30; 39:39) and the "altar of God" (Psalm 43:4). And it is called the "table of the Lord" (Malachi 1:7, 12), for in the peace or fellowship offering, the altar becomes a table. The offerer received back a portion of his sacrifice.

As you may have noticed, the tabernacle can be divided into two sections. The eastern section, 50 cubits square, contains the entry, the brass altar and the laver. The western section, also 50 cubits square, contains the Tabernacle structure with the Holy Place and Most Holy Place. The eastern half represents preparation for His presence. The western half represents our participation in His presence.

In the center of the court of the eastern half stands the altar. In the center of the western half is the Most Holy Place, and at its center is the ark of the covenant. One is a place of death, the other the essence of life. Blood ties the two together and water stands between them. As we approach the altar, God welcomes our access from the bloodstained mercy seat, over the ark of the covenant. The commitment of ourselves to God at the brass altar is somehow connected to the resources of His covenant at the golden ark and mercy seat. The two are bound together.

The altar, standing at the center of the court, dominates the eastern half of the sanctified ground. The centrality of this altar is purposeful. It demands reverent action. The altar symbolizes Calvary. There is no way into God's presence apart from the Cross. And no one should ever enter into the Holy Place without pausing at the altar to consider the blood of the slain Lamb on the altar.

I fondly remember the old Lutheran church of my grandparents. The doors of that church were painted a deep-red color, symbolizing the blood of the Lamb. We enter into His presence by the blood. Catholics kneel in the sight of the Cross and make the sign of the cross as they enter the church to participate in Mass. That is a reenactment of the principle of the altar. They dip into the holy water, a reminder of the laver. And yet, painted doors and symbolic actions cannot be a substitute for transforming encounters with the blood of the Lamb. Holy water cannot compensate for the sacrificial commitment to righteous living. The symbols are only symbols. Spiritual substance is required for spiritual transformation.

The altar was "to make reconciliation upon" (Leviticus 8:15). The Hebrew word for this altar is *mizbeach*, meaning "slaughter place."[66] Here, sin and sinner were consumed. Even the ashes of the sin offering were carried outside the camp. No residue of sin or sinner was allowed to remain inside the parameters of the linen partition. The altar represents the principle of sacrifice, which is foundational for worship that genuinely transforms. The altar today is too often one of convenience, not sacrifice.

Bring An Offering

The offering is a high point of any worship service. No one under the Old Testament economy was to come to God empty-handed. An offering was always commanded. The offering is a reflection of the Cross, of God's gift in Jesus to us. Our offering is our response to Him. It is not money that God is after—He is after our hearts. At every offering, we are to place ourselves and everything we have and are on the altar. There is a radical difference between giving to meet the needs of the church and giving as an act of total surrender to God. Our misunderstanding of the importance of offering as an act of worship and our characterization of it as a means of bill payment cheapens worship.

By His placement of the altar immediately in front of the gate, God makes it clear that sacrifice and offering are primary principles to be understood if we are to advance into His presence. God wants a giving people. And simultaneously, a people who have the humility to acknowledge their needy state.

Romans 12:1 has in view the burnt offering of the Old Testament: *"I beseech you therefore, brethren, by the mercies of God, that ye present your bodies a living sacrifice, holy, acceptable unto God, which is your reasonable service."* Dedication in

---

[66] C. W. Slemming, *Made According to Pattern* (London: Marshall, Morgan and Scott, 1938) 61.

Hebrew is *chaunkah*. It means "pressing in." It was used in the dedication of the Temple in 2 Chronicles 7:5. It is the idea of participation, of not standing back, of aggressively pressing into God—"I dedicate myself to You, God. I press into You. I want to know You." The Greek word is *egkainia*, meaning "renewal." Renewal comes by the personal action of pressing into God. "I am climbing on the altar. I am giving myself to You, God."

Consecration is from the Hebrew word *charam*, meaning "to devote, separate and set apart." It is also from the Hebrew *yad*, meaning "to fill the hand." The idea may be that consecration fills the hand of God with my yielded life, or that as I consecrate myself to God, He fills my hand, empowering my doing and my works, with tools and the means necessary to accomplish His purposes. Thus, true consecration is a life where I become a tool in God's hand and God puts tools in my hand. True consecration is evidenced by deeds that demonstrate my yielded devotion to God.

The Altar

As we come face-to-face with the altar, we realize it is too big to go around without noticing it. The altar was 5 cubits square by 3 cubits high (7.5 feet square by 4.5 feet high). It was massive—the largest piece of furniture in the Tabernacle.

It was made of wood, covered with brass (copper). Skeptics have argued that the metal would conduct the heat and the wood would be burned, given the temperature to which it was exposed. Tests have indicated that wood overlaid with copper and hermetically sealed is absolutely fireproof.[67] This altar was twice the size of the ark of the covenant. The ark could have been placed inside it, as could the table or the altar of incense. In a sense, every piece of furniture rises out of the altar. It gives birth to all the others.

The altar had four horns, one on each corner, pointing in

---

[67] Slemming, 63.

four directions.[68] Though the sacrifice was dead when it was placed on the altar, the sacrifice was tied to the horns (Psalm 118:27). Horns are typically symbols of power. Here, they appear to be symbols of God's wrath and judgment. Since the sacrifice was dead when it was placed on the altar, it was not the horns that held the sacrifice down; it was the sacrifice that restrained the horns. So we would say it is sacrifice and repentance of sin that hold back God's wrath.

Later in the Old Testament, these horns were the contact point for criminals. If one could lay hold of the horns of the altar, he would escape judgment (1 Kings 2:28). Criminal activity is understood as a life devoted to sin and self. At that lifestyle and unacceptable behavior, God has aimed His horns of wrath. But, if the criminal ran to the Tabernacle and

Image courtesy of Melvin Poe

laid hold of the horns of the altar, he was symbolizing repentance and the redirection of his life. He was committing himself to a lifestyle change reflecting righteousness. By laying hold of the horns of the altar, he was signaling a commitment to no longer live in sin or for himself, but to live according to the Law. His action was the binding of his life to the altar, as the lamb was bound to the altar. He would count himself as dead and live by higher principles from that time forth. So wrath was restrained and mercy was given. Genuine repentance and sacrificial commitment always restrain the wrath of God.

In a sense, this altar was a beast complete with horns. It was not an untamed creature, but a disciplined beast of righteousness. With horns pointing in diagonal directions, it was ready

---

[68] James Strong, *The Tabernacle of Israel* (Grand Rapids: Kregel, 1987) 24. Note: Strong sees the horns as an upright, tapered or triangular projection at each corner.

to execute the wrath of God upon sin and sinner—to destroy both. It guarded the Holy Place, God's house, like a vigilant watchdog. It was a terrible, fire-breathing, smoking beast of righteousness. No one with sin dared try to pass through the court blindly ignoring the righteous demands of this altar. The beast would slay them. When an animal was offered, the blood of the slain animal was placed on the horns of this altar (Exodus 29:12). It was a picture depicting the end of a battle. The slain sacrifice—whether it be bull, goat or lamb—lay at the foot of the altar with its blood on the horns of the altar, as

if God's beast of righteousness and this animal had met in God's courtyard and fought, and the altar had pre-

Image courtesy of Melvin Poe

vailed. Sin and sinner had died before this righteous beast. God's holiness will not be compromised. Their blood was on the altar's horns. Their bodies were at his feet. The altar is a reminder of the awesome and consuming holy nature of our holy God.

CONSTRUCTION OF THE ALTAR

A part of the altar construction was the grate—the *mikbar*, meaning "twisted or plaited." The term is unique to the altar.[69] Most scholars interpret this article as being inside the altar. It would then be a removable metal grate upon which the sacrifice was placed. Beneath the grate, the fire burned. There is reason for debate here. Several points need to be considered. In Exodus 27:4-7, the grate, or "twisted metalwork," was placed

---

[69] Slemming, 63.

under the compass, which was actually a band that surrounded the altar. Let's note two scriptures that describe this band:

> *You shall put it under the rim of the altar beneath, that the network may be midway up the altar.* (v. 5). *And he made a grate of bronze network for the altar, under its rim, midway from the bottom.* (38:4).

This band (or compass) was on the outside of the altar, "to the midst" (middle), indicating that it was halfway, midway, down the side of the altar. It may have been a shelf-like structure on which items were stored. Or it may have been a walkway where 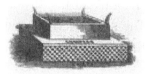 the priests stood for better access to the altar. The metal network, or grate of brass, was below this compass, to the middle of the altar. The metal network was then not inside the altar, but outside. Further, the rings into which the staves were inserted for transportation were attached not to the altar itself, but to the twisted metalwork (again indicating that it was outside).

These two facts lead us to believe that the twisted metal network was not a grill-like structure designed to hold the sacrificial animal roasting over the fire, but a protective metalwork for the outside of the altar. It may have been designed to protect the hermetic seal of the altar from live animals brought near the altar.

Exodus 27:8 indicates that the altar was hollow—*"You shall make it hollow with boards; as it was shown you on the mountain, so shall they make it"*—which may mean a hollow space between the exterior and interior walls of the altar structure itself. Or, it may mean that there was nothing structural on the inside of the four walls of the altar—no grate. We would then understand the twisted metal network to be exterior to the altar. But that also presents a problem. What would an offering be placed on?[70]

---

[70] Slemming, 63.

> *An altar of earth you shall make for Me, and you shall sac-*
> *rifice on it your burnt offerings and your peace offerings,*
> *your sheep and your oxen. In every place where I record*
> *My name I will come to you, and I will bless you. 25 And if*
> *you make Me an altar of stone, you shall not build it of hewn*
> *stone; for if you use your tool on it, you have profaned it. 26*
> *Nor shall you go up by steps to My altar, that your naked-*
> *ness may not be exposed on it. (Exodus 20:24-26)*

Here God explicitly demands that the altar be earthen in construction. Sacrifices were offered on a pile of uncut stones. Is the brazen altar an exception to this earlier command? Or could the altar be both brass and earthen? A recent archaeological discovery may provide insight. It appears the very altar constructed by Joshua has been discovered by archaeologist Adam Zertal. This is the altar built upon Mount Ebal. From the summit of Ebal, the snows of Mount Hermon to the north, the mountains of Gilead to the east, the hills of Jerusalem to the south, and the Mediterranean Sea to the west can be seen. Here is a panoramic view of the land to be conquered. This is where Joshua built an altar upon entrance to the Land of Promise (Joshua 8:30-31).

Archaeologists first assumed that the "filling" inside the altar was rubble collected from the centuries past and was essentially debris. Upon excavation and examination, they concluded the filling to be deliberate layers of material placed inside the altar at the time of construction. The filling consisted of ash and stones, earth, shards and bones. No bones of horses, donkeys, pigs, dogs or cats were found. The analysis of the bones by the Hebrew University indicated the 4,000-or-so bones discovered were primarily those of sheep and goats, acceptable sacrificial animals. The filling has been dated as belonging to the period of the Exodus. The filling is an important clue to us. It was actually a part of the structure. The structure of the altar is similar to the restoration

Temple altar described in the Mishnah. If this altar was built by Joshua, we believe it would have been patterned after the brazen altar. Since it was "filled" as it was, the indication is that the brazen altar also must have had an earth-and-stone filling upon which the sacrifice was placed and not a metal grate.[71]

The grate then would have been a protective metal network outside the brass altar, designed to assure that the copper seal was not punctured or damaged as multiple priests accessed the altar in the sacrificial ministry. The inside of the altar would have been filled with earth and natural, uncut stone each time the Tabernacle was again reassembled. The altar would have been a box, designed to contain the fire burning on a bed of uncut stones inside.

The band (or compass) would have been a ledge around the altar that allowed access by the priest to the topside of the altar. Some illustrative drawings depict this ledge as accessed by an earthen ramp. Exodus 20:26 specifically forbids steps leading to a raised altar. Others illustrate the ledge as being attached to the side of the brass altar itself. The ledge and the band must have been one in the same. We do note in Leviticus 9:22 an expression describing Aaron as coming down from the altar. The priest wore a pant-like undergarment beneath his linen robe. He was to attend the altar in a way that guaranteed modesty. That principle, true then, it is true now.

Rings were attached to the four corners of the protective metal network for the purpose of transport. Wooden bars overlaid with brass were inserted into the rings, and the altar was borne by men.

Sacred Areas

Around the altar, two areas were set apart and declared holy. The first was the area around the gate, east of the altar,

---

[71] Milt Machlin, *"Joshua and the Archaeologist," Reader's Digest*, Sept. 1990: 135f.

where hands were laid on the sacrifice and where the peace offering was slaughtered (Leviticus 3:2, 8, 13; Numbers 6:18). The wave offering was also executed here (Leviticus 7:29, 30; 14:11, 12, 23, 24; Numbers 5:16-25; 6:10-20; 8:9-13). A second special place was on the north side of the altar area, near the linen curtain, where flaying tables were set up to facilitate the actual sacrifice. Animals were skinned and prepared for the altar here. In some cases the slaughter of the animal took place here (Leviticus 1:11; 7:2).

The role of the priest was to catch the sacred blood (1:5). They then flayed and meticulously divided the animal (v. 6). The next step was to prepare the altar by stirring the fire and adding wood (v. 7). They washed the sacrificial parts that were to be placed on the altar, and then laid the parts of the animal on the fire as a sacrifice (v. 9). The final act was to put on different attire (6:10) and carry the ashes outside the camp and put them in a clean place (v. 11).[72]

Garments of the priest were also purified after being contaminated by the blood of a sin offering (v. 27). Ashes that were eventually removed from the Tabernacle were placed temporarily on the north side of the altar (vv. 10, 11). Additional utensils were the copper pans, used for ashes (Exodus 27:3); the shovels, used for tending the fire and removing the ashes to place in the pans; the basins, used to hold the blood of the sacrificial animals; the fleshhooks, used for the arranging of the sacrifice on the altar; the firepans, called censers, used to transport or hold live coals.[73]

A HOLY BLOCKADE

In one sense, the altar was really a blockade. Its invisible sign read: "Holy, authorized, sinless people only beyond this

---

[72] David M. Levy, *The Tabernacle: Shadows of the Messiah* (Bellmawr, NJ: Friends of Israel Gospel Ministry, 1993) 114-5.

[73] William Brown, *The Tabernacle—Its Priests and Its Services* (Peabody, MA: Hendrickson, 1996) 50.

point!" It is a reminder that sin separates mankind from God! Imagine that you are standing in the court of the Tabernacle. You can see the priest part the curtain entering or exiting the Holy Place. You say to yourself, "I think I see the lampstand. I see the golden altar. I see the veil, the entrance into the Most Holy Place, the very presence of God." You may gain a glimpse, but you know you can never go there! You can only return to this brazen altar. And, you will have to do it again and again. You will never go further. You are a victim of sin, inherently; and, of your own sin, specifically.

Now, in the marvel of God's grace revealed in the New Testament, the blockade is removed. As you approach the altar, in the polished brass you see a reflection of the problem—you. Then, on the brass altar you see a solution—a Lamb. The sign warning you from passing beyond the altar is now gone. Following the trail of bloody footprints, you are led through the doorway into the Holy Place, past the candlesticks and the table, beyond the altar of incense and through the freshly torn veil. Then, in the Most Holy Place, you discover that the slain Lamb lives. Transformed into the Lion of the tribe of Judah, He breaks the yoke of the curse and looses upon us the power of regeneration.

THE PRINCIPLE OF SACRIFICE

Under the Old Testament requirements, my sin would require me to bring to the altar a sin or trespass offering appropriately, one without spot or blemish. I would meet the priest at the door of the Tabernacle, lay my hand upon the head of the sacrifice, confess my sin to the priest and then I would slay the lamb. Note carefully, I—not the priest—would execute the lamb, taking its life away. The Hebrew verb that indicates the laying of the hand on the lamb means more than merely "touching." It means *"to lean heavily upon"* the victim. Psalm

88:7 says, *"Your wrath lies heavy upon me,."*[74]

Here we learn a New Testament principle: *"The wages of sin is death"* (Romans 6:23). Sin weighs heavily on us. Because we are so accustomed to viewing the lamb in a Christological sense, we miss something here. The Old Testament worshiper did not know that the lamb was Christ. He saw the lamb as a substitution for himself. He had sinned and should die, but the lamb was dying in his place! This act of substitution reaches forward to Christ, but to understand it more clearly, we must see that it reaches all the way back to the Garden of Eden.

THE PRICE OF SIN

Let's go back to that Garden for a moment. God had commanded: *"But of the tree of the knowledge of good and evil you shall not eat, for in the day that you eat of it you shall surely die,"* (Genesis 2:17). In 3:6 we read: *"And when the woman saw that the... food ... was pleasant to the eyes, and . . . to be desired... she took... and did eat, and gave also unto her husband with her; and he did eat."*

God had said, *"In the day you eat ... you shall die."* They ate. They should have died! But, they didn't! Ah, yes, we often say, "They died spiritually." Wait! Is that what God had said—"In the day you eat, you will die spiritually?"

I believe that God meant exactly this: "In the literal 24-hour day that you eat of the fruit of this forbidden Tree in an act of disobedience, you will die—spiritually, cognitively, volitionally, emotionally, and physically! Within 24 hours after you sin, you will curl up into a heap on the ground and you will experience death in all of its dimensions. Your eyes will not see. Your ears will not hear. Your mouth will not taste. Your tongue will not speak. Your nose will not smell. Your mind will not think. Your heart will not beat. Your lungs will not breathe. Your feet

---

[74] S. H. Kellogg, *Studies in Leviticus* (Grand Rapids: Kregel, 1988) 53.

will not walk. Your hands will not touch. You will be dead!"

God was warning Adam and Eve, "Sin is so poisonous, so toxic, so destructive, that the day you sin, all your systems will shut down and you will die!" Nothing on the planet is more deadly than sin. Again we insist, they didn't die. Why? Implied in Genesis 3:21 is the introduction of the concept and practice of sacrifice: "*Unto Adam also and to his wife did the Lord God make coats of skins, and clothed them.*"

Only in the burnt offering were the skins given back to the people. That alone suggests that the sacrifice in Eden was a burnt offering. That offering was not an offering by Adam—that would have necessitated an offering for sin. Rather, this was an offering by the Father, in behalf of Adam, as a prophetic type of the last Adam, Jesus Christ, who would reverse the Curse and take away all sin. In a remarkable parallel, the seamless robe of Christ is taken from Him and given to a sinful, gambling Roman soldier. He would wrap himself in the covering of Christ, as Adam and Eve had been wrapped in the covering of sacrificial animal skins. Christ had no need to offer to the Father a sin offering for Himself. He was without sin. His perfect life, His sinless state, allowed Him to skip the sin and trespass offering and give Himself as a burnt offering, an act of selfless, total surrender. That burnt offering was counted for us as a sin offering—and it covered us! And it did what no sin offering before could do—it cleansed us as well.

THE ILLUSION CREATED BY MERCY

In an act of mercy, God suspended the sentence of physical death over Adam and Eve and covered their sins. He slew an animal, deflecting man's deserved judgment onto an innocent victim. For the first time, man saw something die. And he witnessed the consequences of his sin. He saw a living creature cease to live, to breathe, to move; one he had been given responsibility for, one he named. He saw blood. The innocent world had been invaded by the ultimate disease—sin. And sin had claimed its first victim. It all happened so quickly. The day they ate, death came. Man was spared physical death, but he was not totally exempted. God suspended judgment over him! Man would live under the potential of death, in bondage to sin. Certainty now gave way to uncertainty. Man was always one step, one breath, one heartbeat away from the effect of sin—death. All mankind continued under that anvil of judgment, until the perfect Lamb rescued us from judgment and placed us under the grace of God. As Christians, the time of death is still uncertain, but the doorway through which death will take us is certain.

At the Cross, the last Adam, Jesus, became sin *"who knew no sin; that we might be made the righteousness of God in Him"* (2 Corinthians 5:21). When He took our sin upon Him, an eternal connection between Father and Son, never broken before, was temporarily severed. Jesus immediately recognized the change in the relationship. He cried out, *"My God, my God, why hast thou forsaken me?"* (Matthew 27:46). At that moment, God had released upon Him the judgment He had suspended over man for all human history. Every sin of man—past, present and future—was funneled into that moment. The result was the cry of Jesus, *"It is finished: and he ...gave up the ghost"* (John 19:30). He died, not from the wounds of the cross, but from the toxic poison of imputed sin. The hour our sin was imputed to Him, He died. He died just as Adam would have died had it not been for the mercy of God and the substitutionary sacrifice pointing to Christ. Adam, and every man after him, lives longer than one day because the Lamb, Christ, died in his place.

The curse of sin affected not only man but his habitation,

the earth. At the time of the crucifixion of Christ, the earth shook. The sun was darkened. The entire planet and the solar system are connected to the curse of sin and cry out for the redemption of His coming kingdom and the end of the curse.

You and I, unless we have come to the Cross, live under the suspended judgment of God. Even if we are believers, we will still experience the consequences of sin in our body. Eventually, we will experience the death of our flesh. We are born dying, and we will live an average of 70-plus years in bodies that were created to renew themselves and last for eternity.

Death is a reminder that sin left its consequences in the earth. Mercy did not remove the toxic effect of sin on our body. Death jolts us. It unsettles us, particularly when it claims in an untimely way the godly and good-natured among us. On the other hand, the mercy of God actually creates an illusion. God's law demanded that sin bring death immediately. But Adam and Eve sprung the trap of sin, and God caught the falling anvil of death and sent mercy tumbling down on man instead of judgment. He spared man the full consequence of his sin.

The result is that we may sin with no apparent effect. The anvil of God's judgment does not fall immediately. Lie and nothing seems to happen. Cheat and perhaps no one will know. Steal and if you do not get caught, you may appear to get ahead. Violate all of the laws of God and there may be no thunder or lightning, disapproval from heaven.

The illusion is established—sin has no effect! Is that true? No, sin brings death. Something is happening to the inside of the man who persistently sins. He is self-destructing. He is killing himself. Inner dissonance reigns. His conscience aches. He denies the pain. Psychosomatic symptoms appear. He carries his toxic disease into relationships. He is a taker, not a giver. He scatters the seeds of distrust by his lies. He destroys others with his anger. He inflicts pain by his insensitivity. He is sick! He is dying. In his blindness, he concludes that there is no God. He sees neither the mercy of God nor the judgment he so narrowly averts. He becomes a god to himself. He has been deluded by misinterpreting the mercy that came when judgment should have fallen.

He unwittingly and naively passes under the shadow of judgment. Multitudes now dance into the Holy Place (God's sanctuary), having ignored the beast of righteousness. They have not repented. They are not sorry for their trespasses. Musicians lead celebrations with unholy hands and proud hearts. Preachers break the bread with polluted hands. Worshipers lift soiled and sinful hands to a holy God. Strange fire is offered on the altar. A carnal church complains that the service is boring, the message irrelevant and the bread tasteless. Their spiritual senses are dull. They have no idea how narrowly they escaped death after having insulted a holy God with inattentive and insincere worship.

Why does the judgment not fall? The horns of God's wrath are now restrained by the sacrifice of Christ, the Lamb. For this season of time, the Holy Spirit, through the instrument of the church, pleads with humanity to come home to God. Soon, God will untie His beast and the earth will see the wrath of God as described in the Revelation of John. May God have mercy on us now. And may that mercy lead us to grace through repentance.

THE CRUEL PRACTICE OF SACRIFICE

Why did God require sacrifice? It seems so cruel to kill an innocent animal as God commanded. And, it is inhumane. That is exactly why God commanded the practice of sacrifice. It would have been so easy for man to forget that sin had consequences. So God instituted sacrifice to remind us of the horrible reality that sin destroys life.

As we remember the Cross, we should see it as the greatest reminder of the destructive nature of our sin. Light came among us, and we snuffed it out. Love blossomed, but we choked it with hate. Innocence moved in our midst, and we slaughtered it. God came to us, and in our blindness, we did not know Him or receive Him (John 1:7-12).

Why sacrifice? God wanted us to learn that every sin destroys. Though we do not always and sometimes cannot see the consequences of sin, due to His mercy, God did not want us to forget the destructive nature of sin. To forget is to become comfortable with sin. To forget is to neutralize sin. To forget is to embrace it and redefine it as acceptable. He wanted us to see that spilled blood equals the wasting of life—and that we waste our own life by irresponsible, sinful and selfish behavior. Sin is a life-waster! And, sin always leads to bloodshed. He wanted us to see the cost of sin. Every time an individual sinned, they were to bring a sacrifice. The higher the position, the more costly the sacrifice.

Sin does cost. It cost God His Son! It costs us our families and marriages. For some, the price is their reputation, their marriage, or their career. For others, the price is their soul. He wanted us to see that sin destroys innocent victims. The sinner would bring his lamb. He would meet the priest and confess his sin. He would look at that lamb and raise the knife. He would hear the innocent "baa ... baa!" He would look into the unsuspecting eyes and sink the knife into the throat of the lamb. The priest would assist in the catching of the blood, but the taking of the life would have been the action of the offerer. God wanted the offerer to come to understand that he was the perpetrator, the victimizer, the priest of death. The lamb stood in his place, just as the ultimate Lamb stands in our place. The act then was one aimed at self—an act of self-destruction. Ah!

At the altar, I need to see that sin is killing me; it is destroying me and it is my sin that destroyed the innocent Christ.

This should create a legitimate anger in us over sin and what sin does. God wanted more than an animal sacrifice; He wanted something to happen in the human heart. At the altar, I am to learn that sin is repulsive, that sin is ugly. That should create a heart change! God wanted the worshiper to leave the altar saying, "I never want to come here to this place and do this again—to slaughter another innocent lamb, to take another life. I do not want blood on my hands again!" It should have done this, but it didn't. So God provided the ultimate sacrifice—His only Son, Jesus, the Lamb. To stand before this slain lamb, and capriciously sin, is the ultimate insult to the love of God, the ultimate indication of a hard and unchangeable heart.

The altar cannot be the place where the mercy of God is exploited time after time without lifestyle change. The altar is the place of life transformation rooted in deep contrition and genuine repentance, and in unspeakable gratitude in view of the depth of God's love. The altar is a place of judgment—no, of mercy! Henry Soltau reminds us, "His anger endures but for a moment! Judgment is 'His strange work,' for 'He delights in mercy!'"[75]

---

[75] Henry Soltau, *The Tabernacle, the Priesthood, and the Offerings* (Grand Rapids: Kregel, 1972) 8.

Image courtesy of Melvin Poe

Image courtesy of Melvin Poe

Image courtesy of
www.tabernacleman.com

CHAPTER SEVEN

THE OFFERINGS OF CONSECRATION

When we think about sacrifices, we tend to view them all through the lens of the Cross and see them all as fulfilled in Christ, as offerings for our sin. But all sacrifices were not the same. All were not for sin. There are five basic and distinctively different sacrificial offerings mentioned in the first five chapters of Leviticus. All of these have relevance to our worship today. And all of them are reflected in the offering of Christ in our behalf. So, there is an application of these principles to the life of the believer and in the life of the church.

CONSECRATION AND REPARATION

Of the five offerings in Leviticus, two are offerings of *reparation* (chs. 4, 5). Three are offerings of *consecration* (chs. 1-3). The two reparation offerings are sin and trespass. They are mentioned last. Reparation offerings were designed to repair the damage to broken relationships. The sin offering restores my broken relationship with God. The trespass offering is designed to restore my broken relationship with God and another. In these two offerings, damaged relationships are healed.

The three offerings of consecration do not repair or heal damaged relationships, they advance relationship with God and others on the back of the reparation offerings. In the burnt offering is the idea of personal consecration to God, the giving of the self totally to God. The meal, called the meat offering, is actually an offering of grain. It is the idea of the dedication of one for service—bringing to God the fruit of the labor of my hands, the offering of my capacities in the harvest field.

Work is a sacred thing to God. In the first two chapters of Genesis, we meet a blue-collar God, a divine Workman. Our culture seeks to avoid work, to retire from it, but God calls us to work. My whole life is an act of worship unto God, including my work. There is no sacred and secular divide. The grain offering is the labor of my hands, given to God as a whole-life offering. The peace (or fellowship) offering celebrates the newly healed relationship with God by sharing a meal with God and others. It is the only offering in which the worshiper gets back a portion. Here, the altar is transformed into a table.

The Book of Leviticus is the manual for Israel's worship. Psalms may be its hymnal, but Leviticus is its canon for worship. Of the 613 commandments noted by rabbinic Judaism, 247 are in Leviticus. God cares about how His people worship.[76] The key word is *qadosh*, translated "holy, holiness, sanctify." The word occurs 152 times. The word translated "unclean" is found in the book 132 times, which accounts for more than half of its occurrences in the Old Testament. The

[76] Gary Demarest, *The Communicator's Commentary: Leviticus* (Dallas: Word, 1990) 17.

word translated "clean" appears 74 times. Together, clean and unclean occur 206 times. Holy, clean and unclean occur 358 times. God seems to be concerned about the purity and holiness of His people. In Hebrew, everything is either clean or unclean—there is no in-between. The key verse may be *"that you may distinguish between holy and unholy, and between unclean and clean, and that you may teach the children of Israel all the statutes which the Lord has spoken to them by the hand of Moses"* (Leviticus 10:10, 11). If worship doesn't result in the discrimination between holy and unholy, it is not Biblical worship.[77] Worship mediates every aspect of life. There is no distinction between the sacred and secular here.

Now let's examine the three consecration offerings one by one. In the next chapter, we will look at the sin and trespass offerings.

1. THE BURNT OFFERING (1; 6:9-13)

The burnt offering is the *'olah*—"that which ascends." It is Yahweh's portion, given to Him as a sweet fragrance.[78] At the Tabernacle and later at the Temple, a burnt offering was given for the nation twice a day, morning and evening.

The morning sacrifice would have marked the beginning of the day—the third hour (about 9 a.m.). It was at the time of the morning sacrifice that Christ was nailed on the cross. And it was at the time of the morning sacrifice that the Holy Spirit descended in Acts 2. The evening sacrifice at the ninth hour signaled the closing hours of the day (about 3 p.m.). These times show up at several points in Biblical history. It was at the time of the evening sacrifice when Elijah stood at the altar on Mount Carmel and prayed and the fire fell (1 Kings 18:36-38).

---

[77] Demarest, 27.
[78] John Ritchie, *The Tabernacle in the Wilderness* (Grand Rapids: Kregel, 1982) 40.

It was at the time of the evening oblation that Gabriel came to Daniel with a message about the future of Israel (Daniel 9:21). It was the ninth hour, the time of the evening sacrifice, when Peter and John came to the Beautiful Gate approaching the Temple when the lame man was healed (Acts 3:1-10). It was the ninth hour, the same time, when Cornelius had the angelic visit that marked the season in which the Gentiles first were invited to the altar (10:30, 31). And it had been at the ninth hour, the exact time the burnt offering would have been laid on the brass altar, that Christ cried out from the cross and the veil in the Temple was *"rent in twain"* (Matthew 27:45-51).

Symbolically, in the burnt offering, the whole nation was daily set aside unto God as an offering, a vessel for His use, day and night. Israel was to be the servant nation to the nations. The offering was to symbolize their perpetual surrender and dedication to God. As a nation of slaves, they had been freed by God's mighty hand. They had been liberated without a fight from the most powerful empire on earth. They walked out free, the gods of the mighty empire powerless to stop them. Their military was buried in the Red Sea. Out of gratitude, they would surely now gladly and freely serve their Liberator. The burnt offering was for the purposeful, daily consecration of the whole nation to God.

Individuals could also bring a burnt offering. Life consecration is the central message of the burnt offering, but the burnt offering could never be a substitute for a sin offering. Giving the burnt offering assumed that the sinful condition had been righted, the damaged relationship repaired, restitution paid. Only then was a burnt offering meaningful.

Speak to the children of Israel, and say to them: 'When any one of you brings an offering to the Lord, you shall bring your offer-

ing of the livestock—of the herd and of the flock. 3 'If his offering
is a burnt sacrifice of the herd, let him offer a male without
blemish; he shall offer it of his own free will at the door of the
tabernacle of meeting before the Lord. (Leviticus 1:2, 3).

First, notice that the burnt offering was to be without blemish.
Crippled or imperfect animals were unacceptable. Wholeness
was and still is a prerequisite for the burnt offering. There were
three grades of animal sacrifices: (1) a bull, (2) a lamb and (3) a
dove. Each represents different thoughts. The *bull* is an offering
of strength, untiring patience and labor. The *lamb* is an offering
of quiet submission, surrender without a battle. The *dove* is a
symbol of vulnerability, innocence, our fragile state. In the surrender of our lives to God, we offer all three things—the
strength of our labor, quiet submission of our lives to God, and
a peaceful innocence of heart.[79]

The sinner could not offer the burnt offering and find acceptance. His sin left him less than whole. Only after finding personal healing for our sin-sick soul is dedication to God
acceptable. The offerings of consecration are meaningful only
if they are proceeded by the offerings of reparation.

Second, note that the personal burnt offering was voluntary.
The offering that symbolizes self-consecration must be freely giv-
en. I give the gift of self, not because I have to do so, but because
I want to. This transformation of attitude is related to my having
been changed. Even though the burnt offering is voluntary, worship cannot take place unless it is given. As marriage cannot be
sustained without love, my relationship without God cannot exist
without the burnt offering. And in the same way, as love cannot
be demanded, this offering is commanded, but not demanded by
God. It must be a freewill action.

The burnt offering and the sin offering always stand

---

[79] Andrew Jukes, *The Law of the Offerings* (Grand Rapids: Kregel, 1966) 66, 67.

together. From a New Testament perspective, God's love in Christ calls out my love. His commitment to me calls out my commitment to Him. He has given Himself, and it was counted as a sin offering for me, I have given myself as a burnt offering for Him. This is what Paul had in mind when he wrote, "*I am crucified with Christ: nevertheless I live; yet not I, but Christ lives within me*" (Galatians 2:20).

The act of self-crucifixion is the burnt offering. It comes in response to the sin offering of Christ. I stand at the altar and I see the Lamb slain from the foundation of the world. I then climb on the altar and surrender myself completely. Christ has a cross, and I have a cross. He has taken, not His cross, but mine to Calvary. Now, I take up His cross and follow Him. He gave Himself for me in death. Now, I give myself to Him in life. He took my cross so that one day I could live in heaven. I take His cross so that this day He can live in the earth in my body. In heaven, He represents me before the Father. He is consumed with my interest. On the earth, I represent Him before man. My passion is to do His will. He went to heaven as a man, touched with the feelings of our infirmities. He left us on the earth, having put heaven in our souls and having clothed us with His glory, to be His body.

The burnt offering is the commitment I make to Him to allow Him to finish His work on the earth through my body—to touch through my touching, to speak through my speaking, to care through my caring, to love through my loving!

> *Then he shall put his hand on the head of the burnt offering, and it will be accepted on his behalf to make atonement for him. He shall kill the bull before the Lord; and the priests, Aaron's sons, shall bring the blood and sprinkle the blood all around on the altar that is by the door of the tabernacle of meeting.* (Leviticus 1:4, 5).

The act of touching the head of the animal is symbolic identification with the animal. It is the recognition that representatively I am dying today. The execution of the bullock or the lamb is also my responsibility.

Image courtesy of Melvin Poe

I am the only one who can stop myself from living for self and live my life in total dedication to God. The term slaughter or kill is literally "to slit the throat." It has strong ritual connotations.[80]

After sprinkling the blood and skinning the animal, it was then cut into parts and washed. Three things were laid on the altar: the head; the fat and the entrails; the legs.

This is a clear demonstration of how I am to give myself. I lay my head on the altar for a change of thinking. Paul connects this with the "renewing of our minds" (see Romans 12:1, 2). The entrails represent the seat of emotions, my feelings, gut instincts. The fat symbolizes the health and vitality of the animal. The feet represent my walk, my behavior. After the presentation of these three—head, vitals, and feet—the whole animal was then quartered and laid on the altar.

In Numbers, we note that the burnt offering was given for the nation at regular intervals—twice daily (28:4), on the Sabbath (v. 9), at the beginning of each month (v. 11), and at the annual feasts (vv. 16, 19, 27; 29:2, 8, 13, 16, 19, 22, 25, 28, 31, 34, 38). Combined with the burnt offering is the drink offering.

As noted earlier, Christ gave Himself as the essence of the burnt offering. His blood was poured out at Calvary, fulfilling the prophetic type of the drink offering. Here are the elements of communion—flesh and blood, bread and wine. Calvary was both a burnt offering and a drink offering, counted for us as a sin offering.

---

[80] Philip J. Budd, *New Century Bible Commentary: Leviticus* (Grand Rapids: Eerdmans, 1996) 48.

> *And its drink offering shall be one-fourth of a hin for each lamb; in a holy place you shall pour out the drink to the Lord as an offering. The other lamb you shall offer in the evening; as the morning grain offering and its drink offering, you shall offer it as an offering made by fire, a sweet aroma to the Lord.* (Numbers 28:7, 8).

This offering of wine was poured out in the Holy Place as a part of the daily burnt offering. The giving of myself at the altar demands the pouring out of my lifeblood, symbolized by the blood-like liquid of the wine, in the Holy Place. This is the image of lifestyle worship. That adds additional meaning to the burnt offering. It is the gift of my life energy to God, the commitment to pour out my life as an act of worship (see Leviticus 23:13, 18).

> *Command Aaron and his sons, saying, 'This is the law of the burnt offering: The burnt offering shall be on the hearth upon the altar all night until morning, and the fire of the altar shall be kept burning on it. And the priest shall put on his linen garment, and his linen trousers he shall put on his body, and take up the ashes of the burnt offering which the fire has consumed on the altar, and he shall put them beside the altar. Then he shall take off his garments, put on other garments, and carry the ashes outside the camp to a clean place. And the fire on the altar shall be kept burning on it; it shall not be put out. And the priest shall burn wood on it every morning, and lay the burnt offering in order on it; and he shall burn on it the fat of the peace offerings. A fire shall always be burning on the altar; it shall never go out.* (Leviticus 6:9-13).

The fire of total consecration "shall ever be burning." This is the fire that burns through the night, that "shall never go out." When the fire of sacrifice goes out, we have violated the most basic law of worship. When Israel packed the Tabernacle and prepared to move, the live coals were placed in fire pans, which were carried by the priests. Each priest had the personal responsibility to carefully keep the fire alive while the nation journeyed. These coals were used to ignite a new fire upon the altar when the Tabernacle was again reared up in a new location (v. 13; 10:1; Ezekiel 8:11).

The responsibility of every believer-priest is to gather live coals from the altar and keep them alive during the week, day and night. When the lively stones of God's true tabernacle are reassembled for worship, there is then fire on the altar, God's fire. Too often, the fire is left to burn out. When no one tends the fire during the week or wakes in the night to stir the coals on their personal and private heart altar, you can expect no fire in the sanctuary. God has started His fire on innumerable altars in countless churches, but the fires have not been nurtured. They are too often abandoned. The result is a cold and lifeless church. Sacrifice keeps the fire going.

2. THE MEAT OR MEAL OFFERING (Leviticus 2; 6:15, 16, 20, 21)

"When anyone offers a grain offering to the Lord, his offering shall be of fine flour. And he shall pour oil on it, and put frankincense on it" (2:1). The meat offering is actually a grain offering. The word meal (*minchah*) means *"gift."* The meal had to be crushed 13 times to become fine flour.[81] The burnt offering is the giving of a life, and the grain offering is the fruit of that life.[82] It represents the results of my labor in the fields. This labor has produced the primary ingredient for bread, which is now offered to God in an act of worship. Labor in the fields involves backbreaking work, sweat and toil, calluses and commitment. The evidence of my giftedness flows out of sacrifice. The meal offering is one of service, of works offered to God. I give Him my talents and abilities, my gifts and callings. My worshipful and sacrificial work is the stuff that "feeds"

---

[81]   David M. Levy, *The Tabernacle of Israel* (Grand Rapids: Kregel, 1987) 118.
[82]   Jukes, 77.

others. My giftedness is the way in which God meets the needs of the hungry and the hurting. My labor, for and with others in the harvest field, is offered as a sacrifice to God.

The grain could be offered uncooked. It could be offered as unleavened cakes (v. 4), created by kneading the flour, placing it in a pan (griddle) and baking it in an oven. It could be green grain, dried over a fire and then beaten to remove the grain (v. 14).

Frankincense was sprinkled over the bread. And then oil was poured on it. Frankincense was the staple ingredient in the incense to which three perfumes were added. And incense is a symbol of prayer; oil, a symbol of the Spirit. So, here is the symbolic meaning we would suggest. The laborer works and prays, and prays as he works. Oil, a symbol of the anointing, is poured over the bread. As I work and pray, I ask God to saturate my work in the oil of the Spirit. As He does, the anointing of the Spirit is poured out on my labor. Work birthed out of prayer and anointed by God is acceptable as a gift to Him.

The meat or meal offering is the natural sequel to the burnt offering. In Scripture they are partners, inseparable one from another. The bull, ram and lamb of the burnt offering are to all have their meat offering. It is one thing to make a declaration of sacrificial commitment, it is another to go into the fields, plow and plant, prune and have patience for the harvest.

How does one give himself to God? Symbolically, the burnt offering is the gift of oneself and of the nation to God. But, that is meaningless unless it is followed by devoted sacrificial service that is saturated with prayer and has the oil of the Holy Spirit poured upon it. This kind of sacrifice is a "sweet savour" (v. 2) unto the Lord.

The common man, any Israelite, could offer grain offerings. His offering was given to the priests. So, the offering of labor was under the control of the priests.

> *He shall bring it to Aaron's sons, the priests, one of whom shall take from it his handful of fine flour and oil with all the frank-*

incense. And the priest shall burn it as a memorial on the
altar, an offering made by fire, a sweet aroma to the Lord (v. 2).

Only a portion was burned on the altar. It was mixed with oil and frankincense. It was a sweet- savor offering. God delights in our labor in His behalf. The offering that came from this season and field of our labor was for only a moment in time. But, offered to God, it establishes a memorial that God remembers. What will be forgotten by others on earth will be remembered by God in heaven for eternity. Our labor in His behalf is timeless. What is burned on the altar as a symbol of our labor is owned by heaven and memorialized there. *"The rest of the grain offering shall be Aaron's and his sons'. It is most holy of the offerings to the Lord made by fire"* (v. 3; see also 6:14-16).

The practical remainder, after the memorial is offered, belongs to the priest who was allowed to benefit from the offering of service. First, a portion was given to God. Then, the priest could retain the remainder. However, this was not the case when he offered his grain offering for himself. *"For every grain offering for the priest shall be wholly burned. It shall not be eaten"* (6:23).

When the priest offered his own meal offering, it had to be wholly burnt. He could retain none for himself. So the offering by the priest, his service to God, was not to be self-promoting or self-enhancing. His service was to be totally sacrificial—a life given completely to God. Nothing I do in the Kingdom should be for a self-serving cause.

Neither leaven nor honey could be mixed into the meal offering. Leaven is symbolic of sin. The absence of leaven here probably symbolizes purity. This is an offering of works that is uncompromised, not morally tainted in any way. Also, leaven puffs up, or exaggerates the size of the loaf. No offering of works is to be exaggerated, overreported, or made to look more impressive than it is in reality. Leaven fills the bread with hot air. Sometimes the reports of works offered to God are half hot air and half credible. That is unacceptable to God.

Honey was disallowed. It corrupts quickly. It cannot stand the fire. It sours.[83] So the sweet thing that sours in the heat was disallowed in the labor offering. It was, however, offered in the abominable practices of the pagans around them.[84] The meat offering was to be a sacrifice traceable to the work of man's hands. And honey was not something produced by man's own labor. The prohibition against the use of honey is a call to offer the plain and simple bread of our labor. No sweeteners or additives are allowed. Christ's great labor in our behalf was the Cross, and there was no sweetness there, only the bitterness of vinegar, the taste of death.

Further, the bread was seasoned with salt. Salt may have been added for taste and as a preservative. It is important that our labors are also preserved! This may reference the covenant of salt. Salt, the king of minerals, is the only mineral taken directly into our bodies. On our tables are meat (the animal kingdom), vegetables (the vegetable kingdom) and salt (the mineral kingdom). Without minerals, we could not exist or survive.

So, our sacrifice of labor has to be anointed by the oil of the Holy Spirit; it is to be offered with incense—prayer; absent of leaven—sin or that which puffs up; without honey—another's sweetness; and seasoned with catalytic mineral salt—flavorful and preserved! Salt's greatest use may be as a chemical catalyst.

A MORNING PRAYER

The meat offering was also given daily, each morning along with the burnt offering (Numbers 28:3-5, 9). As the people began their labor for the day, the sweet savor of the grain offering was being given in their behalf at the Temple.

---

[83] Ritchie, 46.
[84] Levy, 120

Life is more than the monotony of a job. It must be more than meaningless labor. My whole life is an offering to God. Everything I do, I do with all my might as a gift to God. So, as I begin my daily activity in the morning, I enter into a covenant of service with and for God. In God's kingdom, work and sacrifice are sacred.

- *Flour:* I offer my gifts and talents. I commit myself to labor in the vineyard today. I will let my acts of servant-hearted love feed others.
- *Incense:* I will pray without ceasing today, sprinkling every hour with communion with God.
- *Oil:* I pray, "God, pour on me the oil of Your Spirit and saturate me with Your presence."
- *No Leaven:* I will stay pure lest my testimony be contaminated by the leaven of sin.
- *No Honey:* I will not offer a phony sweetness in the place of sincerity. I pray that the heat of trials this day, the conflicts with those who are enemies of faith, will not cause me to quickly sour. Preserve my sweetness.
- *Salt:* May my words be seasoned with salt. May my labor be preserved. May my lifework be memorialized in heaven.

The priests rose early in the morning. They removed the ashes of the evening sacrifice and piled fresh wood on the altar. As the morning burnt offering was laid on the altar, three priests had taken live coals into the Holy Place to attend the altar of incense. Another priest would tend to the lampstand.

The people would be gathered near the gate, ready to begin their day. The burnt offering represented the giving of their lives to God. The grain offering indicated that even their labor during the day was an offering, given as worship unto God. The presiding priest walked toward the people with his hands raised and pronounced the benediction:[85] *"The Lord bless you and keep you; The Lord make His face shine upon you, And*

---

[85] Paul Zehr, *God Dwells With His People* (Scottdale, PA: Herald, 1981) 117.

be gracious to you; The Lord lift up His countenance upon you, And give you peace" (Numbers 6:24-26).

3. THE PEACE OFFERING (Leviticus 3:1, 2; 7:11-16, 20, 21)

The word for "peace offering," *shelamin*, is kin to the familiar Hebrew word *shalom*. It references both the nature of the offering—peace, fellowship, relationship—and the resultant peace that followed the offering.[86] In the peace offering, the worshiper received a portion of the sacrifice back for personal consumption. He could gather family and friends around for a festive meal, a celebration of peace. This is the highest level of worship available through the sacrifice. In this moment, mankind ate with God, joined in fellowship. This was a meal with God! Here, the altar is transformed into a table. At first, this altar demands of me; it appears to "take" from me. Now it gives something back to me and, ultimately, gives someone back to me. I invite friends and family to join me in the eating of the peace offering. This is relational. But in every peace offering, God is served first. God and the worshiper are now united. Sin had alienated us from God and from one another. But now, we are together again. Friends, we are having dinner at God's house.

Notice how the relationship progresses in the offerings to get us to this point. In the sin offering an individual stands alone at the gate needing reconciliation with God. He offers the sin offering. He may also be required to offer a trespass offering, to right a wrong in order to complete restitution. He does so, but he wants to do more. He wants to consecrate himself to God. So, he brings a burnt offering. He gives himself, having dealt with his sins and trespasses. And then, he gives a grain offering. His consecration cannot be "lip service." He must work for God. He will plow and plant, cultivate and harvest. He will offer his abilities as an offering to God. Now, in the crowning offering, the peace offering, reconciliation is not

---

[86] Levy, 126.

only complete, it is celebrated. Man is no longer alone. The individual is now in community again, fellowship with God and his brothers restored. This is a family meal.

In this offering, the fat could not be eaten. It was completely burned up on the altar. Only then could the meal begin. The fat was God's portion. He shared in the meal. He was served first, as the honored guest. After the fat was burned, the meal commenced for the offerer and his guests (1 Samuel 11:15).

> 'When his offering is a sacrifice of a peace offering, if he offers it of the herd, whether male or female, he shall offer it without blemish before the Lord. 2 And he shall lay his hand on the head of his offering, and kill it at the door of the tabernacle of meeting; and Aaron's sons, the priests, shall sprinkle the blood all around on the altar" (Leviticus 3:1, 2).

The peace offering could be male or female, but it had to be without blemish—no crippled or deformed animal was acceptable. The offerer placed his hand on the head of the offering, identifying with it as in other offerings. After it was killed, the priest would distribute its blood as an offering before the Lord. God is a silent participant in the process. He watches our acts of consecration. They are always before Him.

> If he offers a lamb as his offering, then he shall offer it before the Lord ... This is the law of the sacrifice of peace offerings which he shall offer to the Lord: 12 If he offers it for a thanksgiving, then he shall offer, with the sacrifice of thanksgiving, unleavened cakes mixed with oil, unleavened wafers anointed with oil, or cakes of blended flour mixed with oil. 13 Besides the cakes, as his offering he shall offer leavened bread with the sacrifice of thanksgiving of his peace offering (v. 7; 7:11-13).

The peace offering might be given under the theme of "thanksgiving" or celebrated as an act of thanksgiving (v. 12). It was combined with a grain offering of unleavened cakes, mingled with oil, and prepared in a variety of ways. Or it could be in conjunction with a fellowship "vow" (v. 16). The thanks-giving offering had to be consumed that day. It could not be saved for another day.

Thanksgiving is a daily thing. The thanks of today cannot stand for that which is due God tomorrow. If it was a vow, then it would be eaten in part or in whole on the day it was offered, but a portion could be saved for the next day. Vows are meant to endure beyond a day.

> *And from it he shall offer one cake from each offering as a heave offering to the Lord. It shall belong to the priest who sprinkles the blood of the peace offering. 15 'The flesh of the sacrifice of his peace offering for thanksgiving shall be eaten the same day it is offered. He shall not leave any of it until morning. 16 But if the sacrifice of his offering is a vow or a voluntary offering, it shall be eaten the same day that he offers his sacrifice; but on the next day the remainder of it also may be eaten (vv. 14-16).*

It is the peace offering that becomes a *"heave"* offering (v. 14) and a *"wave"* offering (9:21). The wave offering was effect-ed by lifting the breast of the peace offering and moving it backward and forward before the Lord. The heave offering was swung vertically up and down before the Lord. The word heave is from the Hebrew *terumah,* which means "to be lifted up." The *wave breast* was said to represent love and affection; the *heave shoulder,* strength.[87]

The peace offering assumes a prior sin offering and thus a right relationship with God.

> *But the person who eats the flesh of the sacrifice of the peace offering that belongs to the Lord, while he is unclean, that per-son shall be cut off from his people (7:20, emphasis added).*

To eat the peace portion and therefore posture as being at peace with God, but have sin that had not been appropriately dealt with, was a criminal offense. That soul was to be cut off.

---

[87] Levy, 127, 130.

The point is clear: To pretend peace with God and be in a position of active, ongoing sin without repentance is the ultimate offense to God. Sin places me at enmity with God. I am at war with all He stands for. How can I sit at the table of peace and have dinner with Him? I am a Judas, a traitor, at the table.

Moreover the soul that shall touch any unclean thing, as the uncleanness of man, or any unclean beast, or any abominable unclean thing, and eat of the flesh of the sacrifice of peace offerings, which pertain unto the Lord, even that soul shall be cut off from his people (v. 21).

Now the standard is raised even higher. It is not the soul here that has sinned. He has merely come into contact with impurity. He has touched uncleanness. Another near him has sinned. He has uncleanness upon him. He is contaminated. He can't sit at the peace table. This level of awareness of the sin around us, of the holiness of God, of our own need to be cognizant of how quickly sin can contaminate us is the message we should take from this.

Without purity, the peace offering is presumptuous. And, an individual who attempts to move into fellowship with God without a commitment to righteousness or without repentance is setting himself up to be cut off.

The peace offering completes the sacrificial cycle of worship at the brass altar. It is here that people of God celebrate their harmony, their unity with God and with one another. This unity is foundational if we are to experience the greater dimension of fellowship with God in the Holy Place and with one another at the table. Division in the Holy Place is a result of not taking seriously the peace offering, of not establishing a spirit of harmony and unity. Thus, we mute the joy of the Holy Place and reduce the purity of the family celebration around His table.

Image courtesy of Melvin Poe

CHAPTER EIGHT

THE OFFERINGS OF REPARATION

We now turn to the first of the two *reparation* offerings. These offerings are remedial. They do not advance the cause of consecration, they repair the foundational damage to broken relationships allowing legitimate consecration. *The Lord said to Moses, "Say to the Israelites: 'When anyone sins unintentionally and does what is forbidden in any of the LORD's commands ... he must bring to the LORD...a sin offering"* (Leviticus 4: 2, 3).

The term *sin* is from the Hebrew word *chattah*, meaning "to err from God's way" or "miss the mark." It refers to both the disobedience and the remedy, the sin offering. The words "sin through ignorance" (Hebrew, *bishgagah*) mean "to wander, do wrong." These were not sins of overt rebellion. The difference is not found in the act of sin itself, but the attitude of the heart.[88]

---

[88] David M. Levy, *The Tabernacle: Shadows of the Messiah* (Bellmawr, NJ: Friends of Israel Gospel Ministry, 1993) 135.

The sin committed in ignorance does not change the deadly nature of the sin or the consequences of death, the sacrifice! But deliberate sin reflects a heart resistant to change, one that does not long after holiness. That is a different matter. God forgives sins committed by people who have had a heart change, quickly repent, evidencing remorse over their actions. But those with hardened hearts require more than forgiveness; they require a heart transplant.

The type of animal offered depended upon the rank of the person who had sinned. A priest and the whole congregation of Israel corporately had to offer a bullock (vv. 3, 13, 14). A leader offered a male goat (v. 23). An individual could offer a female goat or sheep (v. 28). The poor could offer two turtledoves or pigeons (5:7), one for a sin offering and the other for a burnt offering. Even a handful of flour could be substituted by the poorest (v. 11). Economic status was not to separate the poorest from dealing with his sin and making peace with God. However, a higher rank demanded a greater penalty for sin. Why? Perhaps to demonstrate that the higher the rank, the more costly the consequences. And that remains true today. Every sin demanded a new offering. Sin is costly.

THE SIN OFFERING FOR A PRIEST

> *"'If the anointed priest sins, bringing guilt on the people, he must bring to the LORD a young bull without defect as a sin offering for the sin he has committed." (Leviticus 4:3).*

Note the phrase "If the priest that is anointed do sin." Anointing does not preclude one from the possibility of sin. Some assume that anointing endorses the character of an individual as perfect or sinless. That is not true! And, it is a dangerous postulate. Anointing is not only associated with the individual, but also with office and function. Most ministers have sensed anointing upon their ministry at times when they knew their spiritual condition was unworthy of such grace and glory. However, God, honoring the office, touched the hurts of others, through them, giving hope and healing, despite the ministers' less-than-adequate personal condition. Some preachers live from the residue of anointing resident in the Word as they preach or minister. They rarely pray.

God's blessings are not endorsements of our character. God's blessings are endorsements of His character, of His love and care for His people. Priests who are anointed do sin! The New King James Version says, *"If the anointed priest sins, bringing guilt on the people...."* What an extraordinary notion. The sin of the priest affects the congregation. His relationship with God tends to impact the relationship of the whole congregation. In verse 5, the blood of this sin offering was taken into the Holy Place and sprinkled there seven times before the veil, indicating that the sin of the leader had defiled the Holy Place and a purging was necessary to make it pure again. Not only was the blood of this sin offering sprinkled before the veil, it was also placed on the horns of the altar of incense (v. 7), indicating that prayer and worship had been compromised by the sin of the leader. When a spiritual leader sinned, here is what was required of him: *"He is to present the bull at the entrance to the Tent of Meeting before the LORD. He is to lay his hand on its head and slaughter it before the LORD."* (v. 4).

As with all of the people, he was required to stand at the door of the Tabernacle, as one alienated from the presence of God by sin. He was given no exemption or special treatment because of his position. He was required to lay his hand on the head of the sacrifice and confess his sin. He was required to kill the sacrifice. And in his case, it had to be a bull—the most expensive of sacrifices. His sin was no different than the sin of any other, but his office made the sin a graver offense. It demanded a higher penalty.

> *But the hide of the bull and all its flesh, as well as the head and legs, the inner parts and offal-- 12 that is, all the rest of the bull--he must take outside the camp to a place ceremonially clean, where the ashes are thrown, and burn it in a wood fire on the ash heap.* (vv. 11, 12).

The remainder of the blood was poured out at the base of the altar (v. 7). The inner parts and fat were offered on the altar. Everything else was dragged outside the camp and completely burned. It was a total loss.

We see sin as such an individual and private matter that we fail to see the corporate and relational implications that are evident everywhere. No sin is a private thing. We learned that from the Garden. At times, a whole church should be called to the altar to deal with sins in the church—even if they, as individuals, are faultless. The same is true for cities and nations. Here is the focus on corporate sin, a concept almost completely lost to us today.

CONGREGATIONAL SIN

> *'If the whole Israelite community sins unintentionally and does what is forbidden in any of the LORD's commands, even though the community is unaware of the matter, they are guilty. ...* (v. 13).

Notice the phrase "if the whole congregation of Israel sin." Here is corporate sin! In the Western world with its emphasis on individualism, this concept is ignored. Families sin. So do churches and denominations. Cities and states sin, as well as nations. When such sin is recognized, corporate repentance needs to take place. This was the function of a solemn assembly. *"When they become aware of the sin they committed, the assembly must bring a young bull as a sin offering and present it before the Tent of Meeting. "* (v. 14).

The whole congregation is gathered in the area around the Tabernacle. A bull, the most expensive of sacrifices, is offered in their behalf. The elders gather around the sacrifice and lay hands on it in behalf of the congregation (v. 15). The priest takes the blood into the Holy Place, as he did in the case of the sin of the anointed priest. It is sprinkled before the veil and smeared on the horns of the incense altar. The Holy Place (the sanctuary), the access to God's presence, has been compromised by the sin of the people. Worship and prayer have been affected, so the altar of incense must be redeemed, and the right to pray and worship must be renewed. Sadly, many congregations sin and never repent. They continue to worship in a polluted Holy Place and at compromised altars. Such prayer and worship are an offense to God. The church slowly dies. The people perish. The Spirit is grieved. Deadness abounds. No one seems to know why. No one is willing to repent.

THE SIN OF A RULER

> 'When a leader sins unintentionally and does what is forbidden in any of the commands of the LORD his God, he is guilty. When he is made aware of the sin he committed, he must bring as his offering a male goat without defect. (vv. 22, 23).

Rulers are subordinate to the laws of God. Though they were rulers, they were to submit to the priest in areas of worship and ministry. That makes them safe to and for the people. They are restored and guided by principles of truth. Without this tethering of authority to truth, leaders are unpredictable, self-serving, and at times, ruthless. Here is the place from which we draw, at least in part, the balance between a free church and a government, under God. The province of faith was under the domain of God, stewarded to the priests. The province of government was also under the domain of God stewarded to the rulers. The priests taught the Law and functioned as relational healers. The rulers led. The priest submitted to the ruler. Faith, with its anchoring and enriching values, served the culture. And the ruler, in areas of faith, submitted to the priest. He, too, came to the Tabernacle to absolve himself of the guilt of sin. His sacrifice was not as costly as that of the anointed priest or of the congregation as a whole. He might have offered only a goat.

> *He is to lay his hand on the goat's head and slaughter it at the place where the burnt offering is slaughtered before the LORD. It is a sin offering. Then the priest shall take some of the blood of the sin offering with his finger and put it on the horns of the altar of burnt offering and pour out the rest of the blood at the base of the altar.(vv. 24, 25).*

The blood of his sin offering was not taken into the Holy Place. He was a ruler of the people, not a priestly spiritual leader. The blood of his offering was placed on the horns of the brass altar and poured out at its base. And like all the others, it was a total waste, burned without the camp. Its inards were offered on the altar after he had confessed his sin over the offering.

THE SIN OF THE COMMON PEOPLE

Now we come to the sin offering for the common people.

> *'If a member of the community sins unintentionally and does what is forbidden in any of the LORD's commands, he is guilty. When he is made aware of the sin he committed, he must bring as his offering for the sin he committed a fe-*

> *male goat without defect. He is to lay his hand on the head*
> *of the sin offering and slaughter it at the place of the burnt*
> *offering.* (vv. 27-29).

From the greatest to the least, from the priest to the pau-
per—all had to come to God and deal with their sins. All had to
confess and bring an offering. All had to slay the sacrifice.

No one was exempt, then or now.

THE TYPES OF SIN

In the early portion of Leviticus 5, we have a description of
various types of sin to which the sin offering might apply.

Social irresponsibility. *"If a person sins because he*
does not speak up when he hears a public charge to testify
regarding something he has seen or learned about, he will be
held responsible (v. 1).

The "voice of swearing" appears to be a reference to the use
of the name of Yahweh in vain or some other inappropriate
language. Or, it could be the violation of an oath—the breach
of a promise. However, that is specifically mentioned later.
The individual here was not guilty of swearing. He was merely
a bystander who was exposed to the unfaithfulness or the act
of sin by another. Although he knew the action of the other
was a sin, a violation of the first commandment, his choice was
evidently to remain passive in the matter. He neither con-
fronted the individual nor reported the matter. By his silence,
he gave tacit approval to the act and he entered into a passive
conspiracy with regard to the poisonous behavior. In no way
did he attempt to differentiate himself from the toxic talk. As a
result, he contaminated himself and bore the iniquity of such
slander by his silence.

All that is required to lower the standard of respect for God and to make personal oaths and promises meaningless is silence and toleration of sin. The moral standard of a nation breaks down when silent conspiracies create exemptions from the law and righteous standards. Love must not muzzle truth. We are our brothers' keepers. Mutual accountability is the backbone of any moral system. Police are no match for holy peers who love us enough to confront us and call us to purity. Here the silent conspirator was charged with the moral failure of the person who sinned in his presence. He is described as an accomplice to the crime.

Environmental sin. *"Or if a person touches anything ceremonially unclean--whether the carcasses of unclean wild animals or of unclean livestock or of unclean creatures that move along the ground--even though he is unaware of it, he has become unclean and is guilty."* (v. 2).

Sometimes, we are exposed to impurity in the social environment. When that happens, the exposure mandates personal purification.

Lyrics shout at us from records and radios. Suggestive messages taunt us from billboards and newsstands. Media input appeals to the flesh and the worldly instincts that we war against. The figure of an overtly sexual image, the hook of the commercial jingle that is worldly to the core, are too easily remembered. Suddenly, in the environment of the world, seeds of the same type we had earlier purged now lodge inside our mind and begin to break open and grow. The environment has contaminated us. At first, the impact was hidden. We may not have seen the deep effect of the world on our thinking and acting. Now, standing at the altar before His presence, it is clear. We must again repent—change our mind and manners. We must again correct our course.

Repentance means "to turn." Like driving an automobile, turning is not a single act that occurs at the beginning of our journey and then ends. It is an ongoing activity that requires constant adjustment.

Relational sin. *"Or if he touches human uncleanness--anything that would make him unclean--even though he is unaware of it, when he learns of it he will be guilty"* (v. 3).

In verse 2, only "things" were considered as sources of pollution. Now we have something different. Relational sin is uncleanness that is transferred from one man to another man. One man has failed to keep himself pure and clean. Another is exposed to him and is thereby defiled. In the ancient world there was the worry of communicable diseases, infectious germs and viruses. Living in such close quarters in the wilderness, it was imperative that every man take the necessary precautions to protect himself, his family and his friends from disease. A few careless actions, and an epidemic could result. No one wanted to be responsible for that. No one wanted to see a loved one or a neighbor die, knowing that they had carried the fatal germ to them, and that it could have been prevented.

Is it any less irresponsible to transmit mental and spiritual attitudes to another individual that cause a soul to wither spiritually and die to God and His will? Isn't it an even greater travesty that we are sometimes the carriers of ideas and actions that destroy lives, wreck the self-perspectives of others, and bring death to the Kingdom dimension of love, joy and peace in their lives?

Not only is the individual who sinned responsible, but any person who is a carrier of the contaminant is guilty. Contamination happens in the transmission of ungodly attitudes, jokes and unrestrained fleshly appetites. It may be a companion or a friend, a work associate or a relative who is the influencer. Whatever the vehicle, we are affected by it and thrown off balance morally. The only preventive solution is the personal and habitual practice of purification.

Sin through violation of integrity. *"Or if a person thoughtlessly takes an oath to do anything, whether good or evil--in any matter one might carelessly swear about--even though he is unaware of it, in any case when he learns of it he will be guilty"* (v. 4).

When an individual pronounces an oath but does not make his promise good, he has violated personal integrity. Note the phrase *"though he is unaware of it."* The possibility of a breach in memory or personal oversight is to be given consideration, but when it is clear that he is aware of his commitment, he is expected to make it right.

Contamination by language, things, persons, unfulfilled pledges are social. All of them affect the quality of integrity, the strength of the social fabric that binds us together. Unaddressed, the sin of these things contaminates the whole. A person's word binds him or her to the pledge. *"'When anyone is guilty in any of these ways, he must confess in what way he has sinned"* (v. 5).

All of these examples are cited as sin! They all require an offering. These are serious breaches in community fidelity. The work of the Tabernacle/Temple is not merely in the arena of the spiritual. It is not merely the work of a privatized faith. It connects us and holds us accountable to our word. The altar and the priest are the arbiters of community health, as well as personal and spiritual health. The two are here connected. These sins have affected the quality of community life. And it is not just the culture that needs to be protected here—though that is important and a point we have missed. These sins are serious enough that God himself has been offended. A reconciliation with Him is necessary.

So no one has heard about your escapade! God knows—and He is offended! So no one has found the dirty stash of inappropriate materials! God knows where the polluted stuff lies, and He sees the pollution working in your mind every time you leave the unholy altar you have built to these things. You are grieving the Holy Spirit.

You may have a friend who is bitter, blasphemous, hurt and angry—and yet a pastor. You watch as he goes deeper into a bottomless pit. You are his confidant. But your silent and passive acceptance of his language, laden with sinful attitudes and unforgiveness, may not be helping him at all. When will you gently confront? When will you take him to the Cross?

The secret loan, though sizeable, was never made a matter of record. Now, the lender is dead. The money was borrowed against his life insurance policy to assist you. It belongs to his wife, his family, but the loan was never recorded, never repaid. No one will ever know—no one but God! Can you live with that? These are the secret sins that violate our relationship with God, one another, and plague the church. They are unaddressed. They pollute the holy places of our lives.

> And, as a penalty for the sin he has committed, he must bring to the LORD a female lamb or goat from the flock as a sin offering; and the priest shall make atonement for him for his sin. (v. 6).

The sin offering and the trespass offering now come together. This is a trespass offering to God. The actions of the individual have offended God. Confession and sacrifice are necessary. The sin and trespass offerings are aimed not only at the removal of sins committed, but also at restraint from future sin. The idea was that man should behave more responsibly and keep himself pure. Note again God's accommodation to the economic status of man:

> *'If he cannot afford a lamb, he is to bring two doves or two young pigeons to the LORD as a penalty for his sin--one for a sin offering and the other for a burnt offering ... If, however, he cannot afford two doves or two young pigeons, he is to bring as an offering for his sin a tenth of an ephah of fine flour for a sin offering. He must not put oil or incense on it, because it is a sin offering* (vv. 7, 11).

THE TRESPASS OFFERING (Leviticus 5)

The sin offering was for moral failure and violations of the law occurring unintentionally or without blatant forethought. The trespass offering was for sin that involved intent, a knowing transgression of the law, blatant sin. In trespass, the individual knew the line was there but crossed it anyway. This is a more serious infraction.

The trespass offering is called the *asham* and refers to the guilt committed against God and the harm done to others. The vertical and horizontal relationships (see vv. 14-16; 7:1-6) are tied together here. The love of God and concern for others are always conjoined. Disdain for others is in some way disdain for God.

The blood of the *trespass offering* never went into the Holy Place. It was thrown at the base of the brass altar by the priest. The casting of the blood at the base of the altar illustrates the throwing away of life. The behavior that demanded this trespass offering was a life-wasting kind of behavior. It caused death to triumph and the very energy to be poured out of the individual in vain. The sin offering deals with position with

God while the trespass offering deals with a personal walk with men and before God. Nothing should be between the two. Sin and trespass create walls of separation that must be removed. It is not so much the person as it is the act that is in view here.[89] *"And he shall make restitution for the harm that he has done in regard to the holy thing"* (v. 16).

The sin offering said, "I am sorry, and I will change this behavior." The trespass offering said practically, "I did you wrong, and I will make it right." In fact, the individual was not only required to "make amends," but to add 20 percent to the loss experienced by the other party: *"... and shall add one-fifth to it and give it to the priest. So the priest shall make atonement for him with the ram of the trespass offering, and it shall be forgiven him"* (v. 16).

Notice that the trespass offering goes beyond the sin offering. In principle, when one wrongs or injures another and is genuinely repentant, he or she is not content to simply repair the damage. Reparations above and beyond must be made. Generosity and sensitivity now replace the callous or careless attitude that prevailed when the breach was committed.

There are various dimensions to the trespass offering.

1. TRESPASS AGAINST GOD

> *If a person sins, and commits any of these things which are forbidden to be done by the commandments of the Lord, though he does not know it, yet he is guilty and shall bear his iniquity.* (v. 17).

Sin, specifically the habitual breaking of the commandments, is a trespass against God. To fail to deal with this causes me to "bear iniquity." I am marked in the sight of God. Sin and

---

[89] John Ritchie, *The Tabernacle in the Wilderness* (Grand Rapids: Kregel, 1982) 35.

trespass place one under a burden. It is a yoke, and ignorance is no excuse. "Though he wist it not"—he did not know it! But he was still guilty and suffered the consequences.

God wants me to acknowledge the sin, repent, and change the behavior. Iniquity is the mark of a lawless life, one out of moral control. The person jumps the fences and crosses the lines. He disrespects the boundaries and treats the rules as being there for others. He exempts himself from the standards set by the Almighty himself. The only brakes that will stop this kind of out-of-control behavior is repentance.

2. TRESPASS AGAINST MAN

If a person sins and commits a trespass against the Lord by lying to his neighbor about what was delivered to him for safekeeping, or about a pledge, or about a robbery, or if he has extorted from his neighbor ... (6:2).

Here, man has offended God by inappropriate actions that have affected his neighbor. He told a lie to his neighbor. He agreed to look after something as a good neighbor does for another. What he agreed to protect was lost, stolen, perhaps even violently. He lied to cover up his liability in the matter, or he broke fellowship with his neighbor. "Anything wrong?" his neighbor might have asked him. He lied in response.

Or perhaps, while his neighbor was away, his house was robbed. He was certain that he knew who did it, but he told his neighbor he knew nothing, he wasn't home. He deceived his neighbor for whatever reason. The nature of the deception or the scenario might have changed, but one thing remained constant—God was angry! God considered it a trespass against Him.

3. TRESPASS OVER THINGS

If a person sins and commits a trespass against the Lord ... or if he has found what was lost and lies concerning it, and swears falsely--in any one of these things that a man may do in which he sins...(vv. 2, 3).

The trespass focuses on things, but the emphasis is deeper. I do have a responsibility for property left in my trust, or accidentally found by me and belonging to someone else. But the principle is deeper than things. I cannot let possessions be more important to me than people. These trespasses are over things, but they are about how people treat one another when things are involved.

4. THE TRESPASS SOLUTION

We can distill this discussion about our neighbor to four obligations:

- We are to be watchful in their behalf. Our integrity will be a guard for them. We are, in New Testament terms, to treat them as we would want to be treated.
- We are to live in fellowship with them. The New Testament demands more. If we fulfill the command of Christ, we are to love them as we love ourselves.
- We are to be a faithful friend in times of neighborhood violence.
- We are to be honest and not deceive our neighbor.

Then it shall be, because he has sinned and is guilty, that he shall restore what he has stolen, or the thing which he has extorted, or what was delivered to him for safekeeping, or the lost thing which he found, or all that about which he has sworn falsely. He shall restore its full value, add one-fifth more to it, and give it to whomever it belongs, on the day of his trespass offering (vv. 4, 5).

All of these are simple ethical principles. The phrase "sin through ignorance" is not found in this section. The wrong choices made here were conscious. In every case, he was not only to make restitution of the whole, he was to do it with interest (5:14-16; Numbers 5:5-8). After the break of relationship with another, I not only say I am sorry, but I am to sacrificially repent. I am to pay for any physical damage caused by my action or inaction.

And, I am to go beyond the restitution and add 20 percent. This is the idea of the second mile in the Sermon on the Mount offered by Jesus (Matthew 5:41). *"And he shall bring his trespass offering to the Lord, a ram without blemish from the flock, with your valuation, as a trespass offering, to the priest"* (Leviticus 6:6).

Here is the restoration of relationships. Both restitution with man (the horizontal dimension) and sacrifice offered to God (the vertical dimension) are required in the case of trespass. A breach in the relationship with man is a breach in the relationship with God. The vertical and the horizontal are inseparable. *"So the priest shall make atonement for him before the Lord, and he shall be forgiven for any one of these things that he may have done in which he trespasses"* (v. 7).

Relationships are important to God. Remember, God is Trinity. God is Father, Son and Holy Spirit in dynamic relationship. He is three, yet one. The very nature of deity is made from the fabric of the integral balance of three-in-one. God is a relationship community of three. The sin of Lucifer was a violation of the relationship unity in heaven, and the original sin of Adam and Eve was one of relationship disruption.

Relationship disorder is not a mere effect of sin, but a part of the very nature of sin. Reversing sin's power and effect requires repentance and restitution, integrity and humility. God is concerned about relational restoration. It is the heart of the gospel.

CHAPTER NINE

THE SACRIFICES
An Application

O f the five offerings, only the sacrifice of Jesus on the cross
can satisfy the death demand of the sin offering. He has
perfectly fulfilled all five offerings: He has given Himself as a
burnt offering; His life was an offering of service (the meal offering); and He has enjoyed unbroken fellowship with His Father—the essence of the peace offering. Finally, the self sacrifice
(the essence of the burnt offering) of His sinless life on Calvary
is counted for us as a sin offering unto God.

We could never offer a sin offering that satisfied. He would
never need a sin offering due to His sinless life. His perfect life
was a substitute for our imperfection—His sinlessness for our
sin; His perfect obedience, unto death, for our disobedience.
The Cross represented His whole perfect life for our less-than
whole imperfect life. Now, we need only go to Calvary and

identify with His sacrifice on the cross for the complete remission of our sins. That does not release us from embracing the principles of the remaining sacrifices. In fact, if one genuinely takes Christ's sacrifice seriously, He is obligated to the principles of the other sacrifices. In view of what He has done, I move to repair broken horizontal relationships (trespasses), offering restitution for previously irresponsible behavior. This is the trespass offering. In the language of the New Testament, I leave my gift at the altar and go to be reconciled with my brother (Matthew 5:23, 24). Notice again, God places the value of restored relationships above the offerings of self or service.

After reestablishing healthy relationships, I may now legitimately offer the burnt offering of the total giving of myself to God. My sacrifice is evidence that His sacrifice on the cross has touched me, indeed, transformed me. I am broken. Readily repentant, I run to opportunities for reconciliation. I forgive and seek forgiveness. I pay debts. I add acts of restitution to genuine repentance. In the meal offering, I give my life as an act of worshipful service. In the peace offering, I now enjoy fellowship with God! The altar has become a table. These offerings all presuppose the sin offering and are meaningless without it.

Notice how we move back and forth in these offerings from the vertical to the horizontal and back again. The sin offering is vertical. It repairs my damaged relationship with God. The trespass offering then insists on a horizontal focus, demanding restitution with men whom my sin has damaged. The burnt offering takes me back to the vertical. I have settled my relationship problem with God (sin offering) and my fellowman (trespass offering), and now I deepen my relationship with God by offering the burnt offering. God's response to my dedication in the burnt offering is a request that I love and serve others; thus, the meal offering and the horizontal dimension again. Finally, in the peace offering, the vertical and horizontal join together as I celebrate a fellowship meal with God and my brothers.

Worship involves a dialectic between the vertical and the horizontal. Touched by God, I touch you. Forgiven by God, I forgive you. Experiencing His love, it overflows toward you. I am at peace with Him. Consequently, I am at peace with you.

Three distinct movements take place in these offerings: (1) the healing of my broken relationships in the sin and trespass offerings; (2) the rediscovery of meaning and purpose for my life in the burnt (consecration) and meal (service) offerings; (3) the celebration of wholeness in the peace offering.

These offerings are around and about the altar, and the altar is about prayer. Prayer is not about acquisition; it is about transformation. Only in prayer is my relationship with God and others kept pure and balanced. At the altar, I am required to move to deeper levels of sensitivity about how my actions affect God and others. Only in prayer do I discover God's will for my life, that He has a purpose and mission for me. Only in prayer do I find the strength to fulfill that mission. Only in prayer do I experience fellowship with God as an intimate friend. Dining with God, filling up on His presence, is what makes for a life of peace!

THE OFFERINGS IN LATER BIBLICAL LITERATURE

A number of Scriptural references help us see how these five offerings were viewed in the later history of Israel (Leviticus 9:1-4, 6, 15-24; Psalm 51:16, 17; Hosea 6:6; Amos 5:21-24). What happens in Israel and to most religious movements is that the symbols get preserved, but the substance, the meaning for which they stand, is lost.

To this point, we have seen priests and rulers. Now the prophets weigh in. They seem to function when the priesthood or kingly role is out of balance. The prophets are the watch-guards of moral and spiritual balance. They speak to kings. They address the priests. They arbitrate the direction of the nation for God.

The Prophets and The Five Offerings

In Amos 5:21-24, the prophet appears to cry out against sacrifice: *"I hate, I despise your feast days, and I will not smell in your solemn assemblies ..."*

God had ordained the feast days. Here, God declares that He has come to "hate" these worship festivals. He refuses to "smell" the incense or the savor of the altar. The worship of Israel "stinks." It is no longer a pleasant aroma to God. The burnt offering, the meat or grain offering, and the peace or fellowship offerings are sweet-smelling offerings to God. The sin and trespass offerings were never called sweet-smelling offerings to God. Sin and trespass have noxious odors about them—at least to God. Consecration has a sweet aroma about it, but here something has soured the consecration offerings, giving them a foul odor!

> *Though you offer Me burnt offerings and your grain offerings, I will not accept them, Nor will I regard your fattened peace offerings. 23 Take away from Me the noise of your songs, For I will not hear the melody of your stringed instruments. 24 But let justice run down like water, And righteousness like a mighty stream* (vv. 22-24).

Notice carefully that not all of the five sacrifices noted in Leviticus are mentioned here. Two are omitted here—sin and trespass. These offerings of reparation are no longer valued by

Israel. They apparently skip repentance and restitution and go straight to consecration. God, through the prophet, is declaring that practice unacceptable. Consecration cannot be a substitute for repentance. One cannot consecrate himself right with God. Redirection is necessary out of redemption and regeneration. Consecration without our humble, dependent heart is meaningless. Here, the sacrifices, though costly, are rejected. The songs are simply noise. God is deaf to the melodies. He commits Himself to send a flood of judgment until the muddy stream of hypocritical worship runs pure with righteousness. Why is God so resistant to their worship?

Any group that ignores repentance, restitution, sin and judgment, are likely to be dismissed by God. The fire of authentic worship calls for the death of sin! Any other is a strange fire. Israel has developed a practice of worship that ignores the concept of repentance. Thus, their burnt, meal/grain, and peace/fellowship offerings are meaningless to God. Listen to Amos taunt Israel: *"Come to Bethel and transgress, At Gilgal multiply transgression; Bring your sacrifices every morning, Your tithes every three days"* (4:4).

Amos charges that *Bethel*, the house of God, has become the capitol for transgression. Israel brings sacrifices, even tithes, but at the same time, they are multiplying transgressions. Worship and illegitimate lifestyle are allowed to coexist. Cynically, Amos is saying, "Come to Bethel and sin!" Here is a religion that does not require lifestyle change. Worship has been separated from "the walk." The Tabernacle and the tablets were given together. They cannot be separated. Sin and religious celebration cannot exist side by side.

Hosea, a contemporary of Amos, gives us another perspective: *"For I desire mercy and not sacrifice, And the knowledge of God more than burnt offerings.   "But like men they transgressed the covenant; There they dealt treacherously with Me"* (6:6, 7).

It is not the formality of sacrificial offerings or ceremonial worship that God wants; rather, He wants mercy. This word is *hesed*. It is the closest Old Testament word to our familiar New Testament term *agape*, denoting God's covenant love. Sacrifice was to affect change. God wanted transformation in the heart of the believer through the experience of sacrifice. Israel sacrificed animals, but they themselves were unchanged. They failed to see the consequences of sin. Instead of tender hearts that honored God and one another, they became hard. Instead of a community that championed moral excellence, they ignored their need for repentance.

THE PRACTICED SACRIFICIAL ORDER

When the sacrifices were introduced in the Book of Leviticus, the order was the offerings of consecration first (chs. 1-3), and then the offerings of reparation (chs. 4, 5). Consecration is God's delight. Reparation is man's God-given remedy for sin. Consecration is a higher order of sacrifice so they advance my life. Reparation is the lower, the foundational order so they repair my life.

In Leviticus 9, we have a different order, the practiced order established for the sacrifices. This is the actual order in which Aaron, freshly installed as the high priest, first executed the offerings. Earlier, Moses had offered sacrifices. But now Aaron, a type of Christ, will offer, for the first time, sacrifices in behalf of the people. This is a historic moment. Watch what happens.

> *Then he brought the people's offering, and took the goat, which was the sin offering for the people, and killed it and offered it for sin, like the first one. And he brought the burnt*

offering and offered it according to the prescribed manner.
Then he brought the grain offering, took a handful of it,
and burned it on the altar, beside the burnt sacrifice of the
morning. He also killed the bull and the ram as sacrifices
of peace offerings, which were for the people. And Aaron's
sons presented to him the blood, which he sprinkled all
around on the altar (Leviticus 9:15-18).

Aaron brings the offering for the people. It is first, an offering for sin. Here is the issue of separation and reparation.
Then, he moves to the offerings of consecration, bringing a
burnt offering, a grain offering, and finally a peace offering.
Note the order: sin, burnt, meal and peace. The blood is sprinkled around the altar by Aaron's sons, the priests, making it a
bloody scene. The trespass offering is not included here since
it is offered for specific sins in a relationship violation either
with God or one's fellowman. That does not apply here for the
first offerings offered at the newly raised-up Tabernacle by its
new high priest, Aaron.

Here we have first sacrifices in their corporate application.
When these offerings are properly practiced, they bring three
things: 1. The blessing of God and His presence; 2. A manifestation of His glory; 3. And then fire of God falls.

In verse 22, we have the pronouncement of blessing: "And
Aaron lifted up his hand toward the people, and blessed them,
and came down from offering of the sin offering, and the burnt
offering, and peace offerings."

Next, we have the revelation of glory: "*And Moses and Aar-*
on went into the tabernacle of meeting, and came out and
blessed the people. Then the glory of the Lord appeared to all
the people" (v. 23).

In verse 22, Aaron lifted his hands and blessed the people.
Then in verse 23, he reentered the Holy Place with Moses. And
when they came out, there was a second blessing. Then the

glory of the Lord appeared, and the fire of the Lord fell.

And fire came out from before the Lord and consumed the burnt offering and the fat on the altar. When all the people saw it, they shouted and fell on their faces (v. 24).

Wow! A direct lightning strike from heaven hit the altar—a bolt out of the blue! No one knew how. What a moment that must have been. Suddenly, the sacrifice on the altar was consumed—wasted, gone. It was as if heaven swallowed it up and left the altar smoldering. The experience was so awesome that all of Israel fell on their faces in fearful reverence.

This sacred fire had come specifically in response to the burnt offering. Remember that this is the offering of the sinless Christ. His offering calls for the joyful and liberated surrender of our blood-bought redeemed lives to God. The acceptance of our sinful lives by a holy God is enabled only by the death of the innocent Christ. It is the offering of ourselves as a living sacrifice. In 6:12, 13, God had commanded:

And the fire on the altar shall be kept burning on it; it shall not be put out. And the priest shall burn wood on it every morning, and lay the burnt offering in order on it; and he shall burn on it the fat of the peace offerings. A fire shall always be burning on the altar; it shall never go out.

This is God's fire—fire from heaven. The sacred fire came in response to sacrifice and was to be sustained on the altar of sacrifice. The basic law of worship is that this fire must never go out! Even in transition from one site to another, the coals upon this altar were carried in the censers of the priests and kept alive until the altar had been established at a new location. When it appeared that God's Tent had been folded and His glory lifted, some faithful priest still had live coals. The fire would burn again, and the glory would again settle over the

Most Holy Place. God's purposes in the earth are sure!

Here is a religion of blood and fire. The blood shed at Calvary is followed by the fire of Pentecost. Sacrifice and Spirit are bound together in the Christian faith. Calvary and Pentecost can never be completely understood apart from each other. The sacrifice of Christ allows for the gift of the abiding Spirit. And sacrifice always draws the fire of God.

The Pattern in Romans

The same pattern of principles seen in the sacrifices can be seen in the Book of Romans, the New Testament treatise on soteriology. The order is, first, the universal condition of sin, the moral devolution of man (ch. 1). Then the universality of sin, its solution and the journey to relationship wholeness is found (chs. 2-8). Next, the trespass of Israel is explained with a warning that we should not follow in the steps of Israel's trespass (chs. 9-11). That is followed by the call for the total giving of self, the principle of the burnt offering. Even the language here is sacrificial (12:1, 2). Next, service gifts (frequently called motivational gifts) are noted. These correspond to the meal or grain offering (vv. 3-8). Finally, the issues of peace and relationship are addressed by Paul (12:9—16:20).

Let's take a closer look.

1. **The sin offering.** Paul establishes the universality of sin and trespass. And he proceeds to call for repentance and justification through faith. Sin is universal. *"All have sinned, and It says, 'Abraham believed God!'"* (See 4:3). The basis of his relationship was not obedience to the Law, it was faith. And the exercise of that faith "was counted unto him for righteousness." So Paul makes the bold application, *"But to him who ... believes on Him who justifies the ungodly, his faith is accounted for righteousness"* Romans 4:5). Salvation is by faith.

He then uses a post-Law example: *"Just as David ... to whom God imputes righteousness apart from works"* (v. 6). Paul argues that David was not saved by the keeping of the Law, but by the gift of righteousness.

All of this and the record of Abraham, David and others *"Now it was not written for his sake alone that it was imputed to him, but also for us. It shall be imputed to us who believe in Him who raised up Jesus our Lord from the dead"* (vv. 23, 24). What God did in the old covenant, He will do in the new, through Christ. He will justify us through faith. *"Therefore, having been justified by faith, we have peace with God through our Lord Jesus Christ"* (5:1).

In one bold sweep, we move from the sin offering to peace with God. How do we get this peace with God? Through faith in Christ. *"There is therefore now no condemnation to those who are in Christ Jesus, who do not walk according to the flesh, but according to the Spirit"* (8:1).

Here we are standing on the mountain of God's grace. And nothing can separate us from the love of God though which we are more than conquerors (vv. 37-39)!

2. **The trespass offering.** Trespass is dealt with in chapters 9-11, where Paul discusses the failure of Israel to be the agents of God in the earth, the nation among the nations, a kingdom of priests. They rejected the Messiah, Jesus, resulting in their being cut off as the natural olive branches. Israel's failure to serve the nations as agents of God is a sin of trespass against God and the world that leaves them relationally alienated. Paul warns the church not to let the same fate happen to them.

3. **The burnt offering.** The next sacrifice to which we come is the burnt offering. *"I beseech you therefore, brethren, by the mercies of God, that you present your bodies a living*

sacrifice, holy, acceptable to God, which is your reasonable service" (12:1).

In the Old Testament, the sacrifices die. In the New Testament, the sacrifices live. We live, to "flesh out" the will of God, to complete the work of Jesus that He chooses to do through His body. The sin offering was a life-waster. It was killed at the door of the Tabernacle and then carried outside the camp. So Christ was crucified outside the camp. The sin offering was not even offered on the altar. In the burnt offering, we have the first sacrifice worthy of the altar—the offering of the self for consecration. *"And do not be conformed to this world, but be transformed by the renewing of your mind, that you may prove what is that good and acceptable and perfect will of God"* (v. 2).

4. **The meal offering**—service.

> *Having then gifts differing according to the grace that is given to us, let us use them: if prophecy, let us prophesy in proportion to our faith; 7 or ministry, let us use it in our ministering; he who teaches, in teaching; 8 he who exhorts, in exhortation; he who gives, with liberality; he who leads, with diligence; he who shows mercy, with cheerfulness* (vv. 6-8).

Here are the motivational gifts, our most native leanings. The sacrificial commitment we make cannot be a symbol of consecration. It must be practical, or it means nothing. So the burnt offering is now given practical meaning in the meat or grain offering. Our life is transformed by His grace. In the crushing and humbling experience of salvation, we taste death and life. We then may become bread to minister to the needs of others. We offer words of exhortation, comfort a n d edifica-tion. We serve one another, demonstrating practically our sacrificial commitment. We offer the bread of insight through the gift of teaching. All these are ways in which we serve practically.

5. **The peace offering**—relationship. Now Paul concludes the sacrificial cycle by focusing on relationships. We are to *"Be kindly affectionate to one another with brotherly love, in honor giving preference to one another"* (v. 10). We are to *"bless, and curse not"* (v. 14). If we have an enemy, we are to feed him and give him drink (v. 20). We are to model citizenship in the way we relate to governmental authorities (13:1, 2). Our only obligation to one another should be love that fulfills the Law (vv. 8, 9). Whatever makes for *"peace and the things by which one may edify another"* (14:19)—that is what we are to do.

The conclusion of Romans is consumed with relationship wholeness. This is the essence of the peace offering.

In Romans we find the outline of the sacrificial order taken from Leviticus. First, sin (chs. 2—8) and trespass (chs. 9—11) are dealt with. Then and only then, can we give the gift of self (12:1, 2). Out of this giving flows God's giftedness (vv. 3-8) through us, concluding in peace and ministry that produces healthy relationships (12:9—16:20). Our peace with God has altered the way we relate to one another. Why do Christians fail to live this way?

We have treated the offerings one by one. We have done so to define their various aspects. Now, we should acknowledge them as an organic whole. If we dissect these, separating consecration from genuine, ongoing repentance and restitution, we should hear the voice of Amos, the prophet, telling us how meaningless the pieces are apart from one another. Repentance needs consecration to be complete. Conviction needs to find a resting place in the peace offering. Brokenness in relationship needs the fellowship offering. We need a whole altar experience—one that deals with sin and self, which affects the transformation of relationship with God and others. It combines repentance and restitution with consecration and healthy relationships. It moves from alienation in and by sin, to consecration and celebration with victory over sin. The offerings are whole, just as Romans is a whole. One cannot claim the justification of 5:1 without embracing the consecration of 12:1. One cannot claim peace with God (5:1) without living in peace with others (12:18).

In Romans 1, we see a world out of control in rejection of the Creator and in the process of self-destruction. In chapters 12-14, we see men and women as they were meant to live—in sensitive service to God and one another, with relationships that reflect the Christlike character. It appears that Paul is following the five offerings as an outline for the Book of Romans.

Sacrifice and Lifestyle—A Lesson From The Psalms

Lifestyle and worship are inseparable. Let's note Psalm 50 for that lesson.

1. **God has not been silent.** *"The Mighty One, God the Lord, Has spoken and called the earth From the rising of the sun to its going down"* (Psalm 50:1).

   There has been a revelation of God in nature itself. He has spoken. In fact, He is speaking every day, all day long! All around in nature are evidences of His existence, of His might.

2. **He is neither silent nor secluded.** *"Out of Zion, the* perfection of beauty, God will shine forth" (v. 2).

   He has manifested Himself. This is not the general

revelation of verse 1, rising out of the witness of nature. He has devoted Himself to Zion. He has revealed Himself to them and through them. Israel is without excuse. God has been perfectly revealed, beautifully made known in and out of Israel. The nation has seen His beauty. The manifestation of God has come out of Zion. How could they not know Him? The situation must be addressed. God will confront Israel in a way that cannot be denied.

3. **God is coming as a disciplinarian.** *"Our God shall come, and shall not keep silent; A fire shall devour before Him, And it shall be very tempestuous all around Him"* (v. 3).

God is on His way. He is already on the road. Israel has an unavoidable appointment with Him. He has something to say! The meeting will not be pleasant. He will now speak in a way that will allow no one to accuse Him of being silent. Fire will go before Him. He will come surrounded by a storm. The heavens will roar with thunder and the earth will tremble. *"He shall call to the heavens from above, And to the earth, that He may judge His people"* (v. 4).

THE SUMMONS

This call to the heavens and earth is really a summons—courtroom terminology. Heaven and earth are being summoned by God to serve as the jury in a trial against His people. God has brought charges against them. A pronouncement of judgment is about to take place.

1. **An assembly of covenant people is called.** *"Gather My saints together to Me, Those who have made a covenant with Me by sacrifice"* (v. 5).

A solemn assembly is being ordered! Those who are called the covenant people are being summoned! They have been sacrificing, but something is wrong. They have forgotten what God has said (see v. 1). They fail to see Him presently shining forth among them (see v. 2). So, God will no longer allow for general revelation. He will speak to them in a formal setting, one that records and weighs His words. He will speak to people who supposedly worship Him, but neither hear Him nor see Him.

2. **The first witness is called.** *"Let the heavens declare His righteousness, For God Himself is Judge. Selah"* (v. 6).

   The heavens are declaring His righteousness before the covenant people. Wait! That was the role He created for them, for Israel. They were to be witnesses of His character in the earth. As a result of their negligence, the only witness left in the earth is that of creation. This is obviously not God's idea. It wasn't then; it isn't now. Nature bears the fingerprints of God, but man bears His image. Yet at times, nature—fickle as she is, unstable as she is under the curse—is a better witness than God's own covenant people. It should not be this way.

3. **The second witness is called.** The first witness was overwhelming—the heavens! But now, the Judge Himself will take the stand. This is bad news for Israel! *"Hear, O My people, and I will speak, O Israel, and I will testify against you; I am God, your God"* (v. 7).

The word "hear" is more courtroom terminology, a reminded of the formal and accusatory nature of this encounter. The chief witness against the people, it turns out, is God himself! God now takes the witness stand. Here is His formal testimony: *"I will not rebuke you for your sacrifices Or your burnt offerings, Which are continually before Me"* (v. 8).

God's charge is not for sacrifices withheld at the altar. It is not a reproof for the lack of formal and ceremonial worship. The burnt offerings have been continual. The Temple is open. Worship is ongoing—at least superficially. The people have been worshiping—at least ceremonially. But ritual is not what God wants. He wants more. He wants a healthy and holy relationship.

> *I will not take a bull from your house, Nor goats out of your folds. 10 For every beast of the forest is Mine, And the cattle on a thousand hills. 11 I know all the birds of the mountains, And the wild beasts of the field are Mine* (vv. 9-11).

God does not need the sacrifices. Israel is giving Him what is already His. He knows the sparrows. The wild beasts are His as well. His delight is not in birds and beasts offered as sacrifices. That practice was only to provide a vivid lesson of the nature of death's connection to sin. He does not need to be fed. *"If I were hungry, I would not tell you; For the world is Mine, and all its fullness. Will I eat the flesh of bulls, Or drink the blood of goats?"* (vv. 12, 13). He wants man. He wants man to whom He gave the gift of autonomy, a free will, now enslaved to sin, He wants him.

Israel believes that in merely offering their sacrifices, they are fulfilling their obligation to God and somehow meeting a need that He has. Nonsense. He needs nothing from them. Instead, what He elicits from us is for our good. *"Offer to God thanksgiving, And pay your vows to the Most High"* (v. 14).

God does not need the sacrifices; instead, we need the lessons they teach. And that is, that we need Him. What God wants is thanksgiving as an offering! God wants a grateful people who honor their vows. He wants an attitude alteration, not merely a ritual act. But, their sense of obligation to Him is gone! Even in the days of trouble, they are no longer praying.

They are utterly self-absorbed. Even in trouble, they have no need of God. They are self-sufficient. God wants the focus off of them and back onto Him. They have wrongly assumed that their accomplishments are their doings; thus, the lack of thanksgiving. And thankless worship is no worship at all. *"Call upon Me in the day of trouble; I will deliver you, and you shall glorify Me"* (v. 15).

"Call upon me," declares the Lord. He wants a people who manifest faith and trust by active dependence upon Him. In times of trouble they pray, and prayer becomes the occasion by which He shows Himself gloriously alive. "Glorify me," He requests of the people. He wants a bond with them. True worship is an evidence of that bond.

4. **The specific charge.** Now we come to the specific charge. This is the heart of the court case. What is the problem? *"But to the wicked God says: "What right have you to declare My statutes, Or take My covenant in your mouth, Seeing you hate instruction And cast My words behind you?"* (vv. 16, 17).

"To the wicked?" The unimaginable has happened. The holy people called to represent their holy God have become "wicked"! The problem is twofold. First, they take the covenant in their mouths. They use the language of faith. They give God lip service, but the actions of their lives displace any real dependence upon God. The principles no longer serve as a navigational guide for their lives. Hypocrisy reigns. They declare with their lips what they no longer live. What they demand of others, they resent when it is demanded of them.

Second, they hate instruction. They are intolerant when others impose on them the values of the Law. Personal liberty has triumphed over personal responsibility. Private actions are not seen as having public impact. They have cast the word of the Lord away. They have discarded the foundations. The root of their problem is the attitude toward the commandments. They are in a posture of rebellion!

The charges are before the court. The witness will now enter into evidence the specific examples that serve to prove the charge.

Example one: Complicity in another's sin. *"When you saw a thief, you consented with him, And have been a partaker with adulterers"* (v. 18).

"You saw a thief and you consented with him!" How? Not by being a partner in his crime, but by inaction. The attitude of rebellion against God is manifest as indifference to sin. The result is that it neutralizes one's moral influence upon others. How can this individual say to others, "That is wrong!" when they themselves are not coming under the influence of the Commandments?

Example two: Corrupt conversation and speech. *"You give your mouth to evil, And your tongue frames deceit"* (v. 19).

A holy people should be holy in their speech. These people are not! The language is evil. They speak in deceptive and fraudulent ways. They cannot be trusted. They violate truth. They bend honesty. Their tongue, an instrument intended for righteousness and edification, is now used for evil and deceit. Life should be in the tongue. Here, the tongue is an instrument of evil.

Example three: Slander creates division. *"You sit and speak against your brother; You slander your own* *mother's son"* (v. 20).

Brother is against brother, if it helps his own cause.
The heart of a mother is broken over feuding sons.

Notice that each Scriptural example above actually builds on the one before. We have a picture of sin escalating, of relationships deteriorating and, in the larger scheme, of a culture breaking down.

The first example (v. 18) involves the sighting of wrongdoing followed by silence. Let's assume that the individual did not want to get involved in the matter. He witnessed the thievery but did not come forth with convicting information. He chose neutrality. The charge of God is that such neutrality is nonexistent on moral ground. But let's argue for the accused! He stayed neutral. He was not active in the crime; he was just an innocent bystander. It was unfortunate that he was there at the time, but God will not allow such neutrality.

The second example (v. 19) reveals a not-so-innocent individual. Here, the accused is discovered saying things that reflect inner rebellion. In the first example, he said nothing—to attempt to maintain moral neutrality. Now, the mouth that would not be given to declaring righteous standards is given to evil, to deceit. Whatever neutrality was alleged in the first example is now dissolved.

In the third example (v. 20), relationships begin to come apart. And these are not distant relationships. The relationships that are unraveling are those with whom this individual should be closest—their family! It is the slander of a brother. Where is God when this is happening? *"These things you have done, and I kept silent; You thought that I was altogether like you; But I will rebuke you, And set them in order before your eyes"* (v. 21).

God has also been silent, but, He will be silent no longer! The problem? A faulty perception of God! "You thought I was like you!"

The Warning: *"Now consider this, you who forget God, Lest I tear you in pieces, And there be none to deliver"* (v. 22).

Again, notice the progression. First, a people allow themselves to slip into a pattern of shallow and ceremonial worship. Sacrifice and vows are treated lightly. Today, some people no longer take seriously the implications of their worship and liturgy, the meaning of their confessions, the message in their songs, nor even the exhortations of the Word. It is not that the shift is intentional. At first, it may be imperceptible, but it has devastating consequences.

Watch the progression:

- Shallow worship and a ceremonial worship experience (vv. 8-15) manifest themselves practically in a disregard for the Word on a daily basis (v. 17).
- Rebellion against God's standards subtly take root in the heart.
- The next step is moral neutrality (v. 18). They see evil and say nothing.
- Then, neutrality is signally gone when the mouth begins to reveal a corrupt and deceitful heart (v. 19). What one has only allowed himself to think, he now says!
- Unedifying and insensitive speech now destroys bonds. Relationships begin to deteriorate (v. 20).
- The consequence is that their lives are in disarray.

Shallow worship has produced a life that is no longer rooted in Biblical actions and attitudes. That led to moral neutrality, then to verbal patterns that revealed the inner moral sickness. These deadly speech patterns began to destroy significant relationships. All the while, God appears silent, but He has a message for Israel: *"Think about this ... lest I tear you to pieces!"*

(See v. 22). This is tough talk.

But then, God offers a gracious alternative. *"Whoever offers praise glorifies Me; And to him who orders his conduct aright I will show the salvation of God"* (v. 23).

Here is God's alternative: "Offer praise and reorder your behavior!" Offer is a worship word. Praise is the acceptable sacrifice that pleases God, but praise must be sincere. It must reflect the discovery that God is great, incomparable and worthy of praise. To praise is "to testify in behalf of another." Here, God had to take the stand for Himself. His voice in the earth, Israel, is silent in its witness for Him. He is looking for a people who will witness in the earth. They will declare His greatness. They will exalt Him.

Praise must not stand alone. The offerer also needs to order his conversation right. Conversation here means more than "talk;" it refers to a lifestyle. When both worship and walk are in harmony, then the worshiper will see God's salvation. This is really the same principle we noted earlier: worship, walk and warfare—always tied together!

The dichotomy between worship and walk happens when the priests leave off instruction but continue leading public worship. After a time, such worship loses its meaning. Detached from the principles of holy living, worship is meaningless.

THE PUBLIC AND THE PRIVATE

The Book of Leviticus is largely given to worship—sacrifices and ceremonies. The Book of Deuteronomy is given to the Law. Both books were gifts of God to Israel through Moses at Sinai. Both are critical for Israel's health. Leviticus invites them into God's presence in legitimate ways. Deuteronomy preserves the integrity of their lives before the nations. In *worship* (Leviticus), they meet a holy God. In *walk* (Deuteronomy), they exhibit what a difference the relationship with God makes in the way they live.

The priest had the public responsibility of leading worship (the Leviticus tradition) and the less public and more tedious responsibility of teaching the meaning of worship and the incumbent responsibilities of being the people of God (the Deuteronomy tradition). His public worship role eventually provided robes and regalia, pomp and prestige. His teaching role in moral guidance was more tedious and less glamorous, more confrontational. His public worship role gave him the status of presiding over the superficial altar. But the teaching role called for the principle of sacrifice to be modeled and practiced among the people.

The ceremonial public role was much more inviting than the personal character-building responsibility. So in time, the public role became the all-important function of the priest, and the teaching role was diminished. The consequence was meaningless worship.

The same tragedy is repeating itself in popular megachurch worship centers that are not appropriately tethered to discipleship processes.

CAIN AND ABEL'S OFFERINGS (Genesis 4:3-8)

I believe Cain knew that blood sacrifice was the only sacrifice that was acceptable, but he chose to substitute his own way. That belief is based on the implied sacrifice of God from which He made clothes for Adam and Eve. But there is something deeper.

We know that there is only one way. Why? From the very beginning, Satan has set forth the pluralistic proposition, the lie of Genesis 3:4, 5: *"Then the serpent said ..."You will not surely die ... your eyes will be opened, and you will be like God."* The Serpent was saying, "There is another way! God is holding out on you." Sin deposits itself in the heart, and its most fundamental form is a spirit of independence, of defiance, even rebellion. God said to Cain, *"If you do well, will you not be accepted? And if you do not do well, sin lies at the door"* (4:7).

The real determination as to whether or not God accepts my sacrifice and my act of worship is deeper than the sacrifice it-self. The condition of my heart is the real issue! We could paraphrase the passage, "If you do well . . . if your heart is right, you will be accepted! If not . . . there is a sin problem!"

Cain could have brought a lamb, but if his heart had not been right, he would have still been rejected. On the other hand, if his heart had been right, he would have brought the right offering. Cain enters into worship, but he is not changed in worship. For Cain, worship is a ritual. For Abel, it is the ex-pression of a relationship. Relationship problems with God that are unresolved always end up as relationship problems with others. *"Now Cain talked with Abel his brother; and it came to pass, when they were in the field, that Cain rose up against Abel his brother and killed him"* (v. 8).

Cain leaves the altar and kills Abel. He leaves church and commits a murder. The absence of peace in the relationship between these two brothers is traceable to the sin issue in the heart of Cain. The wages of sin are always death, in one way or another! People who do not repent become ministers of death!

JESUS AND HIS OFFERING
The Old Testament sacrificial lamb did not atone, it only bought more time. It only deferred the suspended judgment. *"Both gifts and sacrifices ... cannot make him who performed the service perfect in regard to the conscience"* (Hebrews 9:9).

The sacrifice offered on the Day of Atonement allowed Israel to spend one more year knowing that God dwelt among them but never knowing that God could dwell in them. Now, Jesus has strapped Himself to the altar. The veil of separation has now been removed. Because of His sacrifice, we can now come to the brass altar and pass beyond it. Now we can draw near to the presence of God. Now that Jesus has offered His perfect sacrifice for our sins, we can follow the bloody footprints of Christ right into the Most Holy Place. *"But Christ came as High Priest of the good things to come, with the greater and more perfect tabernacle ..."* (v. 11).

He is now the High Priest of the tabernacle in heaven. *"Not with the blood of goats and calves, but with His own blood He entered the Most Holy Place once for all, having obtained eternal redemption"* (v. 12).

The earthly high priest entered twice into the Most Holy Place—first for himself and then for his people. Jesus entered into heaven's holy place only once. He had no need to purify Himself, He only needed to enter as a representative of you and me. That He was accepted means we are accepted.

> *For if the blood of bulls and goats ... sanctifies ... the flesh, how much more shall the blood of Christ, who ... offered Himself without spot to God, cleanse your conscience from dead works to serve the living God? ... He is the Mediator of the new covenant ... that those who are called may receive the promise of the eternal inheritance* (vv. 13-15).

> *Previously saying, "Sacrifice and ... offerings for sin You did not desire, nor had pleasure in them" (which are offered according to the law), then He said, "Behold, I have come to do Your will, O God." ... we have been sanctified through the offering of the body of Jesus Christ once for all. And every priest stands ministering daily and offering repeatedly the same sacrifices, which can never take away sins. But this Man ... offered one sacrifice for sins forever, sat down at*

the right hand of God, ... For by one offering He has perfected forever those who are being sanctified. (10:8-12, 14).

Let us therefore come boldly to the throne of grace, that we may obtain mercy and find grace to help in time of need (4:16).

A tremendous price has been paid for our sins to be remitted. Today, if we came to the gate, we would realize that we have no offering for sin that is acceptable. There is no way to pay for the penalty of our sin. Then, upon the ground, we would notice the stains of blood. We would be greeted with the wonderful news that a Lamb has been provided for our sins by another. A blood offering has been given to expiate our sins. We would see it now upon the altar—a Lamb, perfect and spotless, now slain. Once lively and innocent, the Lamb is now limp and lifeless. Suddenly and mysteriously, the earth would shake. Strange sounds would fill the air. Light would give way to darkness. A cold and frightening feeling would be almost tangible. It is as if nature's groans were traceable to the death of that innocent Lamb. Our eyes would go from the horizon back to the altar, back to the Lamb. But the Lamb is no longer there—He has disappeared. Beyond the altar is the blood-stained trail that marks His exodus toward the laver, into the Holy and Most Holy Place. Into the presence of God, we are following the bloody footprints of Jesus Christ, the Lamb. Can His blood cover our sins?

What can wash away my sin?
Nothing but the blood of Jesus!
What can make me whole again?
Nothing but the blood of Jesus.
O precious is the flow,
that makes me white as snow;
No other fount I know,
nothing but the blood of Jesus!
— Robert Lowry

Into the Holy Place we go. We are looking for the Lamb who has disappeared from off the altar. He is not in the Holy Place. But the trail of His bloodstains are on the ground. We notice the beautiful veil. It is rent from the top to the bottom down the middle. It, too, is stained with blood. The Lamb must have

gone into the Most Holy Place, so we venture boldly and faithfully through the torn veil into that room containing the ark and the mercy seat. But we find not a slain Lamb, but a Lion. The Lamb lives—as the Lion of the tribe of Judah! (Revelation 5:5, 6). He has broken the power of sin. He has divided the veil. He has invited us into the presence of the Holy Father. We are home again.

Corrie ten Boom said, "He has cast our sin into the sea of His forgetfulness and put a sign on the bank that says, 'No fishin' allowed!'" In the words of the old gospel song, He has washed us:

> *Whiter than snow, yes, whiter than snow.*
> *Now wash me and I shall be whiter than snow.*
> — James L. Nicholson

CHAPTER TEN

THE LAVER

The Principle of Sanctification

Now, having passed the altar, I again encounter a second piece of furniture. It stands between the brass altar and the entrance to the Holy Place. It is a huge basin made of copper, bronze or brass mirrors and filled with water. No worship is conducted here, no blood sacrifice offered. And yet, there could have been no true worship without this laver. It is an essential at the very heart of worship. It is described in Exodus 30:

> *Then the Lord spoke to Moses, saying: "You shall also make a laver of bronze, with its base also of bronze, for washing. You shall put it between the tabernacle of meeting and the altar. And you shall put water in it,* (vv. 17, 18).

THE LAVER DESIGN

The laver had two parts—a bowl and a base. Some suggest

that the base itself was a bowl; thus a kind of two-tiered arrangement. The upper bowl would have been used to draw water; the lower, probably wider, to catch water. The priest probably did not wash *in* the laver, but *at* the laver. Typically, Eastern custom prefers running water for cleansing, not still water. Speculation leads us to believe that water may have flowed through specially designed spouts or primitive faucets from the upper basin to a wider lower one. Water for washing would be taken from the upper reservoir. Like a saucer and a cup, the lower base, with a broader diameter than the upper reservoir,[90] would have caught water that would have otherwise spilled on the ground, creating a muddy mess in the court area near the laver. Jewish commentators note that no special water was used, but that it was changed daily.[91] This would include constant, but sparing use.

There are no dimensions given for

the laver. Paul Zehr, in his book *God Dwells With His People*, estimates the diameter of the bowl at 2 cubits (3 feet) and the height as 1 cubit (18 inches).[92] William Brown says the upper portion of the laver was a cistern large enough to hold a day's supply of water.[93] The material for the laver was from *"the looking*

---

[90] William Brown, *The Tabernacle—Its Priests and Its Services* (Peabody, MA: Hendrickson, 1996) 54. See also C. W. Slemming, *Made According to Pattern* (London: Marshall, Morgan and Scott, 1938) 70.

[91] See Stephen Olford, *The Tabernacle: Camping With God* (Neptune, NJ: Loizeaux Brothers, 1971) 100. Also see James Strong, *The Tabernacle of Israel in the Desert* (Grand Rapids: Baker, 1952) 19; and Moshe Levine and N. Levine, *The Tabernacle: Its Structure and Utensils* (London: Soncino Press Limited, 1969) 120.

[92] Paul Zehr, *God Dwells With His People* (Scottsdale, PA: Herald, 1981) 52.

[93] Brown, 54.

glasses of the women assembling, which assembled at the door of the tabernacle" (38:8). It would have been made of highly refined brass with a mirrorlike quality. The mirrors represent the need for self-examination as a prerequisite for His presence. The water represents the need for self-purification as a prerequisite for His presence.

THE LAVER IN USAGE

> *For Aaron and his sons shall wash their hands and their feet in water from it. When they go into the tabernacle of meeting, or when they come near the altar to minister, to burn an offering made by fire to the Lord, they shall wash with water, lest they die* (30:19, 20).

A priest was never to come into the Holy Place without having stopped at the laver and completed the ceremonial and practical action of looking and washing. No priest was to attend the altar without checking the purity of his hands and his feet.

Notice the contrast of the altar and the laver. The two represent the multidimensional grace of God. The altar comes first, the laver second. At the altar, we see what God has done for us, justifying us in the cleansing gift of His Son, Jesus Christ. At the laver, our appropriate response is to cleanse ourselves. At the altar, I am sanctified legally (justified); at the laver, I am sanctified practically. Attendance at the laver was critical. In fact, it was a life-and-death matter. Note the words: *"Aaron and his sons shall wash their hands and their feet in water from it ... when they come near the altar to minister, to burn an offering ... lest they die"* (vv. 19, 20).

Note the term "from." Westerners tend to wash by immersing their hands into water. Easterners washed in running water, or tried to prevent polluting stored water by drawing water out and pouring it. They washed *from*, not *in*.[94] Aaron and his

---

[94] Slemming, 69.

sons were to wash their hands when they went into the Holy Place. And when they came near the altar to minister, they were to wash again. Ministry to God in the Holy Place demanded holy hands. Ministry to men at the altar also demanded holy hands.

They were to wash their hands "when they go into the tabernacle"—that is, when they went into the Holy Place to attend the table, burn incense, attend the candles, or any other activity. They were also to wash when they "came near to the altar to minister." Ministry to God in the Holy Place and ministry to men in the court both demanded holy hands. No matter which altar they aimed themselves toward, the bloody brass altar or the sweet golden altar, they could approach only with freshly washed hands.

The washing of hands symbolized the cleansing of works—our doing, our acts. Paul wrote to Timothy urging that men pray, *"lifting up holy hands"* (1 Timothy 2:8). It is not just posture that Paul is addressing here. Rather, he is encouraging people who commune with God to do so having examined their hands (their works), and having found them holy, to lift up holy hands unto God. The forward view is that in prayer, I also offer sanctified hands to God to do His work. Thus, as I pray about needs, I offer God sanctified tools through which He might meet these needs. The washing of feet (Exodus 30:19) symbolizes the cleansing of ways—behavior and lifestyle patterns.

In later years, the Jews developed a blessing for the washing of the hands: *"Blessed art Thou, Lord our God, King of the universe, who sanctified us with His commandments and commanded us concerning the washing of hands."*[95]

As the priest washed at the laver at the beginning of every day, every man throughout the camp in the same manner was to wash his hands at the beginning of each new day as an act of

---

[95] Hayim Halevy Donin, *To Pray as a Jew* (New York: Basic Books, 1980) 185.

consecration. Sanitation and sanctification, cleanliness and holiness are bound together. Any blessing was delayed until after the hands were washed. No blessing could be conferred by unclean hands. No blessing uttered by one with unclean hands could be considered an authentic blessing.

The conventional Hebrew word for washing is *rohetz*, and so the washing of hands would be *al rehitzat yadayim*. But that is not what Jewish men were taught to utter at the washing of their hands. Instead, they said, *al netilat yadayim*, which means not the washing, but "the lifting up of the hands." Washing, making the hands clean, lifted them to a higher purpose. It consecrated them for nobler deeds.[96] The lifting was in the purity.

At the gate, Aaron and his sons were *wholly* washed. The laver was for specific and *partial* cleansing. It assumed a prior more complete purity. Here, only hands and feet were washed. In John 13, Jesus told Peter that if He did not wash him, he could have no part with Him. Peter suggested a total bath. Jesus replied that if he had been cleansed, there was only the need to wash his feet.

Jesus used two different words for washed and wash (v. 10). He told Peter that he who is wholly washed (*louo*) does not need to be bathed, only to partially and specifically washed (*nipto*).[97] Everyone who lived in the New Testament and required the use of the public bathhouse could understand what Jesus meant. On the way home from the bathhouse, having been completely cleaned, yet now following the donkeys and camels on dung-packed roads with open sandals, the feet would again need to be cleaned again before entering the home. If you have been to the bathhouse of Calvary, you don't need to be saved again. But on life's road, it is so easy to pick up the pollution of this world, just as the priest would have

---

[96] Donin, 185-6.

[97] David M. Levy, *The Tabernacle: Shadows of the Messiah* (Bellmawr, NJ: Friends of Israel Gospel Ministry, 1993) 36.

dirtied or bloodied their bare feet in Tabernacle service. This was the purpose of the laver—partial, specific and persistent cleansing. Practical sanctification.

THE LAVER AS THE WORD

This sanctification is accomplished in relationship to the Word. Paul says that God sanctifies and cleanses the church *"with the washing of water by the word"* (Ephesians 5:26). In writing to Titus, Paul uses the term washing of *regeneration*, which he associates with the *"renewing of the Holy Ghost"* (3:5). This term literally translated is *"laver of regeneration—* a reference to the tabernacle."[98] The Word has a cleansing re-generating effect. The psalmist asked, *"How can a young man cleanse his way? By taking heed according to Your word"* (119:9, NKJV). Jesus prayed, *"Sanctify them through Thy truth; Thy word is truth"* (John 17:17). He told His disciples, *"Ye are clean through the word which I have spoken unto you"* (15:3). The Word of God gives balance to our lives.

It is in the Bible that we see what man should and could be and we attempt to match the image we see in the Word. One of our greatest temptations is rationalization. There is a tenden-cy to say, "I am as good as..." or, "That behavior was not as bad as..." or, "What I did in no way compared to what they did to me," or, "I am certainly more spiritual... loving... more mature than...." Paul says to the Corinthians, *"They. . . comparing themselves among themselves, are not wise"* (2 Corinthians 10:12). Compare yourself with Jesus!

THE LAVER IN THE NEW TESTAMENT

Self-examination. The importance of self-examination is

---

[98] The phrase "By the washing of regeneration" (*dia loutrou palingenesiav*) oc-curs only here. The word for washing, *loutron*, appears only here and in Ephesians 5:26. It does not mean the act of bathing, but the bath, the laver. See M.R. Vincent, *World Studies in the New Testament,* Vol. 2 (Macdill Airforce Base, FL: Macdonald, 1958) 1081.

a New Testament issue (James 1:22-25; John 15:3; 1 Corinthians 11:26-32). James, the brother of the Lord, says the Word is like a mirror. The road to self-deception involves exposure to the Word without change. *"For if anyone is a hearer of the word and not a doer, he is like a man observing his natural face in a mirror; for he observes himself, goes away, and immediately forgets what kind of man he was"* (1:23, 24).

Cleansing. *"You are already clean because of the word which I have spoken to you"* (John 15:3). The Word of God is also to have a cleansing effect. We wash with the "water" of the Word! Or it will indict us.

Examining the attitude. Notice the issue of self-examination in 1 Corinthians 11: *"Therefore whoever eats this bread or drinks this cup of the Lord in an unworthy manner will be guilty of the body and blood of the Lord"* (v. 27). The word *unworthily* is not an adjective, but an adverb. It modifies action. It describes the way in which a person eats and drinks—not our unworthy condition, an unworthy attitude. None of us are worthy, but He has declared us worthy and invited us to the table. Having been declared worthy and given such an honor, we must now show reverence and respect. How do we do that? *"But let a man examine himself, and so let him eat of the bread and drink of the cup"* (v. 28). We wash our hands and feet before we attend the table.

Discerning the body. *"For he who eats and drinks in an unworthy manner eats and drinks judgment to himself, not discerning the Lord's body"* (v. 29). Some translations say, "not discerning the body." This absence of discernment, of understanding and moral discrimination, is ultimately devastating. It brings damnation. To participate in communion or worship in a light, nonreflective and non-soul-searching way transforms worship into a celebration of our own damnation. By our attitude we are indicting ourselves. We may feel good, leave satisfied, enjoy the fellowship, but we are headed for judgment.

Preparing to sit at the table. Let's go back to the Tabernacle for a moment. Where is the table? It is in the Holy Place, right? This is the place where the family of God meets for fellowship and breaks bread. What piece of furniture is located immediately before the entrance into the Holy Place? The laver!

Let's recall. In the Old Testament narrative, if the priest did not stop at the laver and examine himself, wash his hands and his feet, what would happen to him? According to Exodus 30:20, he would die! But, that is in the Old Testament. Is that true in the New Testament?

The deadly omission. In Corinth, there developed a pattern of worship that allowed an indiscriminate rush to the Lord's Table without appropriate self-examination and self- purification. Or, to use the Tabernacle analogy, without stopping at the laver! Notice the consequences for those living in the New Testament era at Corinth: *"For this reason many are weak and sick among you, and many sleep [die]"* (1 Corinthians 11:30).

Some experienced premature death due to the absence of self-examination and the consequent judgment of God. Failure to stop at the laver produced death both in the Old and New Testaments.

This was the Pentecostal-Charismatic church of the first century. They came behind in no spiritual gift. Yet, they were immoral and under judgment. *"For if we would judge ourselves, we would not be judged. But when we are judged, we are chastened by the Lord, that we may not be condemned with the world"* (vv. 31, 32).

God loves us. He doesn't want us condemned with the world. He refuses to allow us to go on in a less-than-whole condition.

The place between. The laver stands in the open, between the holy and the unholy. It is the pivotal point between the two altars—one deals with sin; the other allows sweet communion with God. We go to two extremes. On one hand, we attempt to isolate ourselves from the world as a solution to purity, but we can't hide from the world's pollution by camping in the Holy Place. The problem of worldliness and the battle with the flesh is as much an inner thing as an outer thing. It's a matter of the heart. On the other hand, if we permit contamination by too close an association with the world, we fail to give evidence that we belong to the Holy Place.

How do you clean up a polluted world and yet keep your heart pure? How do you get deeply involved with sinners who need salvation without becoming involved in their sin? How do you embrace the holy and live in a polluted world? You must keep stopping at the laver!

The priests were to attend the laver when they entered or exited the Holy Place! When they approached God or went to minister to a sinner, it was the same: Go to the laver. Stay clean! When they ministered to the Lord or at the altar to others, it made no difference. They were to be equally clean in the Holy Place and at the bloody altar and the gate.

The laver reminds us that we must keep washing with the Word. Purity at the laver must be a constant! We wash our minds, our wills, our emotions, our habits and our attitudes. As someone has stated, "Dusty Bibles equals dirty hearts." In the world, I am conformed to the image, the shape, the mentality, and the spirit of darkness. In the Word, I am transformed into the image of Jesus!

There is a tendency to substitute the words of Christian leaders for the Word of God. We must not read books about the Word and neglect the Book of God! Only the Word can change us.

CHAPTER ELEVEN

THE HOLY PLACE

The Principle of the Deeper Life

Sixty posts of wood surrounded the courtyard. They were seated in the copper[99] (brass or bronze) foundations buried in the earth and capped with silver crowns. Silver bars connected them together, and cords of goat's hair attached to hooks anchored them to copper stakes to steady them. On the silver bars hung linen curtains separating the common area from the sanctified courtyard.

Remember, an outsider would have seen this fence first. What did it mean? These posts of natural wood in one sense represent Christ, who came by natural birth to give witness to

---

[99] Throughout this book, the terms brass, bronze or copper are used, as if synonymous. Modern brass is an alloy developed later than the Tabernacle. The Scripture will use the term brazen, but most scholars believe the reference is to what we would call copper.

God. In another sense they represent you and me, as we stand before the watching world in testimony to the reality of God.

The wooden posts were taken from trees. Once rooted in the earth, they had been severed, detached, separated from the world. Yet, here they were again, standing. They represent the death, burial and resurrection of Christ and our identify with Him and subsequent witness to the world. We were once rooted in this world, but not anymore. Buried in baptism, now we are raised up. We stand in brass foundations. Brass is a type of judgment. Thus, we stand by our identification with the judgment of God upon sin at the Cross. We adore confessed some altar moment that we were sinners and worthy of judgment. But that is not the end of the story.

Image courtesy of Melvin Poe

At the bottom, the posts touched brass—judgment. But as they reached for the sky, they were capped with silver—a type of redemption. Our flesh—that dimension to our being that reaches to the earth—is judged in the cross of Christ. It is from the earth, and it will be buried in the earth. But our spirit—that dimension of our being that reaches toward heaven—has been redeemed by the sacrificial action of Christ. In our identity with His death, we are both judged and redeemed. We taste death and life.

From each post capped with silver, a rod of silver reached to the other posts on either side. We stand, all of us, joined together by a silver stream of redemption. The vertical posts with their horizontal silver rods formed a series of connected crosses. Upon these rods of redemption hung the linen curtains, gleaming in the bright desert sun, the symbol of our righteousness in Christ. Facing death by sin (the brass foundation), crowned by redemptive grace (the silver caps), connected by our redemptive experience in Christ (the silver rods), we are draped with righteousness (the linen curtain) to give a witness to the watching world. They can't see the glory of the Most Holy Place with the dazzling cherubim. They can neither smell the incense, nor taste the bread from the table. We are witnesses to them, standing as intercessors between our loving Father and exiled sons.

We have been made the righteousness of God that is in Christ Jesus. This is the testimony we give to a watching world. To them we say, "Stand at the Cross. Step into the place of God's judgment. Put your feet on the foundation of brass. Repent of your sin in the sight of the crucified Lamb. And if you choose to recognize that the deeds you have done in the flesh make you worthy of death, and you identify with God's judgment at Calvary, then He will crown you with redemption and drape you in righteousness. And you will be joined by a wonderful stream of redemptive grace, to your brothers and sisters, and called to offer testimony to God's saving grace before the watching world."

The posts that touch brass at the bottom and silver at the top represent the nature of the true Christian. We are a part of this passing world that is under judgment (brass), and yet something in us longs for the sky (silver), for an encounter with God. We are in between this present world and the tabernacle/God; between the darkness of this age and light of God's glory. What holds us here? These posts were held in place by cords of goat's hair connected to silver hooks near the tops of the posts and then to brass stakes in the ground. Here again is the brass and silver contrast. Judgment and redemption are held in tension. The goat's hair represents the flesh. As long as I am alive, I am bound to this world by my fleshy body.

One day, when God is finished with my witness here, the flesh will give way. This dying, doomed body will wear out. It will no longer confine me to this world. The cord that binds me here will snap. My spirit, by the miracle of God's redemptive grace, will be set free to meet my Creator and Redeemer. And my body at His action will be changed and made like His glorious body. Until then, we believers are joined by the stream of redemption that connects us. And together, we hold up the linen testimony of the only righteous Man whose blood could redeem us from our sins and crown us with redemption.

THE STRUCTURE AND THE MOST HOLY PLACE

The Holy Place and the Most Holy Place together were 30 cubits (45 feet) long and 10 cubits (15 feet) wide and high. The Holy Place measured 20 cubits (30 feet) long and 10 cubits (15 feet) wide. The structure sat upon the desert sand or natural stone. Here, heaven touched the earth! (The instructions to build are given in Exodus 26:15-30; the actual construction, in 36:8-38.)

Forty-eight boards (*qerashim*) each a cubit and a half wide (27 inches) and 10 cubits high (15 feet) composed the walls (26:15, 16). These boards stood on their ends in silver foundations called sockets, planted securely into the desert floor. Each of the 96 foundation pieces weighed approximately 125 pounds[100]—a total estimated weight of 5.5 tons.[101] The silver was from the atonement money; everything else in the Tabernacle came from the freewill offering. Every man 20 years and older had to contribute (30:11-16). It represented redemption. Rich and poor alike had to pay. The price of redemption was the same for all. At other times, men

---

[100] William Brown, *The Tabernacle—Its Priests and Its Services* (Peabody, MA: Hendrickson, 1996) 6. Brown calculates that each socket weighed 1,500 ounces, or 93.75 pounds.

[101] C. W. Slemming, *Made According to Pattern* (London: Marshall, Morgan and Scott, 1938) 24.

gave according to their ability—a freewill offering—but not here. This silver was conscripted. The whole structure of the Holy Place, the church, is on the foundational and redemptive work of Christ. "For other foundation can no man lay than that is laid, which is Jesus Christ" (1 Corinthians 3:11). God's church exists in the earth because of redemptive grace. His Holy Spirit dwells on this corrupt earth, insulated by the redemptive work of Christ.

The boards were joined by 15 golden bars, five on each side of the golden walls excluding the east where a curtain hung. Four removable bars on each of the three sides (12 bars) were fastened to the exterior of the panels horizontally through rings. One bar on each of the three sides (3 bars) was placed through the center of the panels, again horizontally (Exodus 26:28; 36:33). These panels were set in bases of silver and made of acacia wood, overlaid with gold (26:15-29; 36:20-34). The thickness of the panels is not known. Estimates range from 3 to 18 inches. The Jewish Talmud indicates that they were 1 cubit thick. If so, we would think that they were probably hollow.[102]

Twelve exterior bars held the Tabernacle together; three internal bars held it together. The passage immediately comes to mind from Colossians 2:19, that of the church as a body "knit together by the joints and ligaments" (NKJV). Here is a picture, not of a structure, but of a living organism—the church. The bars are the ligaments. Like the muscles that hold our bones in place, these bars hold the boards in place. So what are "joints and ligaments"? A joint is a relationship between two or more members of the body. So, what holds the body of Christ together? The covenant of our relational commitment to Him and one another. Paul built on this metaphor in Ephesians, declaring that "the whole building, being fitted together, grows into a holy temple ...

---

[102] Roy Lee DeWitt, *The History of the Tabernacle* (Chatham, IL: Revival Teaching, 1986) 50.

being built together for a dwelling place of God in the Spirit" (2:21, 22, NKJV). There is no doubt that Paul had the Jewish tabernacle in mind here. It is a building that is alive. Paul declared that we are built up by that which the "joints support" (see Ephesians 4:16)! That relational construction sustains His glory. It is the vehicle onto which He loads His purpose.

Relationships sustain us. They nurture us! Our nurture of one another holds us together. Our covenant of love is what helps us become that holy habitation into which the presence of Christ comes. Notice, 12 bars held the structure together. How many tribes were there? Twelve. Here is the reminder of our brotherhood. We are the tribes of God, the people of God in the earth. We are diverse, yet we are one. We are distinct from one another, but ultimately we are of the same stock. We be brothers, and it is in the action of our unity that there is a demonstrable manifestation of oneness. By our active unity, we create the atmosphere for a manifestation of the glory of God in our midst. Our unity invites His presence. Our unity builds a home for Him in the earth. Our unity invites an exponential blessing of our work in His behalf. Ah, but there were three additional bars!

I cannot resist the temptation to speculate that these internal bars—running not on the exterior, but through the heart of the structure itself—are nothing less than the figurative representation of the fullness of God: Father, Son and Holy Ghost. We cannot impose this notion with certainty, but this provides a beautiful picture of a clear and compelling New Testament truth.

Our external unity, our brotherhood, is an essential component to the plan of God. Unity is a gift, a witness in our divided world. How can we preach a gospel of reconciliation unless we who claim to be reconciled with God are also reconciled with one another? But our bonds of brotherhood alone are not enough. We must have within us the same Father, the same redeeming Son and the same Holy Spirit. He who is in you must also be in me, if we are to be one. That stream of fire and purity that flows through me must flow through you. We are also linked internally by the active pursuit of the Father, revealed in the Son and carried on by the Holy Spirit. And we are demonstrating that organic unity by our active participation with one another to see a church rise up in the earth upon which He can pour His glory.

These boards, like the posts of the court, were also made of wood. They, too, were trees. They were felled, fashioned and raised up to be a habitation of His presence. That is our purpose. We were crucified with Him, then redeemed by His death and resurrected to be a dwelling place for Him. We were raised by baptism. We stand now, not by the attachment of roots deeply anchored in the soil of this passing world, but in one linked foundation of silver—line on line and precept on precept.[103]

The term *tenons* (Exodus 26:17, 19) actually means "hands."[104] These boards had hands! And the two hands, placed in the ends of the boards where we might expect feet to be, laid hold to the silver foundation pieces. So we stand now by laying hold firmly to our redemption in Christ, steadied by our bonds of brotherhood, strengthened by our organic unity, overlaid by gold, a symbol of the divine presence! And *"[Christ] is able to keep you from falling"* (Jude 24)!

Ephesians 2:22 declares that saints are "an habitation of God through the Spirit"! We are His body, organically connected to Him. Here is a picture of the church, a "building fitly framed together [growing] unto an holy temple in the Lord: in whom ye also are built together for an habitation of God through the Spirit" (vv. 21, 22). It was the desire of God *"that*

---

[103] John Ritchie, *The Tabernacle in the Wilderness* (Grand Rapids: Kregel, 1982) 63-66.

[104] Ritchie, 61.

he might reconcile both [Jew and Gentile] unto God in one body by the cross" (v. 16). He has made peace for us *"through the blood of his cross"* (Colossians 1:20).

The ark is at the head of the Most Holy Place. The golden altar is the heart of the Tabernacle. It is before the veil and the ark. It is between the table and the lampstand. This "body" holds in one hand bread from the table and in the other fire from the lampstand. It offers truth and life. It ministers the Word and Spirit. The belly of this structure is the cleansing water of the laver. The foot is the brass altar, the foundation and beginning point for our access to God. The Tabernacle is the living Christ, whose feet are like glowing brass from a fire (the altar). Out of His belly flows a river of cleansing life (the laver). In His hands, He offers bread (the table) and life (the ministry of the Spirit, lit with fruit and fire). His heart ever intercedes for us (the altar of incense). His face is aglow with the glory (the Most Holy Place and the ark of the covenant).

THE DOOR

At the east side of the Holy Place, five pillars on bases of brass or copper supported the multicolored curtain that comprised the door. These five pillars were unevenly spaced. Three were on one side of the center and two on the other. A rod of gold was supported by these pillars. On that rod hung the curtain for the doorway (Exodus 26:36, 37; 36:38), or the "hanging." The fabric was called the *masala*, or the screen. It was a mark of separation. The Hebrew *masak* means "to hide."[105] Some believe the dominant color of the door was blue, the same as the *mishkan*, the ceiling, or the Tabernacle proper.[106] The veil separating the Holy Place and the Most Holy Place

---

[105] W. S. Hottel, *Typical Truth in the Tabernacle* (Cleveland, OH: Union Gospel, 1943) 143.

[106] Brown, 34.

was hung on four golden pillars on foundations of silver, not brass (26:32; 36:36). These four additional silver bases made a total of 100 silver foundation pieces.

The material for the door to the Holy Place was exactly the same as that allotted for the gate into the court. The gate was 20 cubits wide and 5 cubits high. But the door was only half the width of the gate (10 cubits), more narrow. And it was twice as high (10 cubits). Any Israelite could approach the gate and stand before the bloody altar, but only a select group could venture into the Holy Place. The way grows narrower and the gaze is pulled upward as we draw near God. Only a small number seem to want to move to that deeper level.

THE COVERINGS

Moreover you shall make the tabernacle with ten curtains of fine woven linen and blue, purple, and scarlet thread; with artistic designs of cherubim you shall weave them. The length of each curtain shall be twenty-eight cubits, and the width of

each curtain four cubits. And every one of the curtains shall have the same measurements. Five curtains shall be coupled to one another, and the other five curtains shall be coupled to one another. And you shall

Image courtesy of Melvin Poe

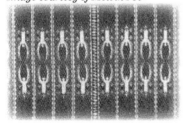

make loops of blue yarn on the edge of the curtain on the selvedge of one set, and likewise you shall do on the outer edge of the other curtain of the second set. Fifty loops you shall make in the one curtain, and fifty loops you shall make on the edge of the curtain that is

on the end of the second set, that the loops may be clasped to one another. And you shall make fifty clasps of gold, and couple the curtains together with the clasps, so that it may be one tabernacle (Exodus 26:1-6; see also 36:8-19, the Scripture passage regarding the actual creation of the curtains).

The fine linen covering was actually the exposed ceiling in both the Holy Place and the Most Holy Place. This covering was comprised of 10 curtains in two sections of five each, joined by 50 blue loops and 50 golden clasps. This covering, called the *mishkan*, means "tabernacle." In the strictest sense, this *is* the tabernacle. All else is structure or attendant principles. Its dimensions were 28 cubits (42 feet) by 40 cubits (60 feet). The width of the Holy Place was 10 cubits and the height was 10 cubits, thus 30 cubits of curtain would have been required to completely wrap the Holy Place from side to side. This linen curtain was only 28 cubits, allowing it to hang 18 inches from the ground on either side of the northern and southern exterior walls of the structure.

On the west, its 40-cubit length would have allowed the covering to extend the full 30-cubit length of the Tabernacle and the full 10 cubits to the ground, completely covering the western exterior wall. This assumes a flat roof structure.

> *You shall also make curtains of goats' hair, to be a tent over the tabernacle. You shall make eleven curtains. The length of each curtain shall be thirty cubits, and the width of each curtain four cubits; and the eleven curtains shall all have the*

> *same measurements. And you shall couple five curtains by themselves and six curtains by themselves, and you shall double over the sixth curtain at the forefront of the tent. (26:7-9).*

The second covering over the *mishkan* was called a tent, or the *ohel* in Hebrew. It was comprised of 11 curtains, each 30 cubits by 4 cubits, thus wide enough to touch the ground on either side of the exterior golden walls. These were in two large sections—six curtains in one section and five in the other. The two sections were fastened together by 50 goat's-hair loops and 50 copper clasps. The total dimensions were 30 cubits (45 feet) by 44 cubits (66 feet). This covering was larger than the linen covering and would have served to completely cover or protect it. The length of the curtain required that it be doubled under at its eastern edge (vv. 9-12) by 3 feet, perhaps doubled to serve as a wrapping for the linen curtain that would have extended almost to the ground at that western exterior wall. The alternative view is that the ceiling was not a flat roof structure but more Bedouin in style, requiring more material for its raised roof.

The goat's hair and the linen were curtains. The ram's and badger's skins were coverings. As noted above, the goat's hair was called the *ohel*, or tent of the congregation; whereas the fine linen curtain below it was called the *mishkan*, or the tabernacle. That points to a very fine distinction often overlooked. The *ohel* was not the tabernacle, but the tent that covered it. The *mishkan* was not a mere part of the tent, but the actual Tabernacle of the Lord.[107]

In a sense, the Tabernacle is a picture of man. He is distinctly individual. Yet, every man was created in such a way to provide a dwelling place for God. God desires to "tabernacle" inside of us. We retain our uniqueness. We are the tent in

---

[107] Slemming, 43.

which He tabernacles.

The goat's-hair coverings were probably from the more common black goat, since white goats in the East were rare (see Genesis 30:25-43). Tents in Scripture, usually made of goat's hair, are typically referred to as being black, as we see in the reference to black tents of Kedar in the Song of Solomon (1:5).

We would believe, then, that the tents of the Israelites were also black. What a contrast then, between the black tents of the people and the white-linen fence of the Tabernacle court, almost glistening in the desert sunlight. *"And thou shalt make a covering for the tent of rams' skins dyed red, and a covering above of badgers' skins"* (Exodus 26:14).

The third covering was ram's skins dyed red. No dimensions are given for this covering. The fourth and final covering was *tachash*, which has been interpreted variously as badger's skins (KJV), sea cow hides (NIV), goatskins (RSV), porpoise hides (NEB) and sealskins (ASV). Whatever the covering, it most likely was an animal whose hides were cured and provided rugged waterproof coverings. Linguistic studies indicate a possible link between the Egyptian term *tj-h-s*, meaning "to tan" or stretch leather, and the term used to denote these hides.[108]

INSIDE THE HOLY PLACE

This was a rough-looking tent viewed from the outside, but inside it was exquisite. Facing west, we would find a golden table set with fresh bread on the north or right side. Immediately before us, in front of the exquisite veil, would be a golden altar, westward, giving off the most aromatic smells. A glistening, golden lampstand would stand to the south, to our left, displaying the emblems of almonds from blossom to fruit stage. Seven dancing flames would rise out of the golden

---

[108] Frank Cross, *"The Tabernacle," The Biblical Archaeologist,* Vol. X, No. 3, Sept. 1947: 62. See also, Paul Zehr, *God Dwells With His People* (Scottdale, PA: Herald, 1981) 76.

almond fruit. Walls of pure gold would be on either side, north and south, reflecting the dancing light of the candlestick. Golden sparkles and shimmers with reflections of the fire of the candlesticks would abound in the room. The colors in the tapestry above and in the veil and the door behind would be brilliant blue, royal purple, scarlet, and a fabric of fine linen. The images and faces of cherubim (angels) are woven into the tapestry above, the *mishkan*—the Tabernacle proper. Woven into the veil would be the images of cherubim. These angels appear to be always looking in on the worship scene as we meet with God in this Holy Place. The eyes and faces of angels tune in on the worship event! We are not alone when we are engaged in true worship in God's holy place.

Here in the Holy Place, one's senses were fully alive.

- **Sight**—The gold, the glitter, the color, the faces of the angels, the exquisite beauty of the lampstand, the table of shewbread, the golden altar.

- **Smell**—Incense fills the air, fresh bread is on the table, lamb or beef is being offered on the brazen altar outside. The aromatic smells mesh together.

- **Taste**—Taste buds come alive at the prospect of a meal with God. The smell of fresh bread, the aroma of the sacrifices on the altar permeate the Holy Place.

- **Sound**—You are so close to the presence of God. He is just beyond the veil. Your ears are alive in anticipation! The bells on the fringe of the high-priestly garments tinkle with happy sounds. The sizzle of the burning incense can be faintly heard.

- **Touch**—You want to reach out and embrace the intangible, to touch the invisible, to behold His glory!

Tragically, this beauty was hidden from everyone except the privileged priests who were allowed in the Holy Place. Only as a priest or Levite could one have seen all this beauty. The beauty was not seen from without, but from within. That remains true today.

From the outside, it looks unappealing, uninteresting. We are reminded, "There is no inherent connection between 'ugliness' and 'holiness.'"[109] Some of us need some motivation to get us in! So, God has a helper named "trouble" that rounds up some of us and gets us into the Kingdom!

BEHOLDING THE BEAUTY

Psalm 27 says it like this: *"One thing have I desired of the Lord, that will I seek after; that I may dwell in the house of the Lord all the days of my life, to behold the beauty of the Lord, and to enquire in His temple"* (v. 4).

Notice the two phrases, "enquire in his temple" and "to behold the beauty of the Lord!" These are two levels of relationship. Some people think the Lord and His Temple are synonymous. They aren't. Going to church and looking for answers is not the same as encountering a beautiful and wondrous God. It may be the beginning point for a life change. However, a relationship with the church is not what saves and satisfies; only a relationship with Him can do that.

Notice also the themes of trouble and tabernacle! War and worship come together in this psalm! Trouble motivates people. It pushes them toward an encounter with faith. Let me paraphrase verses 2 and 3: "When the wicked came, a host encamped against me. When there was war all around me, I said to myself, 'I think I'll go to church and pray about this! I think I'll inquire with some prayer.'"

> *When the wicked came against me To eat up my flesh, My enemies and foes, They stumbled and fell. Though an army may encamp against me, My heart shall not fear; Though war should rise against me, In this I will be confident.* (vv. 2, 3).

These are intensifying problems. Wicked people (v. 2) fail to

---

[109] Dean Stanley, "Lectures on the Jewish Church," 227. Quoted by Brown, 1.

deter the psalmist—they stumble and fall. Next, an army (a host) pursues him (v. 3). The mob of wicked people is now replaced by a well-organized military unit. The foe is more formidable, but his heart does not fear. Finally, he is in the middle of an all-out war. The enemy will not leave. It establishes a camp with the goal of conquest over him. He is a target. He is in warfare, but he remains confident.

His confidence is from the notion that there is a place of triumph in the time of trouble. At the Tabernacle is a secret place beyond the reach of his enemies. Few have known this place. He longs for it now. There, his enemy could never reach him. There he would be safe, beyond the veil, near the ark. It is a daring thought. Perhaps he knows that penetration into the Most Holy Place could cost him his life. The high priest entered cautiously, with blood. The psalmist seems to know that he would be safer in the hands of a holy and awful[110] God than in the hands of sinful men. He will trust God. *"For in the time of trouble He shall hide me...in the secret place of His tabernacle"* (v. 5, NKJV).

Unfortunately, some people live at the "inquiry" level. They experience trouble in their life, and they immediately ask, "Where have You been, God? Why did You allow this to happen to me? How could such a thing have affected me so? What are You going to do about this, God? When are You going to help me?" These are not bad questions. God is not taken back by our complaints, our doubts, our moments of conflict. The problem comes when we do not move to the resolve of faith in the face of these questions, when we do not make the blind leap of faith into His arms when there is no other choice.

Some people are driven into church due to trouble, but they do not move beyond the inquiry level to "behold the beauty of the Lord!" They are self-absorbed, blind. They never see God.

---

[110] *Awful* is a wonderful word that needs to be redeemed. God is called an "Awful and Terrible God" in older English versions. Encounters with Him should leave us "full of awe"—awful!

When the trouble is gone, they usually drop out of church. They actually use God, prayer and faith for their own selfish benefit. Once you have seen the beauty of the Lord, there is no desire to leave and go back to the world!

Trouble may have driven you into the house of the Lord, but trouble is not, nor should it be, necessary for you to stay. You have met your Father. You are at home. This is a wholly different motivation.

CHAPTER TWELVE

THE LAMPSTAND

There are three pieces of furniture in the Holy Place—the golden lampstand, the golden table of shewbread, and the golden altar for burning incense. Imagine that we are standing in the Holy Place. The walls on either side, north and south, are gold-plated. The door behind us (to the east) and the veil in front of us (to the west), as well as the ceiling above us, are all tapestries of linen with the colors of blue, purple and scarlet. In the ceiling (*mishkan*) and the veil (*paroketh*), the designs woven in the fabric are the image of angels. These designs were the thickness of a man's hand giving a three-dimensional appearance.

Let's examine the furniture piece by piece. We begin with the lampstand.

THE LAMPSTAND

The golden lampstand sits in the Holy Place on the south side. The command to build it is recorded in Exodus 25:31-40. Its construction is noted in 37:17-24. Additional notes are found in

27:20; Leviticus 24:1-4; and Numbers 8:1-4. It is called a "candle-stick" (Exodus 35:14; 40:4, 24), the "candlestick of pure gold" (25:31) and the "pure candlestick" (31:8; 39:37; Leviticus 24:4). *"You shall also make a lampstand of pure gold; the lampstand shall be of hammered work. Its shaft, its branches, its bowls, its ornamental knobs, and flowers ..."* (Exodus 25:31).

The lampstand was of "hammered work," that is, it was ham-mered into shape. Its structure was designed like an almond tree trunk with six branches, three out of each side: *"And six branches shall come out of the sides of it; three branches of the candlestick out of the one side, and three branches of the candlestick out of the other side"* (vv. 32, 33). Here is a picture of Christ *"stricken, smitten of God"* for our redemption (Isaiah 53:4).

The Scripture does not give the height of the candlestick. Tradition says it was about 5 feet tall. On top of each branch and the central shaft were bowls. The bowls were made like almonds. Each branch had three sets of knops and flowers. The central shaft had four sets.

The purpose of the candlestick was to provide light in the Holy Place. It was to give light "before the Lord" (Leviticus 24:1-4; Exodus 27:21; 40:25). It was the light for the table and the golden altar of incense (vv. 24-26; see also Psalm 27:1). Each branch is said to have held half a log of oil, a little more than a pint. The oil was produced from hand-crushed and cold-strained olives (see Exodus 27:20), that being the process for producing the purest oil.[111]

FRUIT IN DEVELOPMENT

The knops are buds. The flowers are blossoms. The bowls are the fully developed fruit[112] with six branches each containing three

---

[111] James Strong, *The Tabernacle of Israel* (Grand Rapids: Kregel, 1987) 72.

[112] William Brown, *The Tabernacle—Its Priests and Its Services* (Peabody, MA: Hendrickson, 1996) 70.

sets of buds and blossoms. And the central shaft with four, showing its superiority, makes a total of 22 sets of buds and blossoms (Exodus 25:33, 34). Seven almonds crowned each of the six branches and central shaft. Here is the almond fruit in development. *"And in the candlesticks shall be four bowls made like unto almonds, with their knops and their flowers"* (v. 34).

Each of the branches had *"his knops, and his flowers ... of the same"* (v. 31). That is, all were made of gold. According to 38:24, a talent of gold was used to make the candlestick. It would have been about 94 pounds of gold. The raw value of the gold itself would have been in the range of half-a-million dollars. With the value of the artisanship, that figure would have easily multiplied numerous times. It was designed like an almond tree in various stages of development—from bud, to flower, to fruit stage. Almond means "wakeful" or "to hasten." The almond tree was one of the first trees to put forth in the spring, its blossoms appearing about the end of January. Its blooms announced the death of winter.[113]

There is a connection between the candlestick and Aaron's rod. Both have buds and flowers. Both have almond fruit.

A PICTURE OF CHRIST AND THE CHURCH

Notice the personal language: his shaft, his branches, his bowls! This candlestick is a living thing. It is Christ and His relationship with the church. The central shaft is Christ, the Vine. We are the branches. The Hebrew term used here for shaft is *yarek*. Twenty times it is translated "thigh," twice "loins," four times "side" and once "body."[114] As Eve came out of the sleep of Adam, from his open side, the new Eve—the bride of Christ—comes out of His sleep, from His open side. In the Revelation, Jesus walks

---

[113] W. S. Hottel, *Typical Truth in the Tabernacle* (Cleveland, OH: Union Gospel, 1943) 127, 161.

[114] C. W. Slemming, *Made According to Pattern* (London: Marshall, Morgan and Scott, 1938) 77.

among the candlesticks. There, as here, the candlesticks were representative of the church. The church is the witness of God in the earth—the light of God in the midst of darkness.

A BALANCE—FRUIT AND FIRE

The bowls were designed to look like almond fruit. Inside the bowls was deposited "pure oil olive beaten for the light, to cause the lamp to burn always" (Exodus 27:20). Two symbols emerge prominently here: fruit and fire! Both are symbols of the Holy Spirit's ministry in the life of the church. Fruit represents the character of Christ reproduced by the Spirit. The fire represents the supernatural gifts of the Spirit manifest through the church.

In the visions of Zechariah, the oil symbolized the Spirit and the lamps themselves were the recipients of the Spirit (4:1-6). Notice again, the lampstand is in the shape of fruit, filled with oil and set aflame. Thus, we have fruit and fire. Or, more precisely, we have fire out of fruit on the fuel of oil!

THE FOUNDATION OF CHARACTER

My life is to be in the shape of "love, joy, peace, longsuffering, gentleness, goodness, faith, meekness, temperance"—the fruit of the Spirit (Galatians 5:22, 23). Fruit is to be the foundation, or basis, out of which Spirit manifestation springs.

Dangling from the branches of my life—or the life of the church—is to be the refreshing fruit of the Spirit, available to weary travelers. Others should be able to pull from the branches of my life—love, peace, joy, gentleness, and so forth. They should enter our worship encounters and note that we, the Christian church, are different.

The fruit here is alien to this planet. At what market do you buy unconditional love? Where do you shop for incomprehensible peace or irrepressible joy? Hate and adversity are the native fruits where despair and abruptness grow profusely. In this climate, unconditional love and long-suffering do not fare well. But, the

Holy Place is to be a spiritual greenhouse, a place where the atmosphere of heaven is re-created on the earth. As a result, heaven's fruit is found growing here as well.

In prayer and worship I should notice the fresh buds of Christ-likeness breaking out in my attitudes and soon reflected in my behavior patterns. Like a tree in bloom in the early spring, I should develop a beauty, a fragrance that is both refreshing and appealing. So in the holy place of God's presence, the believer in worship is being transformed by the prayerful worship atmosphere into the character of Christ.

Sometimes, churches and Christians are not filled with love and joy and peace—just the opposite. There is a great deal of foliage, but not much fruit. Worship involves character transformation. If worship is not making saints out of sinners, it is not worship. It may be religious entertainment, but it is not worship.

In Mark 11:12, Jesus is on His way from Bethany to Jerusalem. He is hungry and notices a fig tree. He turns aside and finds that there are leaves, but no figs. So, He curses that fig tree. Some scholars object, noting that it was not seasonally the time for figs. It seems unreasonable that Jesus should then demand it. However, some experts observe that pre-figs, a visible indication that the tree would bear, should have been present. On this tree, even pre-figs are absent. So the tree has neither fruit nor even the promise of fruit.

Jesus is on His way to the Cross. Literally, He is on His way to death, due to sin—our sin. He turns to the fig tree, a symbol of Israel. This is the tree God planted in the earth to nourish the nations. But there is no fruit on the tree, and there is no promise of fruit. There is only foliage, so He curses the tree and makes a declaration: "The kingdom of God shall be taken from you, and given to a nation bringing forth the fruits" (Matthew 21:43). Is the church doing any better than Israel?

So many people are on their way to some crucible of life.

They are experiencing the death of hopes and dreams. In a moment of despair, they turn to the church, but all they find is foliage, no fruit. There is talk of love, but little love. There is talk of joy, but no evidence of it—just foliage, but no fruit. There is a look of life, but the absence of nourishment. That is not acceptable to God. He is committed to have a tree filled with fruit! He comes to our lives and feels through the branches. He is looking for fruit. He isn't impressed with our foliage.

THE DISTINCTIVE MARKS OF GOD'S HAMMER

So, how did the candlestick end up in the shape of fruit? It was not cast in a mold or assembled in pieces. This candlestick was hammered into shape. Paul said, *"I bear in my body the marks of the Lord Jesus Christ"* (Galatians 6:17).

Do you ever feel like you are under God's hammer? What is God doing? Like a master craftsman, God takes a piece of gold from the raw earth. He will try it by fire. He will purify it. He will make of it an object of beauty—one body, with one hope and one Lord, one faith and one baptism. He will heat it to the melting point and shape it. He will cool it and then repeat the process. God has uses for us in eternity. What we are experiencing is not only about here and now. He is fashioning us to reign with Him. If we are content only to make heaven our home, we're missing the greater desires of God for us. He wants us to make our homes like heaven here and now. He wants us to experience mission and purpose in Him.

THE FIRE THAT COMES OUT OF FRUIT

Into the golden bowls of fruit (almond) was placed a deposit of oil. And from each bowl, a flame came forth. This is also a symbol of the Holy Spirit. Here we have a picture of the supernatural gifts or the manifestation of the Spirit (1 Corinthians 12). Out of a life of fruit, the Holy Spirit reveals His supernatural character.

Image courtesy of
www.tabernacleman.com

The lamps were trimmed and re-kindled each day at the time of the evening sacrifice (see Exodus 30:7, 8), which was a burnt offering—an offering of total consecration. This is significant. The time of consecration is the time when God trims our lamps and relights our candle. Every morning, we are to offer ourselves as a consecrated vessel. And every morning, we are again to be refueled with the oil of the Spirit so that we are ever ready to be set aflame with fire from the altar.

The Scriptures state that the lamps were kindled at the time of the evening sacrifice, which would seem to indicate that they only burned at night. However, we are also told that they were ever-burning. This seeming contradiction may be clarified by the following observation. It appears that during the day, only the fruit of the central shaft was illuminated. Josephus believed three of the lamps burned during the day.[115] At night, the fire was spread to the whole candlestick. God's light ever burns. Our lights are on and off; He is constant. We get our fire from His fire. His fire is the fire from the altar. For there, a deposit of the fire from heaven was constantly maintained. The only record in Scripture of the fire going out upon the lampstand is in 1 Samuel 3:3. There it was a prelude to the birth of Ichabod, an indication of the reprobate condition of Israel's priests and the nation.

These were not "candles" in our modern sense. Candles burn by the consumption of themselves. But lamps burn by the consumption of an external fuel. Burnout happens when

---

[115] Paul Zehr, *God Dwells With His People* (Scottdale, PA: Herald, 1981) 82. See also Antiquities III, 8:3.

we, like candles, are consumed in doing God's work. God's fire can depend on nothing less than God's fuel. He is the "burning bush" that does not consume itself.

To have fire, the lamps had to be continually filled with oil. So we are commanded, *"Be ye therefore continually filled with the Spirit"* (see Ephesians 5:18). A classic mistake by some has been the acceptance of a once-for-all filling with the Holy Spirit, a "filling" for life. The Scripture teaches that we are to be continually filled!

WICKS OF RIGHTEOUSNESS

The garments of the priest were consecrated. What happened to them when they were worn out? Rather than discard the sanctified garments, they were dismembered and woven together to form the wick for the lampstand. Remember, the linen stands for righteousness. What a powerful picture. The *fire* of the lampstand burns by the *fuel of oil*, on the *wick of righteousness*, out of the almond *fruit*. So my life burns, not by my fuel or energy, but by the power of the Holy Spirit, on the wick of a righteous life, the fire dancing off a life loaded with the fruit of the Spirit.

Image courtesy of David Hamilton, www.mishkanministries.org

The priests were to trim the lampstand daily, removing the burnt ashes. Desert flies made their way into the Holy Place. They were attracted to the scented oil. The neatly trimmed wicks were a preventative to them. Untrimmed and distended wicks gave them a place to light. But then the dancing unpredictable fire would singe their fragile wings. The dead flies would then pollute the holy oil. Instead of burning pure oil, the lampstand would burn the flesh of the dead flies and create an unsavory odor in the Holy Place (Ecclesiastes 10:1).

We attempt to swat the "flies" in the Holy Place. We focus on them. If daily we would remove the ashes, the burned places of our lives, we would not give Beelzebub, "the lord of the flies," access to our lives. All of us have burned places—unavoidable hurts and misconceptions—that we must carry away. If we don't, the Evil One takes advantage of those wounds and misunderstandings with his unholy deposits.

JESUS AND THE CANDLESTICK

Jesus took 12 men. He worked with them, molding and shaping them into men of love and peace, goodness and gentleness— reproducing His character in them. After His resurrection, He breathed life into them in the Upper Room, saying, *"Receive ye the Holy Ghost,"* (John 20:22)! He put a deposit of oil in them. And then at Pentecost, God lit their fire!

God takes raw human material. He tries it by fire and purifies it. He is building an object of beauty—the true church.

> When the Day of Pentecost had fully come, they were all with one accord in one place. And suddenly there came a sound from heaven, as of a rushing mighty wind, and it filled the whole house where they were sitting. Then there appeared to them divided tongues, as of fire, and one sat upon each of them (Acts 2:1-3).

Here, God was lighting His candlesticks of which the lampstand in the tabernacle was only a symbol. The fire often attracts people to the church, but when they arrive and there is little or no fruit, it is a confusing paradox—a disillusioning experience. Fruit and fire are inseparable. When the church separates these two, there is confusion. The Bible churches emphasize fruit to the exclusion of fire. The Pentecostals have sometimes emphasized fire without adequate emphasis upon fruit! God wants a church that has fruit and fire.

AUXILIARY UTENSILS

Around the candlesticks were auxiliary utensils: golden tongs (always plural in the Hebrew *malkachayim*, literally "double takers, for pulling up the wicks"), snuff dishes (Some translations say "shovels"—actually the same word used for "firepans" at the great altar), and oil vessels (Exodus 25:38; Numbers 4:9). Wicks were made from the worn-out, consecrated priestly garments.[116] They were trimmed with the tongs. Censers were probably used to hold coals from the brazen altar. Oil vessels contained pure olive oil to be used as fuel in the lampstand.

---

[116] Strong, 73.

CHAPTER THIRTEEN

THE TABLE

The Principle of Balance

The command to build the table of shewbread is found in Exodus 25:23-30. This is the first mention of a table in the Bible.[117] In Genesis, fellowship with God had been broken. Now, God commands Moses to build a table. He is going to invite man to His house for dinner. He is beginning the process of restoring fellowship.

Luke reminds us of the living tabernacle: *"Then they that gladly received His word were baptized: and the same day there were added unto them about three thousand souls. And they continued steadfastly in the apostles' doctrine and fellowship, and in breaking of bread, and in prayers"* (Acts 2:41, 42). John Ritchie says, "The doctrine forms the fellowship, the breaking of bread expresses it, and the prayers lay hold on God

---

[117] Kevin Conner, *The Tabernacle of Moses* (Portland: Bible, 1975) 33.

for power to sustain it."[118] The result was an empowered community of Resurrection believers who shook the city.

In addition to being called the *"table of shewbread"* (Exodus 25:30), it is called the *"table of shittim wood"* (v. 23; 37:10), *"the pure table"* (Leviticus 24:6), simply *"the table"* (Exodus 39:36; 40:4, 22), as well as *"the table of gold"* (1 Kings 7:48—the table in Solomon's Temple).[119] Shewbread is a curious word for us. It means "to show" or to "tell forth" and "declare." It is also referred to as the *"bread of God"* (see Leviticus 21:21) and the *"continual"* bread since it was to be on the table continually (Numbers 4:7; 2 Chronicles 2:4; see also Leviticus 24:8). Implicit names for it are *"the bread of presence"* (see Matthew 18:20) and *"the bread of faces"* (see 2 Corinthians 4:6; Revelation 22:4). John Ritchie says, "It was ever in Jehovah's presence, and continually before His face. His holy eye was ever looking down upon it, feasting, as it were, upon it with satisfaction."[120] He declared to Jeremiah, *"I will hasten my word to perform it"* (1:12). Additionally, it is sometimes known as the *"bread of order"* or *"arrangement"* (see 1 Corinthians 11:34).[121]

The Mishnah explains in detail the elaborate changing of the bread each Sabbath:

> Four priests entered the holy place, two of them carrying the piles of bread, and two of them the cups of incense. Four priests had gone in before them, two to take off the two piles of showbread, and two to take off the cups of incense. Those who brought in the new bread stood at the north side facing southward, those who took away the old bread, at the

---

[118]   John Ritchie, *The Tabernacle in the Wilderness* (Grand Rapids: Kregel, 1982) 72.

[119]   Conner, 33.

[120]   Ritchie, 88. (He says the word *shewbread* means "the presence bread" or "the bread of faces.")

[121]   Conner, 36.

south side, facing northward. One part lifted off and the other put on, the hands of one being over against the hands of the other, as it is written, 'Thou shall set upon the table bread of the Passover always before me' (Men. XI, 7). The loaves that were removed were delivered to the priests for their consumption within the Tabernacle, the whole quantity amounting to 75 pounds of bread per week.[122]

The table was on the north side of the Holy Place, opposite the candlestick. A record of the construction of the table is found in Exodus 37:10-16. There are seven features to this table that we will note.

1. It is **an accessible table.** *"You shall also make a table of acacia wood; two cubits shall be its length, a cubit its width, and a cubit and a half its height"* (25:23).

   The dimensions of the table were 1 cubit (18 inches) wide, a cubit and a half (27 inches) high and 2 cubits (3 feet) long. That makes it the lowest piece of furniture in the house. The height of the table emphasizes accessibility. This is a table that has bread that is not out of reach or over the head of anyone. Here is truth that is not out of the conceptual grasp of anyone. It was made of acacia wood and overlaid with gold.

2. It is **a royal table.** *"You shall also make a table of acacia wood; two cubits shall be its length, a cubit its width, and a cubit and a half its height"* (vv. 24, 25).

   This crown was a raised border. The brass altar had no crown. The crown of the golden altar emphasized the royal quality of the table. This is the King's table. It is the table of the royal family. To sit here is a reminder that we were once slaves in Egypt, but we are redeemed to be the

---

[122] Quoted by David M. Levy, *The Tabernacle: Shadows of the Messiah* (Bellmawr, NJ: Friends of Israel Gospel Ministry, 1993) 52-3.

children of God. We are royalty in the ultimate sense. We are the sons of God. Our table is golden! Angels cannot sit here; they hover around and above this table. They may serve the guests of the table at the request of the Host. Those who sit at this table are the King's kids, the bride of Christ, the heirs of the Kingdom, the future rulers of the earth. No one in the family of God should suffer from a self-image problem. We were paupers; now we are rich. We were slaves; now we are free. We were orphans; now we are the sons of God.

And you shall make for it four rings of gold, and put the rings on the four corners that are at its four legs. 27 The rings shall be close to the frame, as holders for the poles to bear the table. 28 And you shall make the poles of acacia wood, and overlay them with gold, that the table may be carried with them. 29 You shall make its dishes, its pans, its pitchers, and its bowls for pouring. You shall make them of pure gold (vv. 26-29).

3. It is **a table always set**. *"And thou shalt set upon the table shewbread before me alway"* (v. 30).

There were to be 12 cakes of bread, like our hotcakes, one symbolically for each of the 12 sons of Jacob, arranged in two stacks of six each on the table. Technically, this bread was reserved for the priests (1 Samuel 21:1-6; Matthew 12:4). And it was to be eaten in the Holy Place, never in the court outside.

There is considerable diversity of opinion regarding the size of the shewbread and the manner of arrangement. We know the measure—two-tenths of a deal. That means each cake was made from a gallon of flour.[123] The ventured guess for the size of each cake of shewbread is 12 inches in diameter and 4 inches thick. Five of them were adequate for David and his men (1 Samuel 21:1-6).[124] These were obviously not dainty morsels, mere symbols. The word here for *row*, noted in Leviticus 24:6, is not the same as that used in Exodus 28:17-20, where horizontally arranged rows are in mind. Thus, stacks is probably more accurate. These stacks would have been some 2 feet high, and that is without shelves or plates for each cake.

Every Friday evening at the beginning of the Sabbath and of the new week, fresh bread was placed on the table (Leviticus 24:8). The bread was not allowed to become stale. Old and moldy bread is not suitable for God's table or God's kids. Fresh bread is commanded. In later years, an elaborate ceremony involved the changing of the bread. The essence of that ceremony required that fresh bread be laid down the moment the bread of the prior week was removed.[125] The table is never to be without bread.

Here is the marvelous picture of a table in the wilderness—a table that never lacked bread. In the worst of times, God's people have bread on their table. God provides! Thus, the bread is a memorial, a covenant that emphasizes His provision, His care and His feeding. Pagan gods needed to be fed. The Egyptian gods were fed three times a day.[126] Our God feeds us!

This is the table of hospitality—of nourishment. It is a place of satisfaction for the hungry. It marks God's con-

---

[123] Roy Lee DeWitt, *The History of the Tabernacle* (Chatham, IL: Revival Teaching, 1986) 54.

[124] James Strong, *The Tabernacle of Israel* (Grand Rapids: Kregel, 1987) 64.

[125] Alfred Edersheim, *The Temple: Its Ministry and Services* (Grand Rapids: Eerdmans, 1969) 185.

[126] G.A.F. Knight, *Leviticus* (Philadelphia: Westminster, 1981) 23.

stant provision. It is a sign of the bounty of the Lord— a table in the wilderness. It is an invitation into divine fellowship, the gathering place of the family around the Father's table. There is always to be fresh bread upon the table in the house of the Lord! And now that the Lord has invited us to come and dine, there is bread on the table for all His sons and daughters.

4. It is **a costly table—with priceless bread.** This bread was made from fine flour or crushed grain. Thus, this is the bread of the crushed One, the crucified One. It is brokenness that feeds. Christ's brokenness at the Cross feeds us spiritually. And, it is often out of our own brokenness that others are most deeply ministered to. The Hebrew term implies that the shewbread was "pierced cakes." They were perforated, with holes. That would point to Christ, the crucified and pierced One (Zechariah 12:10; John 19:34-37).[127]

It is the Cross that draws us to Christ, not His miracles or exploits—not even His teaching. He declared, *"If I be lifted up ... [I] will draw all men unto me"* (John 12:32). The power of Christ and His gospel is the power of the Cross. And, it is out of our cross experiences, the crucibles of life, that our most profound lessons are learned and our most fervent ministry issues forth.

Christologically, the bread is a picture of Christ.

I am the bread of life. Your fathers did eat manna in the wilderness, and are dead....I am the living bread which came down from heaven: if any man eat of this bread, he shall live for ever: and the bread that I will give is my flesh, which I will give for the life of

---

[127] Conner, 37.

the world (6:48-51).

He is the Bread of Life. He is the living manna. Each of the 12 loaves on the table were made of the same measurement—two-tenths of a deal (Leviticus 24:5). The meal offering of the sheaf of firstfruits was made of the same measure (23:13). Also measuring two-tenths of a deal were the two wave loaves used in the Feast of Pentecost (v. 17). And each day Israel gathered two-tenths of a deal (Exodus 16:22, 36).[128] So here is the measure of daily bread on the table. On the day before the Sabbath, Israel was allowed a double portion of manna. That looks to Christ, our double portion. *"This bread,"* He said, *"is my body. Take it, eat it, remember me"* (see Matthew 26:26; Mark 14:22). The laver was the Word in cleansing—remediation. Now, the table is the Word in feeding—edification. Moses declared the meaning of the table in Deuteronomy 8:3: *"That He might make you know that man shall not live by bread alone; but man lives by every word that proceeds from the mouth of the Lord."*

5. It is **an open table**. This is God's table! He has prescribed it and orders it. We are only His guests,

Image courtesy of Melvin Poe

and He can invite anyone home for dinner that He desires to include. There is no denominational label on this table. There are no racial, social, educational or economic quotas or preferential status requirements at this table.

In the Old Testament, there were restrictions on the

---

[128] Conner, 37.

table. A stranger or alien could not partake of the priestly bread—not even a guest of the priest could taste the bread. Anyone who had the status of a slave could not taste the bread, nor could anyone who had the symptoms of leprosy or a running sore, until he was clean (Leviticus 22:4). He was defiled. The table was for priestly covenant people, priestly people who were free, not in bondage.[129] Specifically, this table in Old Testament Tabernacle days was accessible only to the priest. The principle is still true. Those who sit at the table of the Lord have priestly responsibilities and priestly duties—a priestly calling is incumbent upon them!

There are always attempts to regulate the table of the Lord. Some desire to spice up the bread. Let's stick to the pure bread, the plain gospel. Others desire to monopolize the table, but there is no denominational label on this table. We must practice an open table. Still others want to screen off the table.

In the second century, some advocated an exclusive table. Gnostics like Marcion espoused an exalted understanding that had the effect of taking the bread from the common man, since only the enlightened could perceive God's deeper truth. During the Middle Ages, the table of the Lord *was* taken from the common people and made the property of the priests. Today, some postulate "special truth"—a modified form of Gnosticism. They claim to know what others don't know, what others can't know. Their knowledge is not from the discipline of study, nor yet the richness of being a seasoned disciple. It is presumptuous knowledge, so-called special and higher revelation from the Lord, sometimes offered as equivalent to,

---

[129] Ritchie, 92. Note: A lame or blind priest could eat the bread from the table, but they could not come near the veil (Leviticus 21:16-23). A priest showing signs of leprosy was excluded.

or surpassing established doctrine. This spiritual elitism of the "knows" versus the "don't knows" violates the principle of the table—the concept of family unity through our bond with the Father around His table. If you have bread, share it! Don't play games with the Bread of Life.

All around us people are hungry for answers, for meaning in their lives. The Word has those answers. Often it is broken and shared by sincere pastors and teachers, but the church only nibbles at the precious truth. Like children who have spoiled their appetites with junk food, the sickness of the church is evidenced by an absence of hunger for the bread that really nourishes. There is an attitude of inattentiveness when the bread is broken. Far too many services are closed with discarded bread left lying in pews and aisles. The table is not only where I come to feed; it is also the place where I look for answers to the questions those I love and know ask of me. I am to feed myself; then to stuff my heart and mind full of bread for them. Sometime this week, I may meet someone who is hungry and hurting, someone who needs the very bread I received today. They may not sit at the table, but I may be allowed to give them the children's bread! This is the role of the intercessor evangelist—taking bread from the table in the Holy Place to hungry souls in an unholy world and inviting them to come join God's family.

6. It is *a place of revelation.* The table is a place of revelation (Luke 24:15, 30-32). Two disciples are on the road to Emmaus on Resurrection Sunday. There, Jesus came alongside them, walked with them and expounded to them the Scriptures. They were captured by His insights, but blind to His identity. They insisted as they reached their destination, *"Abide with us"* (v. 29).

In the breaking of bread, He was revealed to them. He took bread, blessed it, broke it and gave it to them. And their eyes were opened and they knew Him! They said to one another, "Did not our heart burn within us, while he talked with us by the way, and while he opened to us the scriptures?" (v. 32). Here is holy heartburn! They saw Him, and they felt His lingering presence.

Without the lampstand, the bread would have remained in darkness. No purely rational understanding of the Bible would be acceptable. The natural man does not understand the things of the Spirit. The lampstand illuminates the table. As we break the bread in the light of the candlesticks, the Holy Spirit, Jesus is revealed. It should happen in the believers' meeting. As we break the bread, there is a revelation of Jesus—He becomes real to us. We see Him and sense His nearness. His presence burns within us. That experience should happen to us in our private

Image courtesy of www.tabernacleman.com

times. As we sit quietly with the Word, communing with the Holy Spirit, Jesus rises out of the pages of the Book, becoming real to us, fellowshipping with us.

Remember that the only light in the Holy Place was the light of the candlesticks. So, the bread is to be broken in the light of the candlesticks. Many people break the bread in darkness. They read the Bible without meaning. When the Word is considered under the light of the Holy Spirit, it edifies, strengthens and nourishes!

This bread was sprinkled with incense, a symbol of prayer. So, we approach the Word prayerfully. We pray and read. We read and pray. And, Jesus lives to speak with us. Some read the Bible as a book. Others, in reading, hear the voice of God. Some see facts, while others encounter life. The difference is in how the bread is broken. The Bible must be read in the fellowship of the Holy Spirit, and that reading laced with prayer.

A new model of worship must emerge.

- In the current model, preachers preach; in the new model, people must also be proclaimers.
- In the current model, people are passive listeners; in the new model, people must be active learners and bread breakers.
- In the current model, people eat the bread they want, choosing what the preacher preaches that is relevant to them and leaving the rest of the bread; in the new model, people eat the bread they need, then they box up the rest and take it to the streets for distribution.

7. It is *a place of fellowship.* This is the Father's table. The most important feature of the table is not what is on it, but who is at it. We have come to the table, not merely to eat, but to spend time with the Father in His house, at His table.

Here is a picture of the believers' meeting. The New Testament church had a believers' meeting at least once a week. It included a meal followed by Communion and ministry (1 Corinthians 11). At the climax of the meeting, prophets would speak, two or three, that all may learn (ch. 14). As the church lingers at the table and enjoys fellowship, the prophets begin to minister in the holy place. Words of exhortation, edification and comfort come forth. Numbers 4:7 calls this "continual bread," because it is needed continually.

This picture of fellowship, of lingering at the table of the Lord, is a rich image. There is nothing like family fellowship at the table, and that includes the table of the Lord (God's sanctuary). Today, we have a generation of fast-food Christians. As a result, we are spiritually undernourished. Our altar services barely last more than a few moments. We are quickly back at our pews, ready to rush home and away from the table of the Lord. But it is in the discipline of waiting that we have our deepest, most profound encounters with God.

The eschatological fulfillment of the table of shewbread will be Christ, the Bridegroom, and the church, His bride, around the table at the Marriage Supper of the Lamb (Revelation 19:9). As we meet around the table, we enjoy fellowship, and yet our hearts long for the richer and deeper fellowship with Christ at the heavenly table. The present table is a foretaste of the table above us—the table where we are the anticipated special guests of God the Father and His Christ.

The Table of Utensils

In addition to the bread, four golden utensils were laid on this table (Exodus 31:8; 35:13; 37:16; 39:36).

1. Dishes were used for the bread (Numbers 7:13, 18, 19, 25). These dishes contained the bread. Since there was one loaf of shewbread per tribe, some speculate that there might have been 12 dishes. Our guess is that there were at least two, for two stacks of six loaves each.

2. The Scripture mentions "pans" or chalices and *"flagons"* in association with the table. Some refer to these as bowls and cov-

ers.[130] These were actually cups with handles that held wine to be used in the drink offering (see Exodus 25:29).

3. Oil for the lampstand was placed on the table in the "bowls." This is the oil that replenished the lampstand daily.

4. Incense for the golden altar was on the table. This incense was also sprinkled upon the bread using the special spoons designed in association with the table. Incense for the golden altar was carried from the table to the altar of incense in these spoons.[131]

Oil for the lampstand, incense for the altar, wine for the drink offerings and the bread were all there at the table. The table is the place of the Word. The candlesticks are representa-

Image courtesy of Melvin Poe

tive of the ministry of the Holy Spirit. The incense is a type of our prayer and deep communion with God, but the fresh oil for the lamp and fresh incense for the golden altar rise from the table. The symbolism is powerful. Fuel for both intercession and the Spirit-filled life are anchored to the table—to the Word! It is the discipline of the table that fuels both the Spirit-energized life and one's prayerful communion with God at the golden altar. To say it another way, when we need renewal, or when the fire seems to have gone out and prayer seems a futile exercise—the starting point for personal renewal is found at the table, in the Word.

When your lamp is dark, your flame flickering, and the sweetness of your relationship with God has diminished, go to the table; open the Book. Read! The discipline of the Word is

---

130 Conner, 36.
131 Conner, 35-6.

the key to spiritual renewal. At the table, we find fresh oil to relight our fire. At the table, we find the incense to refuel passionate prayer and worship.

On the Arch of Titus in Rome, the table of shewbread is depicted. And it is shown with the silver trumpets attached to its side, stored in a diagonal way on the side, probably the back side (north side) of the table. Brackets on the legs served to cradle the silver trumpets. One trumpet was estimated to be 3 cubits long (46 inches), the other about 2 cubits long (36 inches). These were most likely a long, single tube ranging from 1.5 to 7.5 inches in diameter.

The silver trumpets were used to signal the camp that a new journey had begun and they were again on the move. They announced special festival days. They were used for command signals in a time of war. Any notable event could have demanded their use (Numbers 10:2-10). They were most likely straight tubes like those on the Arch of Titus.[132]

So the signal to gather, the announcement of seasonal and festival events, even war, was from the table, by the trumpets. The voice of the Spirit is most clearly heard out of Scripture. It is where we are at the table, and bread is being broken, the Word is being preached, that we should hear more clearly a "word" of God.

THE TABLE AND THE LAMPSTAND IN BALANCE

The only furniture not in the straight east-to-west alignment were the table and the lampstand. The lampstand was to the south, the table to the north. The arrangement was

---

[132] Conner, 64, 73.

certainly not utilitarian. Despite the small space in the Holy Place, 20 by 10 cubits (30 by 15 feet), these pieces of furniture could easily have been centered. It is doubtful that the placement of these articles was merely for convenience. This Tabernacle is not about convenience, it is about revelation.

Having suggested that the table represents the ministry of the Word and the lampstand the Spirit, do we have a picture of the balance in worship—in Spirit and in truth? Some churches center on the Word and miss God by emphasis, just as others concentrate on the Spirit and also err by emphasis. The pathway into the Most Holy Place is found as we balance Word and Spirit, as we live in context of both.

Pentecostal churches tend to be experiential and "spiritual" in worship. The Holy Spirit is a vital part of their worship. In fact, He is often the focal point of worship. But the Holy Spirit has not come to testify of Himself. He points to the table, and to Christ! Fundamentalist churches tend to be Bible-centered.

Sometimes they border on bibliolatry, and they ignore or dismiss as relevant the supernatural qualities of the Spirit's ministry in the church. Both extremes are wrong. We need the balance of both the candlesticks and the table.

Image courtesy of www.mishkanministries.org

CHAPTER FOURTEEN

THE ALTAR OF INCENSE

The Principle of Communion with God

The altar of incense is introduced in Exodus 30:1: *"You shall make an altar to burn incense on; you shall make it of acacia wood"* It is a cubit (18 inches) wide, being four-square, and 2 cubits high (v. 2; 37:25). Next to the ark, it was the most sacred piece of furniture in the Tabernacle.

It is called the *"altar of incense"* (30:27; 31:8) as well as the "incense altar" (35:15; 37:25). It is also called the *"altar of gold"* (40:5) and the *"golden altar which was before the throne"* (Revelation 8:3). It is the *"altar before the Lord"* (Leviticus 16:12, 18). Its purpose is seen in the names the *"altar to burn incense"* (Exodus 30:1) and *"the altar of sweet incense before the Lord"* (Leviticus 4:7). First Kings 6:22 calls it "the whole altar that was by the oracle"—a reference to the ark of the covenant.

It had a top surface (18 inches square) where a vessel with live coals was placed, over which powdered incense was sprinkled. The golden altar was higher than the table, being 2 cubits (36 inches) high. The table was a cubit and a half (27 inches) high. The golden altar was a cubit (18 inches) square. You will recall, we do not know the height of the lampstand.

> *And you shall overlay its top, its sides all around, and its horns with pure gold; and you shall make for it a molding of gold all around. Two gold rings you shall make for it, under the molding on both its sides. You shall place them on its two sides, and they will be holders for the poles with which to bear it. You shall make the poles of acacia wood, and overlay them with gold* (Exodus 30:3-5).

The golden altar was made of acacia wood, overlaid with gold on its top and sides. It had four golden horns rising from each corner, a feature that corresponds to the brass altar, also having four horns at its corners. On the sides, at the corners, were rings. Unlike other pieces of furniture, it had only two rings, not four—"*two golden rings ... by the two corners ... upon the two sides*" (v. 4). The passage here speaks of two corners and two sides, but the

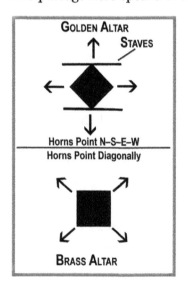

altar had four corners and four sides. It was foursquare. One view holds that at two opposite corners, were two rings, into which specially designed staves were inserted for transport. The staves were also covered with gold. Another view sees them as centered on the two sides of the table. Or even extending along the two opposite sides of the altar, from corner to corner. If the rings were on the corners, the

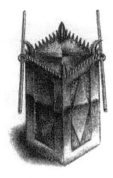 table would have been carried not in a north-south, east-west fashion, but in a diagonal posture. It would have been positioned with its staves parallel to the veil (a north-south orientation), and the altar would have been in a diagonal position. In some arrangements, the rings allow the staves, when the altar is stationary, to pivot to a vertical position. The horns would have been pointed in an ordered north-south, east-west manner, not diagonally as did the horns of the brass altar.[133] In transport, the altar was wrapped in blue, the color of heaven, and covered with goat's skin (Numbers 4:12). "*And you shall put it before the veil that is before the ark of the Testimony, before the mercy seat that is over the Testimony, where I will meet with you*" (Exodus 30:6).

The golden altar was located at the crown of the Holy Place, westward and immediately in front (eastward) of the ark of the covenant, separated by the veil. From the beginning, it seems to belong more to the Most Holy Place than to the Holy Place. The above description ties it more closely to the ark than to the furniture in the Holy Place. Note the phrases *"before the veil," "by the ark," "before the mercy seat,"* and *"over the testimony."* The golden altar is the believer's place of prayer and intercession, of communion with and ministry to God. It belongs in the Most Holy Place, by the ark, before the mercy seat. But sin has separated man from God. A veil still remains.

The veil is not a *what*; it is a *who*. The veil represents Jesus. As the flesh of Jesus was torn, so the veil was torn. Hebrews tells us that we come into the presence of God through the veil,

---

[133] John Ritchie, *The Tabernacle in the Wilderness* (Grand Rapids: Kregel, 1982) 83. (Note: For an illustration of the altar with the bars on the corners, thus a diagonal arrangement, see John Richie's illustration.)

that is, His flesh (10:19). We pray through the veil, that is, through the agency of Christ. At His death, the veil was rent. His sacrifice enabled us to come directly to God. In prayer, we stand before the mercy seat. That is, our God is seated on a bloodstained throne named *mercy*. Glory! The price of our communion with Him is inestimable. It is here, before the veil and at the ark, that God declares He will meet us. It is here, by the ark, with mercy covering *"the testimony [of the Law]"* (see 30:6), that He pledges to hear our prayer. Prayer passes through the veil (Jesus), through the torn veil (His death, the Cross). It is a prayer empowered by our identity with the death of Christ. God sees us in covenant through the blood of His Son.

The golden altar is the bridge between the Holy Place and the Most Holy Place. It is the bridge between this world and the other world. It is the connecting point, between that which is holy and that which is most holy. We stand on the earth in the holy place with its earthen floor, praying, but prayer belongs more to heaven than to earth. By prayer, directed through the veil, we enter another world.

Image courtesy of www. tabernacleman.com

> *Aaron shall burn on it sweet incense every morning; when he tends the lamps, he shall burn incense on it. And when Aaron lights the lamps at twilight, he shall burn incense on it, a perpetual incense before the Lord throughout your generations. (Exodus 30:7, 8).*

The golden altar burned twice daily, morning and evening. It used the fuel of spices and incense, which were stored on the table of shewbread. This incense, apart from fire, had no fragrance, But the fiery coals unlocked the innate sweet fragrance, filling the Holy Place aromatically. Prayer, without passion, does little to change earth's atmosphere. The time of the burning of the altar of incense was parallel to the time the daily morning and evening burnt offerings were given at the brass altar. Here, the two altars smoke together. The time of consecration is to also be a sweet time of communion with God.

Three priests were involved in the ritual. One removed the firepan and the ashes of the previous offering. The second priest set on the altar between the crown and horns another firepan with fresh coals from the brass altar. The third sprinkled the live coals with successive pinches of incense carried in the hollow of his left hand. The substance was highly volatile and capable of producing a thick smoke.[134] *"You shall not offer strange incense on it, or a burnt offering, or a grain offering; nor shall you pour a drink offering on it."* (v. 9).

THE POWER OF PRAYER

Only the incense prescribed was acceptable. We'll look at the ingredients and what they imply. No strange incense was permitted. The golden altar was not the place to offer blood offerings, the meat or drink offering. The two altars had separate but connected purposes. The meat offering was an offering of labor. Both the grain and the grape were the work of the hands. But God wants more than laborers; He wants the communion of a loving relationship. Prayer must be above and beyond either our consecration or our labor for God. Moving to the golden altar is about the sweetness of adoration, our desire to come near His presence. Ultimately, it is not about us; it is about Him! How close can we come? Next to the veil? Near the Most Holy Place?

---

[134] James Strong, *The Tabernacle of Israel* (Grand Rapids: Kregel, 1987) 95.

And Aaron shall make atonement upon its horns once a year with the blood of the sin offering of atonement; once a year he shall make atonement upon it throughout your generations. It is most holy to the Lord (v. 10).

The golden altar required atonement once a year. The right to be in communion with God has a price. Blood makes this place of communion possible. Because sin can contaminate the place of communion, annually the golden altar was sanctified. This was accomplished by placing the blood of the sin offering on the horns of the golden altar.

VERTICAL PRAISE

The golden altar sat in front of the veil. It is the culmination of worship—the high point of communion and intimacy with God. This is as close as any priest could get to God's glory, with the exception of the high priest on the Day of Atonement when he went into the Most Holy Place. Here is the place of petition and intercession, of ministry of worship, praise and prayer!

It is important to see the vertical dimension. We can go through an entire service and never minister to God. There can be warmth, love, grace, anointing, ministry, salvation of souls, healing. All of that is God acting toward us, or our ministry one to another. The altar of incense represents something more—our vertically ascendant ministry to God. The next time you worship, take note of how many songs are directed to God and how many are about us, our experience and feelings. The health of a congregation can be determined by the depth of vertical praise. Worship cannot be merely emotional. It must be a settled, deliberate and conscious act of worshipful prayer and praise! We have created a narcissistic worship mode that focuses on what we get out of our faith. It sees God acting for us, doing for us. We treat God as an errand boy.

- "Fix this, God."

- "A new car please, God—blue, four-door, hatchback, leather interior, plush!"

- "Heal him, God."

- "What's wrong with You, God? Didn't I ask You to do that yesterday?"

- "Touch us, God. Lift us up, God."

He is the Sovereign God; we are His slaves. He speaks; we act. We wait on Him. We serve at His command. He is not bound to answer us or to respond to us. Yet, He does respond. His response is not rooted primarily in our faith or fervency, our goodness or depravity, but in His love and grace.

THE HIGH ALTAR—THE CULMINATION OF WORSHIP

This altar represents the high point of worship. This altar experience does not stand alone. It is built on all the transactions that have occurred before.

- The gate—initial praise, an attitude of praise and worship

- The altar—sacrifice, the concept of surrender and offering for sin and self

- The laver—cleansing, the need for personal holiness

- The lampstand—fruit and fire, the balanced life in the Spirit

- The table—feeding and fellowship, a hunger for the Word and the *koinonia* of the saints

The veil was rent at the crucifixion of Jesus. That veil was 4 inches thick. Access into God's presence is through Christ and His torn flesh. The altar is described as being before the ark, even though the two are separated by the veil. Since it is before the ark of the covenant, prayer is possible because we are in a covenant with God. Prayer is an appeal to that covenant and must be consistent with the design and desire of God's covenant.

Three things were stored in the ark—the tablets of the Law, the rod of Aaron, and a pot of manna. Prayer must be consistent with these three aspects of covenant. To pray without sensitivity to God's righteous demands (tablets), or without faith and dependence (the pot of manna), or without a submissive and obedient heart (rod) is a vain and foolish prayer. Conversely, to pray as a servant-hearted disciple (rod) committed to live according to His godly standards (tablets) in faithful and dependent devotion (manna) is to access the full blessings of God and to come under the mercy of God, facilitating a release of His glory.

To forget these three items and the principles that they represent leads to a frustrating prayer experience. Without a personal commitment to righteousness (tablets), submission to His will (rod), and faith and daily dependence upon Him (manna), time at the golden altar is less than worship. It is less than communion.

To summarize, the discipline of thanksgiving and praise (gate), the crucifixion of sin and self (brazen altar), clean hands and pure hearts (laver), the ministry of fruit and fire (candlestick, or lampstand), and a hunger for the Word (table) all combine at the altar to make prayer a powerful experience of communion with God.

Fire and The Altar

In order to light the fire at the golden altar, one had to get live coals of fire from the brazen altar. These live coals were placed in the golden censer, and incense was poured over them. No other fire was acceptable. No other incense than that which was stored on the table, using the formula given to Moses, was acceptable (Exodus 30:34-38)!

Nadab and Abihu, the sons of Aaron, died before the Lord for offering "strange fire" (Numbers 3:4; Leviticus 10:1, 2). They kindled their own flame. The fire from the brazen altar is the only acceptable fire to light the flame of worship at the golden altar. Korah and his company offered strange incense and experienced God's judgment (Numbers 16).

Christologically, this is the fire of the crucified One that gains us entrance into the presence of God. Personally, it is the fire of the crucified life that lights the fire of true worship. It is the fire of sacrifice that kindles the fragrance of true worship.

Spiritual death occurs whenever we try to kindle the flame of worship instead of getting our fire from the brazen altar of sacrifice. We can start a fire in the Holy Place and create the illusion of worship, but the end result is the same—spiritual death. Fervent worship takes its flame from the fire of the offerings that quench sin, from the fire of repentance and restitution, from the fire of redemption and regeneration, from the fire that consumes the self in total giving to God, from the fire of service, from the crushed and broken life offered to God, and from the fire of sweet fellowship with God.

On the Day of Atonement, Aaron placed the blood of the sin offering upon the horns of the incense altar (Exodus 30:10; Leviticus 16:16-20). It is blood that gives the altar of incense its power. In this act, the two altars came together, united by blood and fire. The blood was placed on the horns of the altar and sprinkled around the golden altar seven times. The place of prayer is a bloody place. A price has been paid to allow us to cry out to God. On the brazen altar, the horns represented the power of God in terms of His judgment against sin. Here, they represent the power of prayer and praise, of worship. In Habakkuk 3:4, God is seen as having *"horns coming out of his hand: and there was the hiding of his power."* The brass altar and the golden altar are inseparable.

INCENSE AND THE ALTAR

The incense that is used in the golden altar is *"holy and pure"* (Exodus 30:35), dedicated totally to use at the altar. Anyone who used this fragrance anywhere else, for any other purpose, would be *"cut off"* (v. 38). Nor could anyone make a duplicate of this incense for his own personal use (v. 37). Prayer can never be an utterly private or personal matter.

The ingredients include three perfumes—*stacte, onycha* and *galbanum*—mixed with frankincense (v. 34). Here sweetness is multiplied.

- *Stacte* came from the myrrh tree growing on the hills around Mount Gilead. When its bark was cut, the sap would flow spontaneously, generously. The word means to "drop" or "distill." It was converted into a powder and crushed fine.[135]

- *Onycha* came from a sweet-smelling shellfish that came from the depths of the Red Sea. It, too, was converted to powder. The smell was detected when its perfume was burned. It was, therefore, a concealed fragrance, only detectable when exposed to fire. So, our sweetness should emerge under fire.

- *Galbanum* came from the juice of a shrub in the high country of Syria. One would break the limbs or twigs of the shrub, or make an incision on the tree, and the juice would flow out through the night. It was a bitter gum resin used to drive away insects, a repellent. As the two

---

[135] Kevin Conner, *The Tabernacle of Moses* (Portland: Bible, 1975) 51.

ingredients above, this too was made into a powder.[136]

- *Frankincense* is a white gum drawn from the incision in a tree. It was pure, sweet and aromatic.[137] The trunk of the frankincense tree has a thin-peeling bark. The trees still grow in Africa, Southern Arabia and India. A cut into the trunk allowed the resin to ooze out. It dried on the tree and was then chipped off and separated from any bark.[138]

Salt was added to the mixture as a seasoning and preservative, perhaps a catalyst.[139] Worship, like incense, is a combination of that which flows spontaneously (*stacte*), that

which comes from the depths of our being (*onycha*), that which is humble and *broken* (*galbanum*), and that which is *pure and sweet* (frankincense)! This is a composite picture of worship. At the golden altar, the analogy is clear. The sacrificial life gives off a fragrance that is pleasing to God. The psalmist prayed, "Let my prayer be set forth before thee as incense; and the lifting up of my hands as the evening sacrifice" (141:2).

Image courtesy of www.tabernacleman.com

The incense has fragrance only because it has contact with the fire. No fire, no fragrance. No passion, no pleasing aroma to God. Here again, the two altars—the brass altar and the golden altar—are brought together. The evening

---

[136] Conner, 51.

[137] See: James F. Spink, *The Tabernacle in the Wilderness* (New York: Loizeaux Brothers, 1946) 79; David Little, *The Tabernacle in the Wilderness* (New York: Loizeaux Brothers, 1957) 37; Roy Lee DeWitt, *The History of the Tabernacle* (Chatham, IL: Revival Teaching, 1986) 39.

[138] David and Pat Alexander, *Eerdmans Handbook to the Bible* (Grand Rapids: Eerdmans, 1973) 100.

[139] Conner, 51.

sacrifice is offered at the first and incense at the latter. Also the two Tabernacles, the Tabernacle of David and of Moses, are brought together. The lifting of hands at the Tabernacle of David is said to symbolize the evening sacrifice of the Tabernacle of Moses. The burnt offering was presented on the brass altar at the beginning of the Jewish day at the Tabernacle of Moses.

The lifting of the hands at the Tabernacle of David was a bloodless act of total consecration, meaning the same thing the burnt offering meant, yet it was offered on Mount Zion. It was a substitute for the burnt offering. Even at the Tabernacle of David, worship was still the giving of oneself sacrificially. And prayer at the Tabernacle of David was like the sweet incense offered at the golden altar at the Tabernacle of Moses.

Prayer and worship go beyond the ritual of reciting words. Worshipful prayer involves sacrificial consecration on the back of repentance of sin. These principles are found in the brass altar. It involves sanctified living. This is the principle of the laver. It necessitates a daily renewing of the Holy Spirit's power— fruit and fire. This is the essence of the candlestick. It means breaking bread and pouring over His Word. This is the table. Communion with God at the golden altar is the culmination of all the other pieces of furniture. It is the heart of prayer, which is worship.

A PICTURE OF WORSHIP

In John 12:3, there is a New Testament picture of worship: *"Then Mary took a pound of very costly oil of spikenard, anointed the feet of Jesus, and wiped His feet with her hair. And the house was filled with the fragrance of the oil."*

Here is a beautiful picture of worship. It is the offering of that sweetness which is costly. Some say a year's wages was the price of the perfume. It was broken and poured out. The offering is humble, personal and fragrant. Mary was at the feet of Jesus in the role of a servant.

Notice the atmosphere transformation! The house was filled with the scent of this sweet fragrance. Such atmosphere transformation doesn't happen without a price. David said, "I will not offer to God that which costs me nothing!" (See 2 Samuel 24:24).

As I give myself as a sacrificial offering of worship, like incense, my praise becomes a sweet fragrance at the throne of God. Praise and worshipful attitudes transform environments.

THE RELOCATION OF THE ALTAR OF INCENSE
The writer of Hebrews says of the Holy Place:

> *For a tabernacle was prepared: the first part, in which was the lampstand, the table, and the showbread, which is called the sanctuary [or the Holy Place] (9:2).*

Here, two pieces of furniture are mentioned as belonging to the Holy Place. Compare this with the Old Testament description of the Holy and Most Holy Place. Remember, in the Holy Place, three pieces of furniture occupied the room. Here only two are located in the Holy Place. What piece of furniture is missing from the Holy Place? The missing piece is the altar of incense. Where is it?

> *And behind the second veil, the part of the tabernacle which is called the Holiest of All, which had the golden censer and the ark of the covenant ... and above it were the cherubim of glory ... (vv. 3-5).*

Here is the golden censer (a reference to the golden altar) in the Most Holy Place. What is it doing here? This is an obvious contradiction with the Old Testament narrative. There, it was before the veil (Exodus 30:6). Has the writer of Hebrews had a lapse of memory? No! After Calvary, our place of communion with God has been moved inside the veil. God has said, "Come on in. You belong in here with Me." The rent veil and the blood of the Lamb allow me to access heaven's throne room!

So the believer's place is now before the ark, in the throne room of God. The altar is still balanced by the golden candlesticks to the south and the table of shewbread to the north. Here is a picture of the Father's presence—the ark; the Son's presence— the table of shewbread; and the Holy Spirit's presence—the oil in the lampstand. The believer's place at the altar of incense is in the center, in direct and dynamic communion with the Trinity— Father, Son and Holy Ghost. As I worship in spirit and truth, I am surrounded by the presence of God. I am caught up into heavenly places. I experience the most holy place of heaven's tabernacle and direct communion with God.

THE POWER OF INCENSE IN THE NEW TESTAMENT

As we enter into prayer, there is enormous spiritual power that is both tapped and released (Luke 1:8-17; Acts 13:1, 2; Hebrews 8:2-6; Revelation 5:8-10; 8:1-5; 11:15-19). In Luke 1:8-17, Zacharias is burning incense in the Holy Place. The time of the burning of incense is also the time of prayer. Outside, the people have gathered to pray.

The Jews believed that corporate prayer had the greatest power. If you could not attend the corporate prayer gathering, the next best thing was to pray at the same time the congregation was praying. The sages taught that the prayers of a congregation carried more

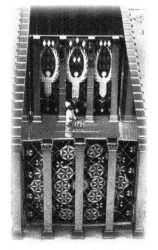

Image courtesy of Melvin Poe

weight than a person praying alone. Psalm 69:13 was interpreted to mean that there was a favorable time for prayer (*eit ratzon*). In that favorable time, prayer was more welcomed, more potent, more likely to be answered. That time was "when the congregation is praying."[140] The Scripture says, *"[Zacharius] went into the temple of the Lord [to burn incense]. And the whole multitude of the people were praying without at the time of incense"* (Luke 1:9, 10). The concepts of prayer and incense flow together here.

> *Then an angel of the Lord appeared to him, standing on the right side of the altar of incense. And when Zacharias saw him, he was troubled, and fear fell upon him. But the angel said to him, "Do not be afraid, Zacharias, for your prayer is heard; and your wife Elizabeth will bear you a son, and you shall call his name John. And you will have joy and gladness, and many will rejoice at his birth. For he will be great in the sight of the Lord, and shall drink neither wine nor strong drink. He will also be filled with the Holy Spirit, even from his mother's womb. And he will turn many of the children of Israel to the Lord their God. He will also go before Him in the spirit and power of Elijah, 'to turn the hearts of the fathers to the children,' and the disobedient to the wisdom of the just, to make ready a people prepared for the Lord (vv. 11-17).*

The two other assistants stepped outside. One had removed the coals of the incense offering from the night before. The other had placed new live coals on the golden altar. The role of Zacharias was then to sprinkle the powdered incense on the live coals. Suddenly, a heavenly visitor stood at the altar of incense with him.

Notice what happens when "incense" is burned—when true worship, praise and sincere prayer are offered. Angels are released. The announcement comes: "Your prayer is heard and Elizabeth shall bear you a son!" Elizabeth is moved from barrenness to fruitfulness. God's purposes are put into process. A

---

[140] Hayim Halevy Donin, *To Pray as a Jew* (New York: Basic Books, 1980) 14.

prophetic voice for the earth, patterned after the ministry of Elijah, is prepared. Changes come that are the prelude to a messianic manifestation. The hearts of the people are going to be changed. Here we have the connection to the Old Testament canon's last prophetic voice, Malachi (4:5, 6). The hearts of the fathers are going to be ignited to engage their children in positive spiritual ways. A generational divide is to be healed. The heritage will not be lost. The earth will be spared judgment. The season of silence is over.

This is a pattern we see over and over in Scripture. As the church prays and worships, God works. When Peter had been jailed and was facing the prospect of death, the church prayed and God acted. Angels were released. Peter was spared, set free. And God's purposes and power were manifest (Acts 12:3-17; see also ch. 16).

ANGELS

We tend to think of angelic activity as confined to the Old Testament. Let's recall that the figures of angels were woven into the fabric of the veil and the *mishkan* in the Holy and Most Holy Place. Angelic activity occurs in both Testaments. Angels continue to attend the holy place today and provide assistance to the people of God according to the purposes of God. They may or may not manifest themselves, but they are nevertheless present.

When Jacob awoke from his dream, he called the name of the place Bethel, meaning *"house of God"* (Genesis 28:19). And he made the pronouncement, *"The Lord is in this place, and I did not know it"* (v. 16, NKJV). In his dream, Jacob had seen a ladder reaching from the earth to heaven. Above it stood the Lord. Jacob stood at the foot of it. Coming and going on the ladder were angels (v. 12). The ladder represents accessibility to God by man.

Wherever there is a deposit, a manifestation of God's presence, Bethel is established. At such a place, angels are coming and going. A connection between heaven and earth occurs, and God allows access to Himself by man. What Jacob dreamed about, Jesus transformed into reality: *"And He said to him, "Most assuredly, I say to you, hereafter you shall see heaven open, and the angels of God ascending and descending upon the Son of Man"* (John 1:51).

What God had wanted to accomplish through Abraham's seed He will accomplish through the church. After the atoning work of Christ, the heavens are now opened to us. Bethel is created, not in a place, but in a people. And angels are coming and going around the covenant people. Peter spoke of the salvation that we preach, that the *"angels desire to look into"* (1 Peter 1:12). The writer of Hebrews asked, *"Are they not all ministering spirits sent forth to minister for those who will inherit salvation? "* (1:14).

Jesus noted in Matthew 18 that disciples who behave like humble servants are never alone: *"... their angels always see the face of My Father who is in heaven"* (v. 10). Angels are coming and going from the throne of the Father to His children, from His children back to the Father. Their concern is the will of the Father in the life of His children, that the purposes of God are manifest in His time.

Joshua and his army had completed the covenant act of circumcision and were ready to follow the ark around the massive walls of the ancient city of Jericho. Before the conquest began, Joshua discovered outside of Jericho that he and his army were not alone. The Angel of Yahweh was present with an army of angels to move above them in the battle (Joshua 5). This is God's air force.

David discovered that the battle went much better when his army moved under the cover of angels.

> *God said to him, "You shall not go up after them; circle around them, and come upon them in front of the mulberry trees. 15 And it shall be, when you hear a sound of marching in the tops of the mulberry trees, then you shall go out to battle, for God has gone out before you to strike the camp of the Philistines* (1 Chronicles 14:14, 15).

The "sound of going in the tops of the mulberry trees" was the audible departure of God's army of angels commissioned to war in the middle heaven against the forces of darkness that

would have energized the enemies of David. God said, "Don't go into the battle and fight in the strength of flesh alone. Come over to the mulberry trees and get under My army of angels. Wait until my Air Force takes off. Go under

Image courtesy of Melvin Poe

the cover of and in coordination with the angels."

The battle that we fight is never a battle purely of flesh-on-flesh. Every encounter is potentially a spiritually charged and dominated encounter. Sometimes we fight as if we are only fighting in the area of the flesh. Our enemies are energized. We come away defeated. What went wrong? Why did God let us down? Why were they stronger? It is simple. We attempted to fight with the energy and resources of the flesh in what was a spiritual battle, and we lost. When David's army moved out with God's army of angels, the battle was won.

The Holy Place is God's conference room. Here, we meet to confer with Him about His purposes in the earth. As we discern direction, we move with God. Moving above us in the heavens are God's angelic hosts. They break the powers of the strong men that war against us and God's purposes. Bethel is the place where heaven touches the earth, where God and man are unified. Angels are all around; a breakthrough is anticipated.

In Acts 13:2, the church is in prayer: *"As they ministered to the Lord and fasted, the Holy Spirit said, "Now separate to Me Barnabas and Saul for the work to which I have called them."*

The word *ministered* is *leitourgeo*, the same word we see in Hebrews 10:11: *"And every priest stands ministering daily and offering ... sacrifices."* It is a worship word. Notice that at Antioch, out of worship, a new direction comes for the church. God speaks. Apostolic ministry is birthed (Acts 13:1, 2). The purposes of God among the Gentiles are set in motion. God's work gets done because we pray. We must move from the weariness of being under the burden of the work of the Lord and learn to enter into His worshipful rest. Worship energizes the work of God.

Image courtesy of Melvin Poe

THE HOLY PLACE—A CROWDED ROOM

We have found in the Holy Place the Church, the Trinity and angels. In addition, the writer of Hebrews declared, *"We also, since we are surrounded by so great a cloud of witnesses, let us lay aside every weight, and the sin which so easily ensnares us, and let us run with endurance the race that is set before us, looking unto Jesus"* (see 12:1, 2).

Who are the witnesses that surround us? He has identified them in Hebrews 11. Among them are Abel, Enoch, Noah, Abraham and Sarah, Isaac, Jacob, Joseph, Moses, Rahab, Gideon, Samuel, David, and more. All around the balcony of heaven are the saints who, through the record of Scripture and the testimony of their lives, encourage us on toward the goal, to the completion of God's agenda in the earth. Somehow, heaven and earth are joined together. In worship, the body of Christ again becomes one—composed of those in heaven and those in earth. It is as if the saints who have gone on join in our worship from heaven, filling this invisible balcony, becoming a grand cheering section praising God with us and urging us onward to the completion of the task! They testify to us from the Scriptural record of God's grace in their lives. They exemplify for us the character of Christ manifest in a hundred and more cultures. Their lives left markers that have aided us in following God.

On the Mount of Transfiguration, as Jesus and the disciples worshiped, the Bible declares that there appeared unto them Moses and Elijah—Old Testament saints (Matthew 16:28; 17:13; Mark 9:1-13; Luke 9:27-36)! A cloud overshadowed them and God spoke. The cloud is clearly a Tabernacle imagery. But, what were Moses and Elijah doing there? Encouraging Him on in the task of bringing the Kingdom to the earth and completing the redemption process? They must have been testifying of the Law and the promises of God, His power and provision. When heaven kisses the earth and the glory of the Lord is revealed, we experience in the communion of the Holy Spirit a sense that we are not alone in this race. The saints who have gone before us are somehow anticipating the consummation of our race.

Angels are coming and going as we move to the end of the present age. But we are looking to neither saints nor angels. We are "looking unto Jesus" (Hebrews 12:2).

The Holy Place is God's conference room. Decisions here affect the earth. When the church incorporates the discipline of praise (the gate), the sacrifice of sin and self (the brass altar), the purity of hands and hearts (the laver), and we acknowledge the place of the table and the lampstand, we are ready to see a release of His power.

INCENSE AND THE TABERNACLE IN HEAVEN

The most powerful example of burning incense is found in Revelation 5:8:

Now when He had taken the scroll, the four living creatures and the twenty-four elders fell down before the Lamb, each having a harp, and golden bowls full of incense, which are the prayers of the saints.

The word *odours* is translated as "incense," which is said to represent the prayers of the saints. These prayers are worthy of an answer, but they remain unanswered. Here is the accumulation of the prayers of God's people throughout history, but the time for God's

Image courtesy of www.tabernacleman.com

action was not yet. They were prayers prayed with fervency and passion, according to His will, but they were out of season. All of us have prayed for God's purposes to be manifest, for revival or for some noble spiritual cause. But we didn't get an answer. We didn't see the result we desired.

At other times, we may have prayed and felt certain in our spirit that we had an assurance from God that He was going to give us a breakthrough, but it didn't come. Precious saints, now with the Lord, have stood among us and declared that God spoke to them of some great coming revival. But, it didn't come. In time, we buried them and walked away from their graves without seeing the answer to their prayers materialize.

Were they wrong? Had they heard amiss? No! It simply wasn't God's time. Did we miss God when we felt the answer was "Yes," but there were no visible results? Why were we so  sure the answer was "Yes"? Because the answer was "Yes... but not yet." What happened to those prayers over which we felt that sense of God's anointing?

Meet the elders of heaven, 24 in number. Some say they represent both the Old and New Testament churches—the 12 tribes of Israel and the 12 apostles. Others see them as a special class of angels. Notice that they hold in their hands golden vials full of incense. The meaning of the incense is specifically interpreted so there will be no doubt as to what it means. It represents "the prayers of saints." The elders then are the custodians of the unanswered prayers of the church. What are they doing with our prayers? We prayed to God the Father, in the name of the Son, by the power of the Holy Spirit. How did the elders end up as trustees of our prayers?

At times, God hears our prayer and commits Himself to

answer it. That is why we felt the assurance in our heart that He had heard us. That assurance is why dear saints made such bold proclamations. Those saints died, but the commitment of God to answer their prayers lives on. Prayer works after we are in heaven's gallery. God receives our prayer, and noting that it is not the season in which He can answer us, He entrusts a heavenly elder with the keeping of the pledge of that unanswered prayer. He won't forget it. There will be some moment in time when God will release the power of that prayer into the earth! There will come a time when that revival will come. There will be a day when the anointing will flow with power and intensity. There will be a time when a city will see His glory, a continent will feel a wave of the supernatural—all because a saint who is now gone on prayed a prayer that God chose not to forget!

The ultimate prayer is for the Kingdom to come in its fullness. In the passage noted in Revelation 5, we are approaching that moment.

> *And they sang a new song, saying: "You are worthy to take the scroll, And to open its seals; For You were slain, And have redeemed us to God by Your blood Out of every tribe and tongue and people and nation, 10 And have made us kings and priests to our God; And we shall reign on the earth* (vv. 9, 10).

Finally, in the midst of worship in heaven, the Lamb takes the book to break the seals. Six seals are broken. We come to the breaking of the seventh seal. *"When He opened the seventh seal, there was silence in heaven for about half an hour"* (8:1).

Here is the silence of anticipation. Something is about to happen that has never happened before. God is about to release a force upon the earth more powerful than any atomic or nuclear energy. It is the power of answered prayer.

THE POWER OF PRAYER RELEASED

John describes the scene:

> *And I saw the seven angels who stand before God, and to them were given seven trumpets. 3 Then another angel, having a golden censer, came and stood at the altar. He was given much incense, that he should offer it with the prayers of all the saints upon the golden altar which was before the throne* (Revelation 8:2, 3).

Here is the golden altar in heaven, of which the golden altar in the Tabernacle is only a symbol. At the time of John's revelation, the Tabernacle of Moses had been folded for over 1,000 years. The second Temple had been destroyed. But God's true altar is still open and functioning. As the writer to the Hebrews said, the earthly Tabernacle was a shadow of the heavenly.

The release of incense upon God's altar in heaven is symbolic of prayers offered by saints on the earth. Our feet are upon the ground, but our spirit is in heavenly places in God's tabernacle. At this altar, heaven and earth connect, angels and men mingle. In this scene, the prayers that are being offered are those that were out of season but still according to God's will. He has not forgotten those prayers. Now, He is getting ready to release the power of those prayers into the earth. *"And the smoke of the incense, with the prayers of the saints, ascended before God from the angel's hand"* (v. 4).

God remembers the prayers of the saints! Not one does He forget! Prayers that have been prayed as He instructed, *"Thy kingdom come, thy will be done in earth, as it is in heaven"* (Matthew 6:10)—those prayers He is getting ready to answer in a powerful way. His Kingdom purposes will prevail. *"The kingdoms of this world have become the kingdoms of our Lord and of His Christ"* (see Revelation 11:15).

"Then the angel took the censer, filled it with fire from the altar, and threw it to the earth" (8:5). The only fire that was acceptable to light the golden altar was the fire from the altar of sacrifice—the altar where sin and self were consumed. This was the fire from the altar of sacrifice. It is the fire of God's judgment that is cast into the earth.

Mercy has restrained God from answering some of our prayers. Now, He restrains His judgment no more. The fire of His judgment is released. *"And there were noises, and thunderings, and lightnings, and an earthquake"* (v. 5).

What is happening here? The power of prayer is being loosed on the earth! Voices, thunderings and lightnings are historically related to Mount Sinai. Mount Sinai is where we meet God's demand for righteousness.

What follows here is reminiscent of the plagues upon Egypt. Those plagues came because Egypt resisted God and enslaved Israel. Into the world that has resisted God, abused His people, rejected His demands and provision for righteousness, a new set of plagues is coming. The seven trumpets sound and the seventh brings the announcement:

> *Then the seventh angel sounded: And there were loud voices in heaven, saying, "The kingdoms of this world have become the kingdoms of our Lord and of His Christ, and He shall reign forever and ever!" And the twenty-four elders who sat before God on their thrones fell on their faces and worshiped God, saying: "We give You thanks, O Lord God Almighty, The One who is and who was and who is to come, Because You have taken Your great power and reigned. The nations were angry, and Your wrath has come, And*

*the time of the dead, that they should be judged, And that
You should reward Your servants the prophets and the
saints, And those who fear Your name, small and great,
And should destroy those who destroy the earth." Then the
temple of God was opened in heaven, and the ark of His
covenant was seen in His temple. And there were lightnings, noises, thunderings, an earthquake, and great hail.*
(11:15- 19).

Now, the veil is pulled back and the earth comes face-to-face
with the reality of the invisible God. The temple is opened—
heaven's temple. The veil is removed. The heavenlies, which
had shielded man from direct exposure to the glory of God for
his own good, are now opened. The ark itself is visible—the
heavenly ark. Suddenly nothing stands between the unholy
earth and its holy Creator. Light and darkness now meet. The
revelation of His glory is too much for the earth. Nature reacts
violently with lightning and thunder. Hail falls, the earth
trembles, voices cry out. The Kingdom breaks into the time-
space world. The Kingdom intentions of God are consummat-
ed in the earth.

God has not abandoned His purposes! The awesome power
of prayer, combined with the passionate fire of Calvary's cross,
will bring redemption into the earth. One great preacher once
said, "Prayer changes nothing!" Such a shocking statement is
a reminder to us of what prayer is and is not.

- Prayer is not a manipulative exercise aimed at God.

- Prayer is not an information session without which God
  is ill informed.

- Prayer is not a report to an out-of-touch God about personal or world events, neither is it a groveling experience
  designed to humiliate man and appease a cruel deity.

- Prayer isn't a process that requires a certain number of names on a petition to get action.

The observation is an overstatement, for prayer does change things. Prayer changes me. Prayer is relational. It is the context in which God allows man to come into His counsel, where God takes us into His confidence. This is where God shares with us His secrets—the place where He transforms us into His agents.

In God's Word, it is written: *"He made known His ways to Moses, His acts to the children of Israel* (see Psalm 103:7). Prayer is a synchronizing experience. Jesus said, *"For I have not spoken on My own authority; but the Father who sent Me gave Me a command, what I should say and what I should speak [the way I should say it]"* (John 12:49). He confided, *"And He who sent Me is with Me. The Father has not left Me alone, for I always do those things that please Him"* (8:29).

The life of Jesus and His ministry was one primarily of prayer. He moved from one place of prayer to the other. And in between, the power of God flowed out of Him. Prayer was not a relief valve or a footnote in the ministry of Jesus; prayer was His ministry. Sometimes we are guilty of working for God, even with God. We are using our agenda for His good. The altar of incense is more than petition or prayer request. It is also communion with God, ministry to God!

CHAPTER FIFTEEN

BEYOND THE VEIL

The Principle of Reverence

The God who inhabits the Most Holy Place is an awesome God, or as the King James Version says, a "terrible God"—what an over-powering concept. To meet Him strikes "terror" in the mortal soul. He is *"awful"*—meaning an encounter with Him fills one with awe. *"Awesome"* is not a cheap word. To be *"awed"* before the "awful" and "terrible" God is to be speechless—to be struck dumb. This God occupies the human heart, and yet the expanding universe is to Him like the cramped quarters of a pup tent. He whispers sounds of comfort into burdened hearts, yet His same voice framed the worlds and created the material universe. He is simultaneously a still small voice and the "big bang!" He is approachable, yet there is a sense in which I must never become casual with Him. He is forgiving, but He will not allow me to exploit His forgiveness. His grace is free, but it is not cheap. His love both liberates and constrains us.

THE VEIL

In the Old Testament, God's glory is separated from man by a veil, the *paroketh*. It is called the veil of covering. Exodus 26:31-35 gives instructions to create the veil, and 36:35, 36 records the actual work. Additional notes are found in 39:34; 40:21; and Numbers 4:5. It covered the ark in transport. And it shielded the ark from casual view when the Tabernacle was stationary.[141] The Hebrew word for *veil* is from an unused verb that means "to break" or "to separate." Of course, that was not only its original intent, but also its destiny. It separated the Holy Place from the Most Holy Place, man from God. And in the end, it was broken, separated, torn in two.[142] Angelic protectors of God's holiness are woven into the fabric of the veil. This veil was 10 cubits (15 feet) wide and high. It completely shielded the Holy Place from the Most Holy Place. The dimensions for the Most Holy Place were 10 cubits by 10 cubits, thus a 15-foot square.

The *paroketh* was made of fine linen. That one material was specifically commanded as the substance of the veil. The colors of blue, purple and scarlet were woven into it. The dominant color was white, representing holiness and purity—righteousness.[143] The the veil itself represented Christ. Like the veil, His flesh was torn on the cross, that the division between God and man could be forever healed.

The veil was woven by a procedure known as *hoshen*, finished on both sides, which allowed the *cherubim* figures to be visible from the holy and the most holy places as if they were peering through the

---

[141] The veil, we are told, was the flesh of Christ. And in the ultimate sense, the ark is Christ. He is, on the earth, the place of the Father's glory. The Tabernacle is layered with multiple meanings. The ark is the place of the Father's glory. It is the symbol of covenant. It is the secret place of the Most High God. It is Christ. And the veil which covers Christ, our testator, our testament, the Word incarnate, is His flesh.

[142] Henry Soltau, *The Tabernacle, the Priesthood, and the Offerings* (Grand Rapids: Kregel, 1972) 26.

[143] William Brown, *The Tabernacle—Its Priests and Its Services* (Peabody, MA: Hendrickson, 1996) 91.

veil. (Exodus 26:31; 36:35). There is incredible speculation about the *cherubim*. No one knows for certain their shape. They are the dominant feature of the veil and on the ark. Their faces are woven into the *mishkan* (the visible ceiling). Their figures rise out of the mercy seat. Tradition says they had four faces—the lion, the ox, the eagle and the man. The *lion* represents the kingly; the *ox*, the servant, enduring labor; the *eagle*, the soaring king of the air, not bound to land; the man, humanity.[144] Strong provides the most detail and speculation about the cherubim. He says, "In shape the cherubim were substantially human, but had the split foot of an ox." They were, he believes, about 4 cubits (6 feet) tall and stood upright (2 Chronicles 3:13). He suggests their color was that of polished copper, although they were made of gold. The man's face was on the proper front, but each side of the head bore another face—the lion on the right, the ox on the left and the eagle behind. "In addition to human hands, they had two sets of wings, one pair always folded for the sake of modesty obliquely downward and forward ... and the other used for flight or for various expressive motions or conditions."[145] On the ark, one pair of wings is spread upward and forward, suggesting a hovering or brooding attitude. With one wing of each reaching upward and the other forward and downward, the wings would have created a "throne-like" enclosure with a back and sides, the mercy seat, itself being the throne. Strong says that Exodus 25:20 provides the picture of the cherubim as a bird fluttering over its nest (Deuteronomy 32:11).[146]

The color of the ceiling—the *mishkan*—was predominantly blue.[147] The color scheme of the veil was a white linen background upon which the colors of blue, purple and scarlet were added. It hung on four pillars, which were overlaid with gold

---

[144] Soltau, 25.
[145] James Strong, *The Tabernacle of Israel* (Grand Rapids: Kregel, 1987) 89.
[146] Strong, 90.
[147] Brown, 34, 35.

and stood in foundations of silver. It fully separated the Holy Place and the Most Holy Place.

BOLDNESS TO ENTER

The writer of Hebrews says now we have *"boldness to enter into the holiest"* (10:19). "The holiest" is a reference to the Most Holy Place. We do not enter this sacred and previously forbidden cube as the high priest entered. We enter by "a new and living way" (v. 20)! Jesus himself is that way. In the Old Testament era, it was a threatening thing to pass from the Holy Place into the Most Holy Place. Now there is a new way, Jesus. *"by a new and living way which He consecrated for us, through the veil, that is, His flesh"* (v. 20). The torn veil finds its true meaning in the torn flesh of Christ. We enter by His death. We enter through the Cross.

At Eden, after Adam's sin, he found the gate to the Garden blocked by the *cherubim* with their drawn sword. If he had attempted to rush to the Tree of Life, he would have been slain. Now we find again *cherubim* at the entry into the Most Holy Place, guarding the presence of God. But here they have no sword. And the veil has been opened. Instead of blocking our entrance, they seem to join our communion with God. What happened to their sword? The sword was used on the Lamb who blazed a new and bloody pathway into the Most Holy Place. Adam's sin and its effect, death, have been banished by the Lamb, carried without the gate. Is He dead, this Lamb? No, we will find Him in heaven's Most Holy Place looking "as it had been slain," yet standing (Revelation 5:6). He cannot be destroyed. He is the Lion of the tribe of Judah! It is He who now invites us into the Most Holy Place for fellowship. Let us be ever aware of the price He has paid and not treat this privilege casually. *"Let us draw near with a true heart ... having our hearts sprinkled from an evil conscience and our bodies washed with pure water"* (Hebrews 10:22).

Despite the "new and living way" and the "boldness" by which we may now enter the Holiest, this is not a casual encounter with God. There are still preparations that are incumbent upon the worshiper. The heart must be true, and it should be "sprinkled," a reference not to the ritual of the Old Testament, but to its fulfillment in the New. On our hearts are the fresh markings of the blood sacrifice of Jesus. The Spirit has sprinkled the believer's heart with the blood of the Lamb, just as the high priest sprinkled blood on the mercy seat on the Day of Atonement.

The believer is "marked" by the sacrifice of Jesus Christ and is under the covering of Calvary's blood. He must be "washed"— and the reference is not merely to the body, but to "the flesh," the rebel principle inside each of us. There is a need for external evidence of inner cleansing in the life of the worshiper. The heart sprinkled with blood is an indication of internal change. The washed flesh, purity of life, actions and attitudes, is external proof of such change. I can now meet with a holy God. Transformational processes have changed me—inside and out.

The phrase "through the veil... his flesh" (v. 20) has even more solemn implications for us. At the death of Jesus, the veil was rent in twain. It was God's invitation into His presence. Thus, the doorway into the Most Holy Place is the Cross. The presence of God is only experienced through death, the death of Jesus Christ on our behalf, and our personal baptism and crucifixion, our death to sin and self in light of the cross. The priest brought blood of both a sin offering and a burnt offering. The crucified believer is welcome in the Most Holy Place, having demonstrated the willingness to pass through the Cross, through death, to get there. Anything of self that is not crucified must die to authentically and transformationally experience His presence.

LIVING IN THE TENSION

Balance is one of our most difficult concepts to grasp in a practical way. Good theology always exists in tension. We live in the tension between the finite and the infinite, the God who can be known, and yet not fully known. He is as familiar as a Father and simultaneously the incomparable Yahweh. We are the finite attempting to comprehend the infinite God. We are mortals; He is immortal. We are transient; He is eternal. We are flesh; He is Spirit. We are confined in space, but all of space cannot contain Him! He is incomprehensible, and yet He can be known.

The revelation of God is like light gleaming through a prism. When light breaks through a prism, it gives off a rainbow of colors. God, who is light, shines into our world with a manifestation of His manifold nature. He may manifest Himself as love and yet, He is Judge. He is peace and yet, He is the warrior God. He is gentle and also terrible. He is our Father, and at the same time an awesome and unknowable King. Though He is forgiving, He will execute judgment. And while He is the Healer, He also sends the curse. He is sovereign, and yet to man, He has given free will. We live in this tension. We may prefer God to be one-dimensional—our Father but not our judge, or a judge to our enemies but not a Father to them. We like Him as our Healer, but not as the One who sends the curse. When He is gentle, we are comfortable with Him; but when He reveals Himself as terrible and awesome, we become uncomfortable in His presence. He cannot and will not be controlled. He defies our caricatures of Him. He cannot be represented by a mere idol or any one form.

THE LITURGICAL CHURCH AND THE BIBLE CHURCH

Nonliturgical Bible churches tend to become familiar with God. They are uncomfortable with formality and liturgy. They resist mystery in faith, preferring a rational and pragmatic faith. They do not construct a cathedral, but a "house" of worship—a simple building for the assembly of believers. Their worship is informal. They may whisper in church. They abhor the solemn. "Be still, and know that I am God" (Psalm 46:10) is not one of their favorite verses. Silent or meditative prayer is not common. They prefer to "make a joyful noise" with action in worship, especially if they are Pentecostal. They like practical teaching if they are a Bible church. This is increasingly true in post-modern church movements.

Other traditions approach God with a sense of awe, a sense of mystery. The lofty ceilings of the cathedrals are to convey the grandeur of God. The liturgical symbolism is to convey the mystery of His grace. The railed and protected table in the liturgical church is to convey His being set apart, that our approach is with reverence. Though we draw near, He is still apart from us. The stained-glass windows with their diverse and rich colors are a parallel to the beauty and glory of God revealed in the colors in the Tabernacle. The rich and impressive vestments of the priest reflect his office and function. They are designed to reflect the beauty and dignity of priestly function. The exalted lectern in ancient churches illustrates the loftiness of the Word when it is read, it is a word from on high, from heaven.

The liturgical church says, "God is mysterious." The Bible church says, "God can be known." The liturgical church says, "God is incomprehensible." The Bible church says, "A simple gospel for the common man." The liturgical church says, "God is King of the earth. Be silent before Him." The Bible church says, "Talk to Him like a Father." The liturgical church says, "Stand in awe and reverence." The Bible church says, "Sing and celebrate." The liturgical church says, "Be silent, words are inadequate." The Bible church says, "Make a joyful noise!"

Who is right? Both are right. We live in the tension. He is God, our Father. And He is also the incomprehensible and awesome Creator. We have the privilege of speaking to Him or standing speechless before His inestimable glory. He is the God for whom the universe is too small, and yet He is the holy and intimate Guest who occupies our heart. Balance is needed.

We need the personal relationship, the closeness that Bible churches have learned that one can have with God, the intimacy and the sense of celebration to which Pentecostals are accustomed. And we need from the high church their sense of the awe, the majesty and the reverence that is due God. We must neither become too casual nor too cold in our worship, neither too familiar nor too detached.

The Issue of Honor and Respect

There is a growing tolerance of the subnormal in terms of lifestyle issues, ethics, and questionable personal activities and values coexisting with comfort in the presence of God (see Leviticus 1:3, 10; 3:1, 6; Malachi 1:6-14; 2:2-5; 4:2, 3). Notice the recurring phrase in Leviticus— "a burnt sacrifice... *without blemish*" (1:3, 10). In 3:1, 6, the sacrifice of a peace offering, male or female, must be *without blemish*.

These sacrifices are not only pictures of Christ, but of us. They are a reflection of our heart. As such, they must be without blemish.

After the Babylonian Captivity, the remnant returned to a decimated Jerusalem and a demolished Temple. But they rebuilt the city and raised a modest Temple. They proceeded to restore the sacrifices and ceremonies, but they had not learned their lesson. As the Old Testament era came to an end, a crisis of healthy worship theology emerged. God asked, *"Where is My honor? As a Father or even a Master? Where is My fear? What has happened to your respect for Me? Your reverence of Me?"* (See Malachi 1:6).

God wanted from Israel the respect that a son should give to his father, but He was not getting that. He suggested a gracious alternative: *"If you can't respect Me at the level of son to father, could you not at least show Me the respect that a slave gives to his master?"* Hear the heartbreak of God: "I have treated you like sons, but I do not even get the respect that a wise slave sincerely offers his master."

The problem was not simply among the people. It was also among the priestly leaders. But they were blind to their own sinful attitude. *"To you priests who despise My name. Yet you say, 'In what way have we despised Your name?"* (v. 6). The prophet Malachi charged that the family name was not being honored. The priests and people did not understand how special it was to be called by the name of God or to be His people. They disdained His name. Notice the blindness to the violation! "How have we despised Your name? What have we done wrong?"

Sin is so subtle, it eventually blinds its victim. The line between right and wrong is crossed so many times, it is blurred. Note how these moral indiscretions alter the perception of God. The transgressor loses his sense of honor and respect toward God. Nowhere is that reflected more than in the attitude toward worship. The Lord says:

> *For from the rising of the sun, even to its going down, My name shall be great among the Gentiles; In every place incense shall be offered to My name, And a pure offering; For My name shall be great among the nations," Says the Lord of hosts* (v. 11).

God wanted a people to bear His name in the earth with dignity, to give witness to His existence before the whole world. Nations were to be discipled. All around the globe, the sun was never to set on God's worshipers. Incense—prayerful worship— was to be offered everywhere unto His name. God was not to be anonymous among the nations. He was to be known and respected! But that was not the way Israel responded to His name. *"But you profane it, In that you say, 'The table of the Lord is defiled; ... its food, is contemptible"* (v. 12).

The altar is God's table. The loving commitment people offer by means of sacrifice is His "meat." But these people hated the altar. They despised sacrifice. They were not motivated to give worship their best.

> *You also say, 'Oh, what a weariness!' And you sneer at it,"*
> *Says the Lord of hosts. "And you bring the stolen, the lame,*
> *and the sick; Thus you bring an offering! Should I accept*
> *this from your hand?" Says the Lord* (v. 13).

Their attitude toward worship was that it was "wearying"— boring! Instead of bringing their best, giving their best, they were offering their leftovers!

> *But cursed be the deceiver Who has in his flock a male, And*
> *takes a vow, But sacrifices to the Lord what is blemished--*
> *For I am a great King," Says the Lord of hosts, "And My*
> *name is to be feared among the nations* (v. 14).

God makes it clear that the quality and nature of their worship should be reflective of who He is. Worship is not about us—our style, our preferences, our cultural tastes. He is a great King, the Lord of Hosts. Crippled animals will not do; lame sacrifices are not acceptable. A covenant with Him demands our best!

Malachi gives a snapshot—the individual had an acceptable lamb, but he chose to give an inferior one. This choice to not give God the first, the best, the purest, the perfect, Malachi says, opens one up to be cursed, not to be blessed. The sacrifice is not accepted by God—it is rejected. The pronouncement of a curse is tied to the attempt to deceive God. In truth, the worshiper himself was deceived not only about God's greatness and worthiness but also about himself. The crippled sacrifice is reflective of his own sick soul.

> And when you offer the blind as a sacrifice, Is it not evil? And when you offer the lame and sick, Is it not evil? Offer it then to your governor! Would he be pleased with you? Would he accept you favorably?" ... I have no pleasure in you ... Nor will I accept an offering from your hands (vv. 8, 10).

Listen to the satire of the prophet: "Take this sick and dying lamb down to the governor's house and give it to him as a gift. See if he won't give you a reward!" Or, "Take this to the mayor. Tell him, 'Look, this animal has been acting a little strange lately. I think he is sick. But, if you kill and eat him fast, I don't think it will bother you.'" God makes it clear that He will not receive lame lambs.

The attitude in and toward worship is an indication of the health of a Christian. When people constantly drag into church late, they are offering a crippled animal. When they default on church commitments, they are offering a crippled animal. When they function without adequate planning for quality, that is a crippled animal. When they stand in the sanctuary but their mind is on the world, that is a crippled animal. We sometimes treat our church responsibilities in a way we treat no other commitments. Tithe is paid after the house, groceries and boat payments. Commitment to church duties is scheduled after other priorities. Convenience is the slogan that governs service to God. That, God makes it clear, is a crippled animal. Now God becomes stern: *"If you will not hear, And if you will not take it to heart, To give glory to My name,"... "I will send a curse ... I will curse your blessings ... Because you do not take it to heart"* (2:2).

Have you ever wondered why some people attend church, seem to pray, give, participate in the life of the church, but never experience the blessings of God? Here is the reason: They are under a curse, God's curse. Blessings and curses are connected to the issue of worship. Specifically, to our giving. And giving is more than gold and silver. The way we wholly give ourselves in prayer and worship opens the door to blessing or to curse! God wants all of us, not merely ten percent of our income!

There are two aspects of this potential curse. First, *"I will corrupt your seed"* (v. 3).

The impact of polluted worship is upon the "seed." In an agricultural society, seed is wealth. It is the potential for the coming year. Corrupt seed means certain poverty, along with hunger and need. A long winter is in store with meager meals. Our capacity to either survive or thrive is bound up in our seed. Worship brings the blessing of God upon the whole life.

The seed here is also the subsequent generation—the children. They are corrupted by the warped values of the parents and the accepted inconsistency between worship and walk. Children see their parents' worship and believe them to be good Christians, acceptable in God's eyes. They also see the lifestyle patterns of their parents. What they don't see clearly is the incongruence between the worship values and the subnormal spiritual walk of those same parents. They tend to adopt the practiced values of their parents as if they were appropriate expressions of God-centered worship. Their parents represent to them "normal" Christianity, but, of course, it is not the normal Christian life. It is an inferior pattern.

Then, in the course of their lifetime, they further compromise the pattern. The disparity between the worship and walk of each generation is further exaggerated. The pattern is soon thoroughly flawed, but imperceptibly so. The seed is corrupt, now producing a deformed church. After the third or fourth generation, it becomes necessary for God to visit the iniquities of the fathers upon the children. The sins of the children are merely the multiplication of the original error. Like a lunar moon mission, a fractional miscalculation in navigation early in the launch can place the mission off target by multiplied miles over the longer distance. Little sins have multiplied in three generations and now they are major cancers, violations of God's holiness.

The fathers set their children's children up for correction by God. It was not intentional. The pattern they passed on was flawed. Now their posterity is disqualified not simply because of the disparity between their own worship and walk, but also because they are blind to it. They have no idea such a dichotomy exists. They may be insulted that someone would call them to repentance. At some point, the dichotomy between walk and talk becomes so great that God visits the generations with judgment. All that would have been necessary to avert the judgment would have been open repentance by the fathers before the children. It is not perfection God expects; He expects perfect honesty about sin. When we recognize our errors and repent, our children can then discern between the absolute pattern of Scripture and the flawed pattern of our lives. But, when we pretend to pass on perfect patterns and fail to repent—pointing to specific flaws in our lives—our children become blind and bitter. Bitter, they reject faith. Blind, they copy our worship and our walk, assimilating the inconsistency. They are blind to the need for repentance. We have set them up for a visitation from God for correction.

Second, God promises to spread "dung" in the faces of worshipers. *"I will... rebuke your descendants And spread refuse on your faces, The refuse of your solemn feasts;"* (v. 3).

That's not nice! It is a picture of utter impurity. It is a disgusting image. God recognizes the great offense of these worshipers in offering crippled animals, a sin to which they are blind. They can't see their contamination. God promises to get their attention by putting dung, a symbol of their contamination, in their own face. Then they will see the problem, or at least smell it! Where will He get this dung? It is the "dung of your solemn feasts." The value assessment that God makes of their worship festivals is "dung." God says, "Your worship stinks!" Dung is the ultimate expression of waste, of refuse, leftovers. And it is given to God in worship. Why is this disgusting analogy used? Worship without honor and reverence is not only unacceptable to God, it is dung. Since they are giving dung, they are going to get dung back in return. Give leftovers, get leftovers. Give your best, get God's best.

Interestingly, it is not that they were not passionate. This was not non-fervent worship. *"You cover the altar of the Lord with tears, With weeping and crying; So He does not regard the offering anymore, Nor receive it "* (v. 13).

They were saying, "What is the problem?" Verse 17 states, *"You have wearied the Lord ... Yet you say, "In what way have we wearied Him?" In that you say, "Everyone who does evil Is good in the sight of the Lord, And He delights in them," Or, "Where is the God of justice?""*

"Everyone that does evil is good in the sight of the Lord!" They seem to have developed the notion that the actions of individuals did not reflect on their essence. Their motto might have been like that you hear in today's world: "Good people do evil things!" Certainly, *"all have sinned"* (Romans 3:23). But their position seems more extreme. They were willing to dismiss evil actions. With such compartmentalization of personal actions, covered by faith in human nature, personal accountability for immoral behavior was dismissed. No one could be held accountable to a standard of holiness and, therefore, called to repentance. "Don't be so hard on him. Sure, that was an evil act, but he is basically a good man!" We hear it all the time in our culture. Increasingly, even in the church, we deny the sinful nature of man's heart and the strength of the carnal flesh.

But there is an even more shocking position being set forth. Not only should the sinful actions of the people be dismissed in light of their goodness in the sight of the Lord, but God actually "delights" in them. A loose translation might be: "God loves everybody!" And that is true. But notice the specific words: "He delights in them," in those who are doing evil. It is clear that the people do not perceive the erosion in the quality of their relationship with God and how their evil actions block the blessings of God.

What does God want to give? *"My covenant was with him, one of life and peace, And I gave them to him that he might fear Me; So he feared Me And was reverent before My name"* (Malachi 2:5).

God says, "I wanted to give you life and peace. But, in order to qualify for that covenant, you have to reverence Me, to honor Me. You haven't done that."

Lest we think that this is unreasonable on the part of God, we need to remind ourselves that our planet was taken over by a band of hostile and renegade angels. God was not at fault. Rather, the defection to Lucifer's kingdom by our father and mother, Adam and Eve, gave him his grip on our planet. God refused to leave us stranded on this planet as hostages to Satan. He decided to offer us an escape. He did not send an angel to attempt redemption; He sent His only Son, even though it cost the life of that Son. And Jesus, His Son, came willingly! God has not spared us the best! He has given Himself in Christ. Now, He asks that we give Him our best! We must give Him no more crippled animals, no more lame sacrifices, no more unrehearsed songs. There must be no more fitting God into our schedule, no more tipping in the place of tithing, no more convenient service. The result will be no more dung and, therefore, no more curses, but blessings, life, peace ... God's best!

CHAPTER SIXTEEN

THE MOST HOLY PLACE

The Principle of Reverence

The dimensions of the Most Holy Place produced a perfect cube of 10 cubits. The walls were made of boards of acacia wood, overlaid with gold as in the Holy Place. Here, the walls on the south, the north and the west were golden. Special corner boards joined the walls on the western side (Exodus 26:15-25; 36:20-30). Four pillars, as contrasted with five, stood at the entrance to the Most Holy Place. They were the supports for the veil, called the *paroketh*. These pillars were unevenly spaced. They had no crowns, but they rested in silver bases, as did the walls.

THE DAY OF ATONEMENT

The Most Holy Place was a dreaded room in the Tabernacle (Leviticus 16; Numbers 4:15, 20). When the high priest came into the Most Holy Place, he did so only once a year, ceremonially—first for himself, then for the people. He came with a basin of blood. This was not a celebration experience, but a time of accountability for sin. It was on the occasion of the Day of Atonement.

> And the Lord said to Moses: "Tell Aaron your brother not to come at just any time into the Holy Place inside the veil, before the mercy seat which is on the ark, lest he die; for I will appear in the cloud above the mercy seat (Leviticus 16:2).

Man's meeting with God was not to be marked with casualness. When worship becomes a casual thing, it degenerates because it fails to respect God.

Aaron was required to bring the evidence of a sacrifice for sin and a burnt offering when he came into the Most Holy Place. *"Thus Aaron shall come into the Holy Place: with the blood of a young bull as a sin offering, and of a ram as a burnt offering"* (v. 3).

The priest appeared in the presence of God with the blood of both a sin and a burnt offering. The first offering obviously deals with human sin, the second with self. So, unless I bring evidence that both sin and self have been dealt with (crucified), I have not come properly into His presence! Of course, I can bring no such offering by myself.

Christ has given Himself as a burnt offering, and that is counted for us as a sin offering. He had no need, unlike any human priest before Him, to offer a sin offering. That allowed His offering to be received not in the earthly, but in heaven's tabernacle itself.

Since Christ has given Himself as a *burnt* offering, and that is counted for me as a perfect sin offering, I should now give myself to Him. God's action for me in the sacrifice of Jesus should call out the giving of myself back to Him. Sin made me a slave to death. The offering of the Lamb sets me free. What shall I do with my freedom? I choose to give myself to God (Romans 6:11, 18).

The dress code. The dress code for the Levites was not prescribed. There were no canonical robes appointed for them, but the dress code of the priest was regulated. Normally, the priest wore a robe or gown of linen. It covered his whole body from his neck to his ankles with full sleeves. It was so fine, it resembled silk. White in color, it was woven on the loom (Exodus 39:27) and was probably seamless. The robe of the high priest was most certainly seamless. The Hebrews knew and practiced the art of seamless garment making.[148]

Under the robe, the priest wore breeches supported by a simple belt-like girdle. The breeches or drawers were a single piece of cloth about a yard wide and long enough to wrap around a body. The ends were sewn together to create a kind of tube. The cord or girdle was stitched into the upper edge like a belt—one with the garment and used to secure the breeches. The bottom center would have been stitched together to create leg spaces.[149] Wrapped around the priest's head would have been another linen cloth, worn as a mitre or head wrap. A plate of gold was placed in the front of the mitre and tied with a blue string upon the head of the priest with the engraving, *"Holiness to the Lord"* (Exodus 28:36).

Image courtesy of Melvin Poe

Over this foundational robe or gown of white that covered the body of the high priest, he wore a robe or coat of all blue (v. 31), symbolizing his heavenly calling and duties. Around the

---

[148] William Brown, *The Tabernacle—Its Priests and Its Services* (Peabody, MA: Hendrickson, 1996) 91.

[149] James Strong, *The Tabernacle of Israel* (Grand Rapids: Kregel, 1987) 98.

hem of this beautiful blue robe were sewn *"pomegranates of blue, and of purple, and of scarlet ... and bells of gold"* (v. 33). The fruit and the bells were alternately placed around the hem of the priestly garment (v. 34). As the priest went about his daily duties, there was the sound of bells, the delightful and cheery ringing associated with joy!

Bells are still associated with churches and are declarations of joy to a community. Unless the priest wore the bells so that this joyful sound was heard, the solemn warning came: *"He will die"* (see v. 35). When the priest went into the Holy Place, God wanted to hear the sound of joy! That principle is still true. When God's priests are in the holy place, there is to be the sound of joy. The silence of our sanctuaries is an indication of spiritual death.

Image courtesy of Melvin Poe

Image courtesy of www.tabernacleman.com

Over the robe of blue, he would have worn the priestly ephod with the colors of blue, purple, scarlet and linen. Attached to it was the breastplate with the 12 stones, each representing a tribe. The breastplate was half a span, about 9 inches square, doubled. Inside the fold, behind the precious jewels, was a pocket that contained the *Urim* and the *Thummim*. The *Urim* is mentioned seven times in the Old Testament. The *Thummim* is mentioned five times (Exodus 28:30; Leviticus 8:8; Numbers 27:21; Deuteronomy 33:8; 1 Samuel 28:6; Ezra

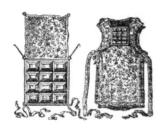

2:63; Nehemiah 7:65).[150] *Urim* means "lights." It is the plural of *Ur*, the birthplace of Abram. In Isaiah 24:15, it is translated as *"fires."* *Thummim* means *"perfections."* It is the plural of *tom*, meaning *"perfection."* It is usually translated *"integrity"* (Genesis 20:5, 6; 1 Kings 9:4; Psalms 7:8; 25:21; 26:1, 11; 41:12; 78:72); *"uprightness," "upright"* or *"uprightly"* (Job 4:6; Proverbs 2:7; 10:9, 29; 13:6; 28:6); *"perfect"* or *"perfection"* (Psalm 101:2; Isaiah 47:9); "simplicity" (2 Samuel 15:11); *"full"* (Job 21:23); *"at a venture"* (1 Kings 22:34; 2 Chronicles 18:33). It is used in the plural only when it is a reference to the *Thummim* in the priestly ephod. The combined meanings of the words would be "perfect (*Thummim*) light (*Urim*), multiplied (thus the plural)." The high priest alone consulted it. No tradition remains about how he used it.[151]

The priestly garments were designed for *"glory and for beauty"* (Exodus 28:40). However, on the Day of Atonement, the priest wore only a simple linen robe and undergarments, without the colorful coat of blue, the ephod or the breastplate.

> *He shall put the holy linen tunic and the linen trousers on his body; he shall be girded with a linen sash, and with the linen turban he shall be attired. These are holy garments* (Leviticus 16:4).

The holy linen material of the coat, trousers, girdle and mitre all symbolize righteousness and holiness. His heart, his legs, his loins and his head were to be wrapped in righteousness when he appeared in the presence of God. He was wrapped up in righ-

---

[150] David M. Levy, *The Tabernacle: Shadows of the Messiah* (Bellmawr, NJ: Friends of Israel Gospel Ministry, 1993) 163, 164.
[151] Strong, 110.

teousness! He had to appear before the Lord clean.

There was no attire for the feet. The priests worked barefoot. God had told Moses at the bush to remove his shoes, for the ground was holy (Exodus 3:5). That example continues here. The priests stood on ground made hallow by God's presence with no insulation between. *"Therefore he shall wash his body in water, and put them on [the holy garments]"* (Leviticus 16:4).

So are we to be wrapped up in righteousness, the righteousness of God in Christ, when we come to worship God. The robe of righteousness was not to be a cover for dirty flesh. He was to clean his flesh before putting on the garments of righteousness. So the righteousness of Christ can never be a cover for "dirty flesh," an excuse for carnal behavior.

The linen was broidered (Exodus 28:39). That does not mean *"embroidered,"* but to weave in squares, creating a subtle checkered design in the fabric itself.[152] Strong suggests that the high priest garment was stored in the Holy Place (Leviticus 16:23).[153] That became his dressing room. What an interesting idea. The high priest would enter the Holy Place and adorn himself with the blue robe of glory with its bells and pomegranates, the priestly multicolored apron-like ephod with its breastplate loaded with precious jewels representing the people of God. He placed upon his head the mitre and the golden plate with its blue thread and emerged from the Holy Place with the regalia of priestly ministry. So should we! Exiting God's holy place, we should emerge wearing priestly attire as the bride—partners of Jesus—wrapped in righteousness and adorned with God's glory.

Sacrifice and atonement. First, he makes atonement for

---

[152] Brown, 91.
[153] Strong, 49.

himself and his house, then for the people.

> *And Aaron shall bring the bull of the sin offering, which is for himself, and make atonement for himself and for his house ... [And he] shall kill the bull as the sin offering which is for himself. Then he shall take a censer full of burning coals of fire from the altar before the Lord, with his hands full of sweet incense beaten fine, and bring it inside the veil* (vv. 6, 11, 12).

Here the two altars are beautifully brought together—the fire from the brazen altar of sacrifice, and the incense symbolizing prayer, praise and worship.

> *And he shall put the incense on the fire before the Lord, that the cloud of incense may cover the mercy seat that is on the Testimony, lest he die. He shall take some of the blood of the bull and sprinkle it with his finger on the mercy seat on the east side; and before the mercy seat he shall sprinkle some of the blood with his finger seven times* (vv. 13, 14).

Note the combination: *blood* and *fire!* In verses 15-19, he repeats the process, this time for the people. He not only makes atonement for the people, but also for the Holy Place itself. The sanctuary must also be purified. A holy people require a holy place. It has been contaminated by the sin of the children of Israel. Unless the place of His presence is kept pure, He will not dwell in our midst!

Atonement means "healing the division." This division is due to uncleanness, contamination of the people. Living in a world of sin, the people tend to pollute the Holy Place. Thus, the Tabernacle is to be annually sanctified so that it is not assimilating the condition of the world in which it resides. The altar is also sanctified (vv. 18, 19). And by the symbolism of the scapegoat, the sin is carried out of the camp and the remains burned (v. 27).

Image courtesy of Melvin Poe

The seriousness of sin and the sacredness of the Most Holy Place are together here. Tradition says that the high priest went into the Most Holy Place with a rope tied around his leg. Should he die in the presence of God, no one wanted to have to go into the dreaded Most Holy Place and remove his body. That practice is not recorded in Scripture, but if true, it only reinforces the idea that an encounter with God is a solemn thing.

And yet, our worship does not stand under some kind of ominous shadow. The veil has been rent. We have been invited into God's presence. Celebration is in order. Rejoicing is appropriate. But rejoicing without regard to the price paid for our admission into His presence, without regard to the judgment of God upon our sin taken to the cross by Jesus—that kind of celebration and rejoicing is sacrilege.

True celebration embraces reverence and awe and the mystery of what has transpired. It is posited on a lifestyle of holiness and renunciation of sin. Even when the cloud had lifted—a sign that the glory of the Lord no longer filled the Most Holy Place—the sanctuary was not to be entered casually.

> *And when Aaron and his sons have finished covering the sanctuary and all the furnishings of the sanctuary, when the camp is set to go, then the sons of Kohath shall come to carry them; but they shall not touch any holy thing, lest they die* (Numbers 4:15).

They were not to be casual with holy things and the place of God's presence! The priests Nadab and Abihu died because they were casual in worship matters (see Leviticus 10:1-3). So, when we come into His presence, we should stand, be silent, take off our shoes and fall on our face. We are in the presence of the Most High God.

AN OPEN DOOR

Of course, the Old Testament Day of Atonement could only defer judgment. Let's remember, the lamb was not merely a type of Christ, but a substitution for the life of man. It was a reminder that man was living under the suspended judgment of God.

When Jesus died, the veil was rent in twain, and God said to man, "Come on in!" The Cross created an open door. The altar of incense has been moved inside the veil; thus, the believer's place is in the presence of God.

Image courtesy of www.mishkanministries.org

CHAPTER SEVENTEEN

THE ARK OF THE COVENANT

The Principle of His Covenant

W hat do we find in the Most Holy Place? The Most Holy Place is the sanctuary for the presence of God. Here, God's exiled glory dwells. The Hebrews called this manifestation "*the Shekinah*." The word never occurs in Scripture, but it appears in other Biblical literature. It means "the One who dwells."[154] His intent had been to dwell in the heart of man, but sin alienated man from God (Romans 3:23). Here, in the Tabernacle, He dwells among men, but not in men. He chooses for His dwelling place an article called the ark of the covenant. This becomes His throne on the earth.

THE PRESENCE OF HIS GLORY

Israel's worship was directed to Yahweh, who dwelt above

---

[154] Kevin Conner, *The Tabernacle of Moses* (Portland: Bible, 1975) 26.

that bloodstained mercy seat (Psalm 80:1). Everything moved toward that spot, that single piece of furniture, the place of His glory. And everything flowed from it as well. The psalmist pleads, "Give ear, O Shepherd of Israel... that dwellest between the cherubim, shine forth" (v. 1; see also Isaiah 37:16).[155] The psalmist declared, *"I will abide in Your tabernacle forever; I will trust in the shelter of Your wings"* (61:4). *"Because You have been my help, Therefore in the shadow of Your wings I will rejoice"* (63:7).

The instructions regarding the construction of the ark and the mercy seat are recorded in Exodus 25:10-22. The record of the construction is in 37:1-9. The ark was at the head of the

Image courtesy of www. tabernacleman.com

Tabernacle. The staves were left in the ark, and they were at the sides (25:12-15). The cherubim were on the ends (vv. 18, 19). The mercy seat faced eastward (Leviticus 16:14), indicating that the ark was placed in the Most Holy Place in a north-south orientation, the wider sides facing east and west. Most likely, the staves then ran east-west along the narrow side of the ark, not its broad side.[156] This would have been the way the ark would be carried—broad-sided. Neither cherubim would have been carried back-first, nor would a back-facing cherubim have been placed forward of the glory between the cherubim. It was the glory that was featured here. Above the ark, between the cherubim (the golden figures of angels) was the glory of God! So the ark, in transport, would have been carried with the *cherubim* on either side, facing the glory. With the staves placed near the base of the ark and borne on the

---

[155] Conner, 26.
[156] Conner, 12.

shoulders of the priests, this would have lifted the ark high above the men who carried it.

The concept of glory. *"Then the cloud covered the tabernacle of meeting, and the glory of the Lord filled the tabernacle"* (Exodus 40:34).

When the Tabernacle was set up in the wilderness, the glory of the Lord appeared—a visible manifestation of the invisible God (v. 34; Numbers 14:21). Practically, the glory was a cloud by day and a pillar of fire by night. In the Most Holy Place, God dwelt in darkness until He chose to manifest Himself as light. The Temple, too, had been full of His glory (2 Chronicles 7:1; Isaiah 6:3).

> *When Solomon had finished praying, fire came down from heaven and consumed the burnt offering and the sacrifices; and the glory of the Lord filled the temple. And the priests could not enter the house of the Lord, because the glory of the Lord had filled the Lord's house* (2 Chronicles 7:1, 2).

In both the Tabernacle and the Temple, there is a manifestation of glory attached to the structure. But when there was sin and the righteous demands of God were not honored, or when appointed leaders were disrespected, the Bible says, *"So the anger of the Lord was aroused against them, and He departed. 10 And when the cloud departed from above the tabernacle ..."* (Numbers 12:9, 10).

God's glory, then, is facilitated by the heart attitude of the people in whose midst He dwells. Rebellion and sin drive away God's presence. Righteousness and a servant heart facilitate His presence. God makes a pledge in Numbers: *"But truly, as I live, all the earth shall be filled with the glory of the Lord--"* (14:21).

The commitment of God is to display His glory in the earth in an immeasurable and unprecedented way (see Ephesians 1;

Colossians 1:27). The fall of man in the Garden and the rebellion of Israel in the wilderness may seem to delay God's plan, but He is committed to His eternal purposes. He will raise up new seed to Abraham. That people, consisting of lively stones, may devolve into the Dark Ages, but He will in time reform the church, bringing it back from Babylon. Even our generation may not realize His plan, but He will wait for the next. The ultimate display of His glory is not dependent on the lives of mortals but on the life of God himself—"As truly as I live!" His oath is predicated on His own life. One generation will finally yield to Him, discover the richness of His proposition—and see His glory. This glory is not to be confined to the Most Holy Place, or even to the Tabernacle. God will break out and flood the earth with His glory! To this, He is committed!

Image courtesy of Melvin Poe

We are to be burden-bearers of His glory. It is not the cares of the world with which we are to be laden, but with the weighty *chabod*, the glory of God. *"We cast our care on Him, for He cares for us"* (1 Peter 5:7). As He cares for our earthly needs, we care about His spiritual purposes. He carries the weight of our problems; we carry the weight of His glory. Man was created for this cause—to bear His glory. All that transpires in the Tabernacle is preparatory to the fresh deposit of His glory on the living temple.

At the brass altar, we learned the value of justification. At the laver, we learned the importance of sanctification. In the Holy Place, we learned the meaning of edification. But, in the Holy of Holies, we will learn glorification. This is not the glorification of our bodies, but the glorification of the church. A transformed people reflect His presence—His character! This theme of glory is echoed in the New Testament. Paul says that sin causes us to "*come short of the glory of God*" (Romans 3:23). In Ephesians, a deposit of glory in the church is the goal of God. He has "*predestinated us...to the praise of [His] glory*" (1:5, 6). He desires "*that we should be to the praise of His glory, who first trusted in Christ*" (v. 12; see also v. 14) and "*that [we] may know what is the hope of His calling, and what [are] the riches of the glory of His inheritance in the saints*" (v. 18).

There is no shortcut to the glory over the ark. You cannot bypass all that is before. The way prescribed is line-on-line, precept-on-precept. To come directly into the presence of God meant death. To throw reverence and heart preparation aside, making encounters with God superficial and common, still produces death.

In Colossians, Paul defines the "mystery" that he spoke of in Ephesians, saying, "*To them God willed to make known what are the riches of the glory of this mystery among the Gentiles: which is Christ in you, the hope of glory*" (1:27).

The Most Holy Place concealed His glory. It had a veil! The writer of Hebrews defines that veil as the "flesh" of Christ (10:20). Jesus was the living tabernacle. In Him was the "*fulness of the Godhead bodily*" (Colossians 2:9). He came to make visible the invisible God. He reflected the glory of the Father, saying, "*He who has seen Me has seen the Father*" (see John 14:9). The Father had given to Him His glory (17:22). But, the glory, like that in the Most Holy Place, had been veiled by the flesh of Christ. Without the veil of flesh, the world could not have survived the exposure to His glory or His presence among men. So God veiled the glory of the Son with the flesh of man. When Christ died on the cross, when His flesh was torn, the world experienced a revelation of His glory. This is what Jesus had prayed for: *"O Father, glorify Me together with Yourself, with the glory which I had with You before the world was"* (John 17: 5).

When the veil of flesh that had hidden the brightness of His glory was rent, the revelation of God's glorious Son was revealed (Matthew 27:45, 51-54). For three hours, the earth was dark. The planet trembled. Men repented. The veil in the Temple, a type of His flesh, was rent. The dead in Abraham's bosom rejoiced at their coming freedom when the grave's prison doors were jolted open. Dead men walked free in the streets of Jerusalem, tasting the fruits of resurrection. For 40 days, Jesus showed indisputable proof of His victory over sin and death, appearing and disappearing supernaturally. Then He ascended, disappearing from the earth, entering heaven's tabernacle. But, He had prayed:

> *And the glory which You gave Me I have given them, that they may be one just as We are one: I in them, and You in Me; that they may be made perfect in one, and that the world may know that You have sent Me, and have loved them as You have loved Me* (John 17:22, 23).

Here is the transfer of this glory to the church! The manifestation of glory through the church is dependent upon the humility and unity of the church. This is the way the "world will know" that God sent Christ—when we are one.

It is upon our lives that God seeks to place a deposit of His glory! His throne is established in the hearts of a church that rightly relates to His tablets, His rod, His pot of manna—and hides under His covering of mercy!

THE ARK

God's presence in the Tabernacle is tied to the ark. There are 185 references to the ark in the Old Testament alone.[157] And the ark is tied to the concept of the covenant. This became the "place" of His presence. It was made of acacia wood and overlaid with gold inside and out. The mercy seat (the lid of the ark) completed the chest, sitting inside its royal border. Rising out of the mercy seat were two *cherubim* facing each other, gazing toward the mercy seat. They are called the *"cherubims*

of glory" (Hebrews 9:5). What is it about this piece of furniture that caused God to attach His presence? If we can discover the answer, we will find the principles that point the way to our facilitating His presence.

The record of the construction of the ark is found in Exodus 37:1-9. It was never exposed to the inquisitive eyes of the people, even in transition. It was always covered, first by the veil itself. The priest would remove the veil from its hooks and, holding it high, they would walk westward and cover the ark.[158] Next, they covered the ark with a layer of badger's skins. Finally, they covered the ark with a cloth of blue. In 30:26, the ark was anointed. And in 25:22 and Numbers 7:89, the voice of God is noted as coming from the ark. The cloud overshadowed it (Exodus 40:34-38).

Exodus 25:10-22 and 37:1-9 describes the ark. It was 2 cubits long (3 feet) and 1.5 cubits high and deep (27 inches). On each corner a ring was fastened into which staves were placed for transport. The Hebrew word for *corners* means

---

[157] Conner, 19.

[158] Roy Lee DeWitt, *The History of the Tabernacle* (Chatham, IL: Revival Teaching, 1986) 79.

"feet." So the ark had four feet to which the rings were attached and into which the staves were placed for transport. This would mean that the ark was always lifted above the heads of those bearing it on their shoulders. It would have been the most exalted piece of furniture in the march, leading the way for the people. The rings would have been placed so that the staves were inserted on the short sides, not on the long sides.[159] This means that the ark was carried broadside! These staves were never meant to be taken out of the ark (25:15). Israel was not at home in the wilderness, just as we are not at home in this world. Only when the ark was moved to the Temple of Solomon were the staves taken out (1 Kings 8:8). The walls on the north, south and west were all solid, necessitating that the staves be drawn out of the rings eastward, under the veil. It would have been impossible to draw them out in any other direction. The staves would have been removed only after the ark had been perfectly placed since the ark itself was not to be touched.

The ark would have sat in the Holy Place in an east-west fashion, broadside, the cherubim facing one north and the other south. The upward and extended wings would have been to the west, the lowered wings of the cherubim to the east, a throne facing eastward, as if Yahweh observed the approach of the worshipper through the veil, over the altar of incense, and before the table and the lampstand, the laver and the bloody brass altar. And every believer at the gate faced toward the ark, and the God enthroned on mercy. The staves would have been on the ends, in an east-west alignment.[160] Their continual presence in the ark demonstrates the mobility, even the unpredictability of God. When God moves, He wants His throne to be

---

[159] William Brown, *The Tabernacle—Its Priests and Its Services* (Peabody, MA: Hendrickson, 1996) 75.

[160] Brown, 75.

moved "under Him." And, He moves spontaneously. If we are going to be burden-bearers of His glory, we have to travel with our staff in our hand, ready to move with Him at any moment!

It is called simply the "ark of shittim wood" (Exodus 25:10); then, the "ark of the testimony" (v. 22). It testifies to the covenant God has established with Israel. It is the "ark of the covenant" (Joshua 3:6). More definitively, it is the "ark of the covenant of the Lord" (Numbers 10:33). It is the "ark of God" (1 Samuel 3:3) and the "ark of the covenant of God" (Judges 20:27), a visible symbol of His covenant. It is later called the "ark of the Lord God" (1 Kings 2:26), "the ark of the Lord" (Joshua 4:11), and the "ark of the Lord, the Lord of all the earth" (3:13). It takes on cosmic dimensions as its history progresses. Psalm 132:8 calls it the "ark of thy strength." It is the "ark of the God of Israel" (1 Samuel 5:7).[161]

This ark is awesome! Rivers dry up before it (Joshua 3:15, 16). The walls of cities cannot stand before its power (6:6-9, 20). The immobile gods of the heathens bow before it and disintegrate in its presence (1 Samuel 5:1-5). A whole nation is beset by an affliction traceable to the presence of the ark (vv. 6-12). Men who touch it die (2 Samuel 6:6, 7).

Given the Hebrew prohibition to idolatry, why would God allow something so sacred and powerful to even exist among His people? Let's recall. The ark is in how many pieces? Two! The chest itself is one piece, but not whole. The mercy seat was made to be one with the chest, a covering for completion. It is the ark of "the covenant," or "testament." How many testaments do we have? Two! Yes, and the Old is not complete within itself. The old covenant was never meant to be ratified. It was a temporary measure, a custodian of the

---

[161] Connor, 19.

Law and a testimony of God. Only when the New Testament came was the Old complete. The two together represent the full revelation of God. The Old was made for the New, and the New was the answer to the Old. This ark, then, is a picture of the Word! No wonder it is so powerful, so forceful. When His Word goes forth, walls fall (Jericho) and rivers dry up (the Jordan), and the gods of this world are toppled (pagan). This ark is no idol. It represents the Word upon which the presence of God rides, and to which angels of the highest order attend.

There is more, for *"the Word was made flesh, and dwelt among us, (and we beheld His glory, the glory*

Image courtesy of Melvin Poe

as of the only begotten of the Father) full of grace and truth" (John 1:14). The ark is not merely the conceptual Word of God, it is the living Word of God—a picture of Jesus Christ Himself. Paul declared in Romans that we were *"justified freely by His grace through the redemption that is in Christ Jesus... whom God hath set forth to be a propitiation"* (3:24, 25). That word *propitiation* is the Greek word *hilasterion*, which literally means "mercy seat." Jesus is our mercy seat. He is the Testator who has forged a new covenant in our behalf with the Father. He is our Covering, our Ark!

Wherever the ark went, there was victory. And wherever Jesus went, He had victory. So the ark represents the place of victory. It also represents a place of safety and protection, or a haven of security. This ark is God's "secret place" (see Psalm 91). In it is His treasure. To secure His treasure, He sits on this chest. One will have to move God to disturb or seize His treasure. And who can do that? His presence over the ark casts a shadow over it. Since the ark is under the shadow of His glory, it is the most secure place one could be on the face of the earth. As we come to dwell under the shadow of His glory, we find ourselves in His secret place, under His security and in safety.

We cannot understand this fully without noting that the Hebrew word *aron*, which is translated "ark," also means "chest" or "coffin." So Israel's most sacred possession is a coffin. They carried a coffin through the wilderness. They enshrined a coffin in the Holy Temple. In the Most Holy Place is a coffin. Strange, isn't it? I want to be in the secret place of God, under His mercy, under the shadow of His presence, under the wings of the awesome *cherubim*. But in order to get there, I must crawl into the coffin. I will have to die! Paul declared, *"If ye then be risen with Christ, seek those things which are above, where Christ sitteth on the right hand of God"* (Colossians 3:1).

How can we be raised with Christ and experience the reality of new life in Him? Paul tells us, "For ye are dead, and your life is hid with Christ in God" (v. 3)! Where does God put us when we surrender to Christ, when we count ourselves as dead in order that He might live in us? He puts us in His coffin, His secret place! It is here, in this place of death to self, of total surrender to God, that we experience the secret of personal and spiritual power.

Many times in the New Testament, we note the phrase "in Christ," particularly from Paul. Where are we when we are "in Christ"? We are buried with Him! But that is not all. *"In Christ shall all be made alive"* (1 Corinthians 15:22). In Christ we are "established," or made strong (see 2 Corinthians 1:21). In Christ we are "made to triumph" (see 2:14). In Christ we are a new creation (5:17). And on and on the list goes.

Arks or chests are designed to protect their contents. But this Ark—Jesus—protects us. But we are not in this box alone. This Ark is not empty. It was designed to carry special contents. Note Exodus 25:16: *"Put into the ark the testimony."*

The ark is sometimes called "the ark of the testimony" (30:6). The altar of incense was always in front of the ark, specifically before the testimony (v. 36). What is this ark testifying of? In Hebrews 9:4, we learn that inside the ark were three things: the pot of manna (Exodus 16:33, 34), Aaron's rod that budded[162] (Numbers 17:10, 11), and the tablets upon which were written the Commandments (Exodus 25:16; Deuteronomy 10:2). These also give testimony to Jesus: the rod reflects the Father's sovereignty; the tablets speak of the truth revealed by God's revelation, the Word; the manna speaks of the appropriation of God to the daily needs of man. So here is the Father's authority, the rod; the Son's revelatory office, the tablets; and the Spirit's ministry of appropriating the grace of God to meet daily needs, the manna. Here is the Trinity. What does this have to do with Jesus?

In Him is the fullness of the Godhead bodily. In the ark, life and death are joined. Here we lose ourselves ... and find an eternal self.

Image courtesy of Melvin Poe

Here we choose surrender ... and find victory. Here we embrace the Cross ... and resurrection power explodes inside of us.

THE TABLETS

The tablets represent God's demand for *righteousness* revealed in the Law and lived out in the life of Jesus! They represent God's

---

[162] When Korah rebelled, the solution of Moses was to lay 12 marked rods before the presence of the Lord. Aaron's rod, marked with his name, came alive in the night. It had buds, blossoms and almond fruit (Numbers 17:1-10). The miracle validated the role of Aaron as the priestly leader of Israel. It was a prophetic sign of our priest, Christ, and of His resurrection. At the ultimate rebellion, the Crucifixion, He was laid before the Father in death, but He came alive. His resurrection makes Him different than the head of any other religion. He is a living Priest, who rose from the dead and offers to us life.

relationship values. The tablets demand healthy relationships. Four of the 10 deal with the vertical relationship with God; six deal with the horizontal relationships of man with man. The first commandment deals with worship—the ultimate value issue. Worship is always directed to where my heart is. I am to love God with all my heart, mind and soul. My life is to revolve around Him. Life energy rises out of worship energy. All the Commandments are mere expressions of the first. My transformed horizontal relationships are indicative of my vertical love relationship with God. His love reaches through me. His covenant demands that I behave differently. Here is a personal love relationship, not a dispassionate arrangement with a distant God. Slaves are now called His sons. He is our Sheikh (chief) who leads us through the earthly wilderness. His tent is among us. But, God demands from us a sensitivity to righteousness. And, God measures righteousness relationally. Keeping His Commandments is an act of love that touches His heart. Violating the Commandments breaks the heart of God.

THE ROD

The rod represents God's anointed *leadership*, His representative authority demonstrated most perfectly in the life of Christ. Just as Aaron's rod budded, so this type of godly authority produces life! Thus, it deals with *headship*! The rod is a symbol of divine authority. This is not the rod of Moses, but of Aaron. As a priestly rod, it represents the mission of ministry—more precisely the ministry of bridge building, of reconciliation. That is what a priest is—a bridge builder. Again, this is the rod that budded. When Aaron's authority was challenged, 12 rods were laid before the Lord in the Holy Place. Aaron's rod was the subject of a miracle. The rod, without roots or apparent life, brought forth buds, blossoms and even fruit. This rod, then, represents priestly authority that produces "life" and brings forth fruit. That is the purpose of spiritual authority—to aid in the production of character and maturity in God's people. But the authority must be Christlike if it is to produce Christlike outcomes. Authority that is anointed carries the buds and blossoms of the spiritual life. Authority that is anointed is weighted down by the fruit of the Spirit. This is the rod that has power, the power to reconcile man to God.

THE MANNA

Manna is a reminder of the provision of God during the wilderness sojourn. Thus, it speaks of the hand of God. Manna was the staple diet in the wilderness. The Hebrew word means "What is it?" In Chaldean, it means "It is a portion." And to us in English, it means "bread." At first, Israel hated it. Later, they called it "angel's food" (Psalm 78:25). It was bread from God's table, rained from heaven. It was the provision for the wilderness. Manna represents the covenant of God to supply our needs, to feed us and to nurture us.

The manna was always sufficient. It is said by some that it tasted to every man as he pleased. It satisfied and gave strength. It never failed. It was small and seemed insignificant in size. It was round. It was white. It was like hoarfrost, crisp. It was like coriander seed, which was an herb that was fragrant when crushed. It was like fresh oil, a daily diet of anointing. It was the color of bdellium, like a white pearl.[163]

The "manna" covenant is echoed in multiple passages of Scripture:

- *"The Lord is my shepherd; I shall not want. He maketh me to lie down in green pastures: he leadeth me beside the still waters"* (Psalm 23:1, 2).
- *"My God shall supply all your need according to his riches in glory"* (Philippians 4:19).
- *"Consider the lilies of the field... they toil not"* (Matthew 6:28).

---

[163] C. W. Slemming, *Made According to Pattern* (London: Marshall, Morgan and Scott, 1938) 114, 115.

When the widow at Zarephath went back to her meal barrel, she found just enough for the day, time after time (1 Kings 17:8-16). That is the manna covenant. When Elijah was at the brook Cherith, the ravens brought food and the brook ran in a year of drought (vv. 2-6). That, too, was the manna covenant.

Here are the dimensions of God's covenant. These three articles—the tablets, manna and the rod—offer a testimony about...

1. God's righteous demands—the tablets
- *Implication for me*: The covenant with God demands that my lifestyle must change.
- *Revelation about God*: This is a look at the heart of God—purity, righteousness, no evil.

2. God's provisional promises—the manna
- *Implication for me*: The covenant has provisions. God has committed Himself to meet my most fundamental daily needs.
- *Revelation about God*: This is a look at the hand of God—powerful in provision, caring, bountiful, creative, nurturing.

3. God's anointed leadership—the rod
- *Implication for me:* The covenant requires my obedient cooperation in His purposes and with His leaders. This is the headship of God. It is not positional authority (kingly) that He offers but relational authority (priestly).
- *Revelation about God:* He wants a relationship with me! In the rod is authority. In the priestly office is a rod that buds and bears fruit. This relationship calls the deadness to live, the barren to bear. This relationship is not static, it is life-giving. But I must yield to it and not fight it. I must submit to it and trust it.

The rod demands of me a right relationship of submission. The pot of manna demands of me faith, dependence and child-likeness. The tablets demand of me righteousness, manifested in my worship and walk. This worship is given only to God. It is an exclusive devotion that results in responsible social relationships with my own family and the community (walk).

The rod meets spiritual needs. The tablets meet the needs of the soul. The manna meets the needs of the body. The rod envisions the Father's sovereignty. The tablets envision the Son's righteous revelation of the Word and truth. The manna envisions the Spirit's executive ministry of appropriating from the estate of Christ whatever I need, to sustain and develop me.

Notice, this is the ark of the covenant. Covenant is the concept of a testament, will or even a treaty. It delineates the nature of a relationship. This is not a contract! Covenants and contracts are two different things! A contract is about things; a covenant is between people. A contract usually involves the exchange of goods and services; a covenant is about the relationship itself. A contract says, "In exchange for this, I will do or give that!" A covenant says, "I will!" A contract is outcome-focused; a covenant is input-focused. A contract is conditional, void if either party fails to perform. The covenant we have in marriage and that which we have with God is unconditional. It is for better or worse. We do not have a contract with God, we have a covenant! But, there are conditions that determine the quality of the relationship the covenant embraces.

Where people respond to God's righteous demands, God is revealed. Where people are submitted to the headship of Christ, God is enthroned. Where people trust God and rely on Him for provision, God is active. And yet, His presence is not a sign of my righteousness, faith or my submission, but of His mercy!

THE ARK AND THE MIRACULOUS

When He is present, things get exciting! The ark divides the Jordan. The ark brings down the walls of Jericho. The ark topples Dagon, the Philistine god. The ark plagues the Philistines. As the people followed the ark, thus honoring the covenant, the power of God was manifest. There is safety and security in meeting the righteous demands of God, trusting Him for provision, and submitting to His life-giving authority.

THE MERCY SEAT— A COVERING OF MY SHORTCOMINGS

What if I fail to trust God completely? I become stubborn? The tablets, the rod, and the pot of manna were all placed in the first portion of the ark, the chest. That is to say, God's demands rise out of the old covenant. His requirements regulating my actions and attitudes are rooted in the old covenant, but we know that obedience to the Law could not save us. The old covenant was incomplete, ineffective. Does that mean the principles revealed in the old covenant are now null and void? Listen to Christ: *"I have not come to destroy the Law but to fulfill it, or to complete it!"* (See Matthew 5:17).

The chest needed a cover. It was incomplete. The blood of bulls and goats was not adequate, meaning there was nothing on this earth precious and sacred enough to redeem us. So Christ came as the covering, the mercy seat. Now, there is a covering of mercy over the Law. The demands of the Law still stand as the principles by which God wants us to live. He still wants a righteous people (tablets), a people of humility and submission to His will (rod), and a people of faith (manna). However, when we fail to achieve perfection in the flesh, mercy makes up the difference between God's demands and the performance of a sincere heart and truly changed believer who sometimes falls short. The good news of the new covenant is that ultimately, it is not my performance that maintains the covenant bond, it is His character, rooted in mercy.

This is living in the tension. There are righteous demands, and yet I am still imperfect, so His mercy covers me. I cannot exploit His mercy with settled unrighteousness, and if I am truly changed, I could not and would not do that.

The mercy seat (*kapporeth*) was a solid cover of gold, perhaps as thick as 3 inches, large enough to serve as a cover for the ark. Made as one solid unit with the lid were two cherubim figures facing each other with outstretched wings (Exodus 25:19, 20; 37:7-9). (Note: *cherub* is the singular form; *cherubim*, the plural form.)

THE THRONE OF GOD ... HIS VERY PRESENCE

Christianity is often misunderstood. Outsiders see the smoke and the fire in the court, the blood and the issue of judgment on sin; they see the laver and the demands for constant cleansing— and they never look further. Their resistance to change distorts their ability to see beyond God's demands for righteousness. So our society quickly writes off our God and our faith and frantically searches for a substitute.

But those who see the wisdom of God in the altar and understand His demands for purity have the distinct advantage of pressing into the Holy Place to see a revelation of His beauty. Does anyone dare venture beyond the veil into the Most Holy Place? Does anyone want to see the God who is there, the God who hates sin and is committed to righteousness, the God who is awesome and to be feared?

Yes, let's venture in. Into the Most Holy Place we go. We've made the preparations. We do not enter casually. But, once on the inside, we are amazed. This God who is to be feared; this awesome being, the Creator of all life, is seated on mercy. And His seat is stained with blood—not the blood of a million goats and lambs, but the bloodstains of His only Son. "Who murdered Your Son, Sir?" Without hesitation, the answer comes back, "You did it!" But, there is no bitterness in His voice, no anger on His countenance, no vengeful spirit in His attitude! Instead, this awesome God takes a closer look at us and declares, "And, you look somewhat like Him! You don't have a father, do you?" "No," we reply. "Then, I'll call you My son!" Instead of a journey that ends in an experience of fear, we have discovered a Father—a Father who always sits on a seat called "mercy." This is a seat supported by a box called "the covenant." There, we climb up into His lap. There, we find a home!

CHAPTER EIGHTEEN

EXITING TO SERVE

The Principle of Transformation

We have made our trip from the outer gate into the Most Holy Place. When we started our journey, we were sinners, aliens from His presence. Now, we are sons and more. We are priests and kings.

In the Most Holy Place, we found "home." Now, we can never be comfortable in our tents, no matter how lavish—not after we have sat with God in His tent. In His presence, we were earthbound in body, but our spirit touched heaven. We realize that deep inside us we have a longing now for another world. Only our bodies are at home here. Yet, He has chosen to leave us here. So we will live in transit between His tent and our tent, between heaven and earth, between the Most Holy Place of His presence and the most unholy world.

Taking the Holy Place into an unholy world! As we leave the Most Holy Place, we do so conscious of the fact that we are missionaries to our world. As we were touched by each piece of furniture in preparation for His presence, we are now touched by each piece of furniture in preparation for His service.

As we exit, we take with us...

- The *glow of His glory* out of the *Most Holy Place*
- From the ark of the covenant: we take the priestly *rod* of *spiritual authority*, the *tablets* of *liberty through righteousness*, the *bread* of *provision by faith*
- From the lampstand, we take the *fragrance of His presence*
- From the altar of *incense* we take the fire of passionate prayer, and the evidence that we have been with Him
- From the lampstand, we take *fruit and fire* with a daily dose of fresh oil—the ministry of *the Spirit*
- From the table, we take the fresh *bread* for a hungry world
- At the laver we pause, we again wash hands and feet, so we can meet the world with *clean hands* and a *pure heart (motives)*.
- At the altar we make a *sacrificial commitment* to be His agents in the earth! There at the altar is the Lamb, slain for us. We climb on the altar and whisper, "You died for us. Give us grace to live for You. From the altar we take the message of the Lamb, redemption by the blood.

He has called us to be *burden-bearers of His glory*! May He touch through our touching, speak through our speaking, love through our loving, and care through our caring.

THE SACRIFICES

SACRIFICE	SCRIPTURE	MATERIAL	KEPT BY MAN	GOD'S PART
Sin and Trespasses	Leviticus 5; 6:1-7, 26-29; 7:1-7	Male and female of the herd and flock, turtledoves, young pigeons, or 1/10 of an ephah of flour	Offerer got nothing. He could benefit in no way from his sin or trespass. Highest grade was burned outside the camp. The lower grade offerings were eaten in the Holy Place by priests.	Blood was placed on the horns of the altar, thrown at the base of the altar and on its side. The fat was burned on the altar.
Burnt Offering	Leviticus 1; 6:8-13	Bulls, goats, sheep, rams, lambs, turtledoves, pigeons	Skin	All burned
Peace Offering	Leviticus 3; 7:11-13	Male and female of the herd and flock, bull, lamb, goat	Heave shoulder; wave breast	All the fat
Meat/ Meal/ Grain Offering	Leviticus 2; 6:14-23	Fine flour, green ears, frankincense, oil, salt	Offerer: none; priests: the remainder after the offering	A portion burned as a memorial

COVERINGS FOR THE FURNITURE

FURNITURE	1ST COVER	2ND COVER	3RD COVER
Ark	Veil	Badger's skin	Blue cloth
Golden table	Blue cloth	Scarlet cloth	Badger's skin
Lampstand	Blue cloth	Badger's skin	None
Golden altar	Blue cloth	Badger's skin	None
Brass altar	Purple cloth	Badger's skin	None
Laver	No cloth	Not covered	Not covered

TOPICAL INDEX

264

H

I

M

V

vertical 138, 142, 146-147, 184, 231, 234, 295

vessel/s 14, 31, 62, 112, 207, 210, 230

vestments 74, 263

victim/s 100, 102-103, 106, 265

victimizer 106

violate/d/s/ing 21, 104, 116, 136-137, 162, 221, 295

violation/s 133, 136, 138, 142, 151, 265, 269

visible 34, 44, 50, 205, 250, 254, 258-259, 285, 287, 291

voluntary 46, 113, 124

W

wagons 61-62

warfare 16-17, 165, 197

washed 41, 99, 115, 171, 175-177, 261

washing 41, 173-178, 181

watch/es/ed/ful/ing 81, 87, 123, 141, 184-185

weigh/ed/ing/s 55-56, 62, 101, 159, 186

weight/ed 55, 62, 80, 186, 243, 248, 169, 286

Wesley 87

western 16, 67-68, 90-91, 130, 192-193, 273

Westerners 175

westward 61, 89, 194, 231, 289

wholeness 113, 147, 153, 156

wholly 119, 177, 198, 268

wilderness 10-15, 17, 19, 29, 44, 58, 60, 86, 111, 135, 139, 189, 214, 217-218, 231, 239, 285-286, 290, 293, 295-296

within 32, 58, 65, 81, 83, 101, 114, 188, 196, 215, 222, 291

without 14-15, 17-19, 22, 25, 27, 35, 38, 41, 68, 70, 82, 91, 93, 100, 102, 107, 112-113, 120-121, 123, 125, 128, 131-133, 138, 142, 146,

149, 157-158, 168, 173, 175, 179-181, 196, 209, 217, 222, 233, 236, 241, 243, 250, 254, 260, 264, 267, 270, 277, 280, 287, 293, 295, 301

witness/ed 26, 102, 158-159, 162-163, 165, 183-185, 188, 204, 265

wooden 67, 70, 98, 184

woolen 48-49

worship/ed/er/ers/ful/ing/s 1, 3, 11-19, 22-30, 32-33, 37, 39-41, 43, 45, 57, 68, 75, 80-81, 83-86, 89-90, 92, 101, 105, 107, 109-111, 113, 116-117, 121-122, 125, 129, 131, 146-150, 152, 157, 159-161, 164-167, 173, 179-180, 195-196, 204-205, 223, 226-227, 234-244, 247-248, 251, 253, 261, 263-270, 274, 278-281, 283, 290, 295, 298

Y

Yahweh 27, 85-87, 111, 133, 245, 262, 283, 290

yellow 51, 54

Z

Zacharias 242-243

Zacharius 243

Zarephath 297

Zebulun 54, 57, 61

Zerubbabel 14, 26, 28, 46

SCRIPTURAL REFERENCES

New Testament

BIBLIOGRAPHY

Atwater, Edward E. *History and Significance of the Sacred Tabernacle*. New York: Dodd and Mead, 1875.

Bright, John. *A History of Israel*. Philadelphia: Westminster, 1959.

William Brown, *The Tabernacle—Its Priests and Its Services* (Peabody, MA: Hendrickson, 1996).

Caldecott, W. Shaw. *The Tabernacle: Its History and Structure*. Philadelphia: The Union Press, 1904.

Corbin, Bruce. *The Tabernacle in the Wilderness*. Enid, OK: Truth, 1951.

Cross, Frank. "The Tabernacle." *The Biblical Archaeologist*. Vol X, No. 3. Sept. 1947.

De Hann, M. R. *The Tabernacle*. Grand Rapids: Zondervan, 1955.

Demarest, Gary. *The Communicator's Commentary: Leviticus*. Dallas: Word, 1990.

Dewitt, Roy Lee. *The History of the Tabernacle*. Chatham, IL: Revival Teaching, 1986.

Dolman, D. H. *Simple Talks on the Tabernacle*. Grand Rapids: Zondervan, 1941.

Edersheim, Alfred. *The Temple: Its Ministry and Services*. Grand Rapids: Eerdmans, 1969.

Epp, Theodore H. *Portraits of Christ in the Tabernacle*. Lincoln, NB: Back to the Bible, 1976.

Fuller, Charles E. *The Tabernacle in the Wilderness*. Westwood, NJ: Fleming H. Revell, 1955.

Hastings, James. *Dictionary of the Bible*. New York: Scribner's, 1963.

Hottel, W. S. *Typical Truth in the Tabernacle*. Cleveland, OH: Union Gospel, 1943.

Jukes, Andrew. *The Law of the Offerings*. Grand Rapids: Kregel, 1966.

Keil, C. F. and F. Delitzsch. *Biblical Commentary on the Old Testament*. Grand Rapids: Eerdmans, 1963.

Kellogg, S. H. *Studies in Leviticus*. Grand Rapids: Kregel, 1988.

Kittel, Gerhard. *Theological Dictionary of the New Testament*. Vol. VIII. Grand Rapids: Eerdmans, 1939.

Knight, G. A. F. *Leviticus*. Philadelphia: Westminster, 1981.

Levine, Moshe. *The Tabernacle: Its Structure and Utensils*. London: Soncino, 1969.

Levy, David M. *The Tabernacle: Shadows of the Messiah*. Bellmawr, NJ: Friends of Israel Gospel Ministry, 1993.

Little, David. *The Tabernacle in the Wilderness*. New York: Loizeaux Brothers, 1957.

Muntz, Eugene and Louisa J. Davis. *A Short History of Tapestry*. London: Cassell and Company, 1885.

Olford, Stephen. *The Tabernacle: Camping With God*. Neptune, NJ: Loizeaux Brothers, 1971.

Rhind. *The Tabernacle in the Wilderness: The Shadow of Heavenly Things*. London: Samuel Bagster and Sons, Paternoster Row, 1845.

Singer, Isidore. *The Jewish Encyclopedia*. Vol. XI. New York: Funk and Wagnalls, 1905.

Slemming, C. W. *Made According to Pattern*. London: Marshall, Morgan and Scott, 1938.

Spink, James F. *The Tabernacle in the Wilderness*. New York: Loizeaux Brothers, 1946.

Stanley, Arthur Penrhyn. "Lectures on the Jewish Church." London: Murray, 1865.

Strong, James. *The Tabernacle of Israel in the Desert* (Grand Rapids: Baker, 1952).

Tenney, Merrill C. *The Zondervan Pictorial Bible Dictionary*. Grand Rapids: Zondervan, 1967.

Unger, Merrill. *Unger's Bible Dictionary*. Chicago: Moody, 1957.

Zehr, Paul. *God Dwells With His People*. Scottdale, PA: Herald, 1981.

Other Books by P. Douglas Small
AVAILABLE AT WWW.ALIVEPUBLICATIONS.ORG

ENTERTAINING GOD AND INFLUENCING CITIES
" Prayer is not about words and requests. It is not even first and foremost about intercession. That will come. Prayer is about hosting God in a world from which He has been excluded. In prayer, you declare God is not only welcome, but He is invited... you host Him in your heart and your home, the church and your corporation."

INTERCESSION:
THE UNCOMFORTABLE STRATEGIC MIDDLE
Doug shows how Adam was created for the middle—a representative of God in the earth. All creation saw in him the image of God. From that place he fell. Only the last Adam, Jesus, coming to re-secure the broken middle, could reconnect creation to mankind. Jesus came to the middle.

PRAYER: THE HEARTBEAT OF THE CHURCH
Whatever the challenge, conditions, or conflict, prayer has transforming power. Prayer has resurrection power, renewal power, and restoration power. Prayer is the heartbeat of the church! This covers three issues: Magnify the divine privilege of prayer; Motivate individuals to develop a disciplined prayer life; and Mobilize the church to create a prayer culture. As we go forward in prayer, we will witness God's transforming power.

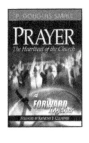

TRANSFORMING YOUR CHURCH
INTO A HOUSE OF PRAYER
Jesus taught on Prayer. When He did, three times in three verses we find the phrase "When you pray..." (Matthew 6: 5, 6, 7, emphasis added). After all He would do for them, it was inconceivable that they would not even talk to Him in prayer after He had gone. It is astonishing that the church in much of the world does not talk regularly.

WET EYES AND CARING HANDS
An excursion through the ministries of 10 churches, plus vignettes of many other churches and ministries led by pastors and missionaries who want to touch the unreached around them. Their stories will inspire you. As members joined them in city or national impacting mission, sparks of new life erupted. The result has been explosive growth in some cases, a culture shift in congregations in other locations, and the transformation of the pastoral leader himself.

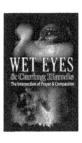

Through the Tabernacle

"I learned the real goal of prayer is my desire to please Him."

"I am now inspired to pray as never before."

"I learned the dynamics of prayer."

"I came away with useful, practical information and have an understanding of the workings of prayer better now than ever before."

"I learned how to structure my prayers to make an appointment with God with many intercessors."

Host a Tabernacle School of Prayer

Take a walk, a prayer walk, through the Old Testament tabernacle with Doug Small. You will learn and then you will pray. You will enter the gate with thanksgiving. Stop at the altar and apply the blood of the Lamb to your heart. Examine and wash yourself at the laver and then enter the Holy Place. The table of shewbread represents the ministry of Christ, the Bread of Life broken for us. The golden lampstand, fruit and fire, represents the ministry of the Holy Spirit in our lives. At the golden altar you'll discover that the sweetness of our lives is to be offered to God in worship and then you'll go into the most Holy Place and put yourself into the ark of the covenant. The blood, the water, the bread, the oil, the incense, and the glory. This will change forever the way you pray.

Schedule your School of Prayer:
1.855.842.5483
www.projectpray.org

ALIVE MINISTRIES

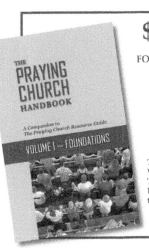